THE HOBO

THE SOCIOLOGY OF THE

HOMELESS MAN

BY

NELS ANDERSON

A STUDY PREPARED FOR THE CHICAGO
COUNCIL OF SOCIAL AGENCIES UNDER
THE DIRECTION OF THE COMMITTEE
ON HOMELESS MEN

Phoenix Books

THE UNIVERSITY OF CHICAGO PRESS

CHICAGO & LONDON

THE UNIVERSITY OF CHICAGO PRESS, CHICAGO & LONDON
The University of Toronto Press, Toronto 5, Canada

© 1923 by The University of Chicago. Published 1923. First
Phoenix Edition 1961. Third Impression 1965. Composed and
printed by THE UNIVERSITY OF CHICAGO PRESS, Chicago,
Illinois, U.S.A.

INTRODUCTION TO
THE PHOENIX EDITION

IT IS now thirty-nine years since *The Hobo* was published and forty years since I began assembling the materials out of which the book grew.

Not long ago I was lecturing at the University of Copenhagen, and I was asked to devote one lecture to the hobo. I was particularly asked to tell about the author, how the book came to be written, how the research was done.

In 1882 my father migrated to the United States after a boyhood in Sweden and some twelve years in Germany. Some labor contractor picked him up on arrival, and he was sent to a railroad construction project. For the next year, until he learned enough English to get along, he went from job to job trying to find German- or Swedish-speaking companions. The effort to get settled enabled him to acquire a facility for getting about. As he gained confidence in this respect, he lost for the time his wish to settle. My father found himself moving about through the Middle West, a real hobo worker: farm hand, miner, lumberjack, building worker, and for a while coachman in Chicago. Once he ventured west as far as Deadwood in the Black Hills during a gold rush. For my father, getting Americanized by this process of moving from job to job was a continuing adventure. He remembered later with pride how he learned to beat his way on freight trains.

Five years later in St. Louis he met my mother,

who had been employed as a housemaid and as a factory worker. After the marriage they went to Chicago, where I came on the scene. While I was still an infant, my father heard about a great fire in Spokane. This opportunity he could not miss. Spokane would need bricklayers, and in 1889 we moved west.

Spokane was *The West;* here was plenty of land and much work. My father filed on a timber claim not far from Spokane. My mother, with two small children, and a third born soon after, lived in a shack on the claim, looking after the garden and chickens. My father worked in town, coming home on horseback for weekends. This arrangement was not satisfactory, so the claim was sold and my family, in a covered wagon, trekked to Lewiston, Idaho. Here my father had an opportunity to farm Indian land on shares in the Nez Perce Reservation. The Indian reservation was not satisfactory either, so the family moved into Lewiston. My father built a good house, our first. He had steady work at good wages. But he wanted land where his family could take root; so after wandering in a covered wagon and sleeping in tents at night, we arrived at the Teton Basin in Idaho. The Teton Basin had rich land but no schools.

Everything was sold, and the family returned to Chicago less than ten years after departing that city. Chicago was disappointing. My father found work, but his wages were not enough. We lived in the worst kind of housing on the edge of Hobohemia. I turned to selling newspapers in the very streets and alleys, saloons and other places I was to study later. There was continuous sickness in the family. One

baby born in Chicago died after a few months.   My
father could think only of finding a farm.

Less than three years after leaving the Teton
Basin we were living on a rented farm in Michigan.
Two years later, in 1903, we had our own farm nearby.   It was my mother who called the halt.   In the
sixteen years since her marriage she had packed and
moved ten times, and, in the course of this wandering,
twelve babies had been born to her.   Nine were still
living when we settled on the Michigan farm.   My
father agreed he would not move again and put the
farm in my mother's name.

When visitors came, if it was not my father telling
his stories, it was Mother telling hers.   My father
usually tried to point out how in America even a
"greenhorn" could get around.   In his own way he
saw the road as adventure.   He never heard of Walt
Whitman, but his thinking about the open road was
no different.

Now that he had finished moving, his attention
was on the dream that came with him from the "Old
Country," to take root in the land.   He would settle
each child on a farm, and each Anderson would stick
together against the world.   In the end only two of
his children became farmers, each of them only after
he had done some wandering.   Four of the boys became migratory workers before settling in other
careers.   My three sisters also left home and did some
moving about before settling.

But none of my family became a drunkard,
gambler, or loafer.   All became self-supporting in
some occupation above common labor.   In that solid
sense my parents did not fail.

I left high school and became a mule driver in central Illinois. I was getting a man's pay, and I felt I had an occupation; besides entering the honorable ranks of the mule skinners, I had entered a select company of hobo workers. We had to widen the grade for doubletracking the Santa Fe railroad from Chicago to Kansas City. Every few miles along the entire stretch were grading camps. We lived in tents, and so did twenty span of mules. We moved the dirt with an elevating grader and dump wagons. Work was ten hours a day, six days a week.

In this crew of good names, the respected old-timer was Shorty Carroll. He symbolized much that "hobo" came to mean to me. He had driven string teams in the West. He had been on all the big railroad construction and canal-digging jobs, and he knew about levee building along the Mississippi. He had been a prospector, a stagecoach driver, and had marched with "Coxey's Army." A good worker and a better storyteller, Shorty had a weakness for strong drink. Four years later when I met him in Montana his health was breaking. He had finished working as a blaster in a railroad tunnel, his money was gone, and he was recovering from drinking his earnings. He said he was going "over the hump," over the mountains to the Pacific Coast. He was really going over the hump in another sense, but he was still a hero to me, and I felt it an honor to lend him money and to see that he boarded a train. There were other good names in that group: Rickety Bill, who talked little but about whom many stories were told; Kansas City Dick; Yellow Kid; Memphis Joe; and other "monickers," each having a character of his own.

Like the student who learns the "theory" of his

occupation in school, I learned how the hobo behaved, or should not behave, in town, how he went about from place to place on freight trains, how he evaded train crews and railroad police, and how he found his work. But I had no experience of my own, and after six months in the outfit I began to feel self-conscious about holding on so long. I had become what the hoboes called a "home guard."

Under this compulsion I went to Chicago, to remain only a few days. I met a man who had worked for the Santa Fe outfit, whose money was gone, and who was ready to ship out on the Chicago, Milwaukee and St. Paul Railroad, then in process of extending its line across South Dakota, Montana, Idaho, and Washington to the Pacific. This was the last big American railroad building project and, as I realized later, the "last roundup" for the hoboes, who had formerly performed such work. For a month I worked for this road in South Dakota.

I decided to move on into Montana, where I found work again as a skinner. My next job after that was on a rock contract, driving a railroad tunnel. Before another year had passed I had also worked in a lumber camp and a metal mine, and another four years were spent in pursuit of experience. I learned to ride freight trains and even passenger trains. I tried my hand at different kinds of work. While I was never given to spending money on drink, I did find myself penniless a number of times. I used these occasions for getting another kind of hobo experience, begging from passers-by on streets ("panhandling") or begging at back doors for food.

Something like five years after leaving home I decided to go to Los Angeles, but I found the going

difficult.   Twice in the course of the night I was put
off the train, but each time managed to get back on.
The third time was at a lonely station near the Utah-
Nevada line.   The station master gave me a drink
of water and told me to move on.   The next water
tank was seven miles ahead.   When I reached the
water-tank station, the station master warned me to
move on.   Another five miles nearer Los Angeles I
came to a small valley with four ranch houses.

I saw a man mowing hay in a meadow near the
track.   When I asked him for a job, his answer was
negative, but he did take me to his home for supper.
The next day I helped him get in the hay, not asking
about money, and learned there was a job some
twenty miles away in Utah.   The rancher from
Utah happened to be present, and I was hired by
him.

On that ranch I liked the variety of the work.   I
was taken in as one of the family.   I found myself being persuaded to return to school.   For the next several years, whether I was away at school or working,
the ranch was my home.   My high-school work was
taken partly in the academy branch of the Brigham
Young University, partly in a school not far from the
ranch.   I earned money as a timberman in mines, as
a maintenance worker on railroads, or as construction worker.   Other students earned their money
herding sheep, working on ranches, working in stores.
I could earn much more through my migratory work.

From 1912 to 1920 I concentrated on getting
through four years of high school and four of college
at Brigham Young.   Although learning was an ab-
sorbing interest, I had no goal except the vague one
that I might later study law.   John C. Swenson,

chairman of the economics and sociology department, suggested that I would not be happy in the law, that I should go to a graduate school to study sociology, and that the most dynamic center for sociology then was the University of Chicago. Going to Chicago was my final effort at riding freight trains.

In Chicago a new way of earning a living had to be found. I knew how to get in and out of cities, but I had never worked in one. Finding jobs was easier than adapting to an upper-level academic life, for which there was so little time.

Then came an unexpected demand on my time. In each class I had to prepare a term paper, which meant field research and reading. I knew the hobo, his work, and his urban habitat, and I was permitted in two classes to do papers about that world so little known to most professors.

Because these initial papers were well received, other possibilities opened to me. I chanced to meet people who were interested in the problem of the homeless in Chicago. I had never thought of the hobo in this way, but in Hobohemia, his Chicago habitat, he was indeed among the homeless. I began reading articles, reports, and books about the homeless and the vagrancy problem. None touched the hobo as I knew him. I came to know Ben L. Reitman, physician to the homeless, friendless, and wicked, who enlisted the interest of Dr. William A. Evans, author of a syndicated medical column, who gave a small sum to start a study. This enabled me for several months to devote my time to research.

From this beginning other support came from the Chicago Council of Social Agencies and the Laura Spelman Rockefeller Fund. I found myself en-

gaged in research without the preparation a re-
searcher is supposed to have. I couldn't answer if
asked about my "methods." In my research efforts, however, I did have two resources that could
be put to good use—a capacity for interviewing and
a capacity for reporting what I had seen and heard.
Still, even after the publication of *The Hobo*, when I
was permitted to take the oral examination for my
Master's degree, I was not able to answer most of the
questions put to me. Apparently some of my answers must have amused the professors. When I
was called back into the room for the verdict, Professor Albion W. Small pointed to the street, "You
know your sociology out there better than we do, but
you don't know it in here. We have decided to take
a chance and approve you for your Master's degree."

To return to the story of *The Hobo*, I took a room
on Halsted Street near Madison, the heart of Hobohemia, and continued my research. Of the guidance
I received at the University of Chicago from Professors Robert E. Park and Ernest W. Burgess most was
indirect. The only instruction I recall from Park
was, "Write down only what you see, hear, and
know, like a newspaper reporter."

At last I had to write a report for the Chicago
agencies which had displayed interest in the study.
I had many "documents" but no idea how they might
be put into a report. The task was one of arranging
my materials into some sort of pattern. When I
delivered it to Park and Burgess for their review,
I had an unsure feeling because it seemed ordinary,
a little naked, and lacking in literary style. But
Park, usually slow to praise, put aside other work to
read it, and without my knowledge, even without my

thinking of such a possibility, interested the University in publishing the report.

Years later Pauline V. Young, writing about non-controlled participant observation as a field research method, described the author of this book as "an intimate participant observer of the life of the hobo on the road, in the 'jungle,' in lodging houses, at Hobohemia, at work and at Hobo College in Chicago. He identified himself with the life of the hobo for an extended period and gained insight into the inner life which would have been almost impossible had he not been able to eliminate social and mental distances through intimate participation."[1]

Although I appreciate the compliment, I must respond. Both Dr. Young and her husband were graduate colleagues at the University of Chicago when *The Hobo* was written. I think at that time that neither she nor I had ever heard the term "participant observation," yet at Chicago that type of research was gaining a vogue. While this method was faithfully followed in my work, it was not in the usual sense of the term. I did not descend into the pit, assume a role there, and later ascend to brush off the dust. I was in the process of moving out of the hobo world. To use a hobo expression, preparing the book was a way of "getting by," earning a living while the exit was under way. The role was familiar before the research began. In the realm of sociology and university life I was moving into a new role.

Perhaps we understand the hobo better today than in 1923, when this book was first published. For example, we have a better understanding of the

[1] Pauline V. Young, *Scientific Social Surveys and Research* (New York: Prentice-Hall, Inc., 1951), p. 203.

frontier, and the role of the hobo on the frontier is more clearly seen today. We need no longer think of the hobo as a problem, for he has just about disappeared. There are still the homeless, but the hobo has moved into frontier history. His counterpart may still be found in other new countries such as Australia, but the American hobo was unique.

Let me now use "hobo" in a collective sense and speak of the "typical hobo." The first observation is that he was American. The foreign-born who moved into that way of life were primarily Scandinavians, Germans, or from the British Isles. While most who entered hobodom moved out within a decade, the foreign-born turned even sooner to a settled existence.

The hobo was American in the same sense that the cowboy was. The cowboy emerged in frontier history for the same reason that the hobo did; there was a labor market need for him. The cowboy was a hobo type.

Again, the hobo was seldom an illiterate person. Even when illiteracy was high among urban and rural workers, the hobo was a newspaper reader and an ardent follower of the sport page. He had a higher degree of mental curiosity and cosmopolitan interest than most workers.

Apparently the hobo way of life was severely selective. Continuation in it called for a capacity to move from one type of work to another and from one place to another. Adapting to the strange and new in tools, work, machines, and scenes was for him a normal consequence of moving. Such resourcefulness was expected of all who went out into the wide areas.

Not uncommonly, the hobo would resolve that on the next job, if not on the present one, he would begin saving money. Each time he quit a job and took his money to a town, he was determined to spend carefully. He would buy clothes, eat well, sleep in a clean room, and take it easy. He would do some reading, see a few shows, and go to ball games. Only a few were able to realize such good intentions, especially if the first stop was made at a "barrel house." Usually all savings were gone by the second day. Then came a few days of begging, then a search for the next job. Few hoboes ever learned how to use leisure time.

The Industrial Workers of the World, with headquarters in Chicago's Hobohemia, was long identified as a hobo organizational activity. This is only partly true. Many hoboes carried "red cards"; most hoboes did not. This does not mean the hobo was antilabor; he was too much of an individual to feel comfortable in an organization whose control was distant. Groups of IWW "organizers" would ride freight trains during harvest time and throw off anyone who did not have a red card. Many would pay the dollar for a red card as insurance, but throw it away later. Perhaps they did the same the next year. Perhaps the only mass expression of hobo labor consciousness was the march of "Coxey's Army" following the depression of 1893. In economic depressions during the frontier period the hobo employed on development projects was usually the first to be dismissed. Significantly, the unemployed "armies" that started for Washington came from the Middle West and the Far West.

Chicago's Hobohemia was only one of several

well-known "main stems." Its counterpart was
found in St. Louis, Kansas City, Minneapolis, and
other western cities. Chicago, being the greatest
railroad center, had the largest Hobohemia. In New
York its counterpart was the Bowery, but the Bowery
was not primarily a hobo street, although an occasional hobo did get that far east. Just as the
private employment agencies, selling distant jobs,
were more numerous in Hobohemia, so the rescue
missions were more numerous on the Bowery.
Hobohemia was the great labor market where the
hobo spent or lost his earnings and started again on
the road. There he was met by the horde waiting for
a "live one": moochers and hangers-on who borrowed
or begged, gamblers and tricksters, procurers who
had prostitutes "working" for them, and a variety of
"jack rollers," who lived by robbing. The narcotic
handler could also be found, since an occasional hobo
was a "snowbird." The same leeching horde could
be found on the Bowery, but much more money
circulated in Hobohemia.

Of Hobohemia's places where the hobo ate or
slept or found religion nothing needs to be added
here. Such institutions continue, whether the hobo
is there or not. It must be kept in mind, however,
that the descriptions in this book are for 1921 and
1922. At that time Hobohemia was brighter and
livelier. Workingmen who were not hoboes would
go there to spend an evening. They found in Hobohemia a type of "downtown" atmosphere with all the
friendly anonymity one might wish as well as any
contact one might desire.

For twenty years I have carried a card announcing that I am a "Knight of the Road," a member in

good standing of "Hobos of America, Inc." I was so honored by Supreme Knight Jeff Davis, "King and Emperor," in tribute to the author of *The Hobo*. But perhaps the only man to acquire anything like a leader role among American hoboes was Jacob S. Coxey. When he was leading the unemployed to Washington, he was "General," and he was never called a king. It was evident in his old age when I knew him that he liked to be called "General." It was reminiscent of a colorful episode in his life.

Finally, a word about "wanderlust," a term that stems from the writings of a German authority on vagrancy. I cannot now find the source, but I think it was a French authority who invented the term "dromomania." Either term seems to assume a type of pathology in chronic wandering. Each term assumes an inborn urge to be mobile, an inability to resist the pull of the road. As Robert W. Service wrote of hoboes, "Theirs is the curse of the gypsy blood, and they don't know how to rest." From science to poetry, this explanation of wandering is heard again and again. But if we use wanderlust to explain the hobo's mobility, it would be difficult not to explain other types of mobility in the same way. On the American scene mobility was imperative, else the frontier would still be wilderness. It was a real asset for the hobo.

Americans are beginning to recognize that the frontier was much more than the movement of land settlement from the east toward the west, a rush to appropriate the natural resources. There was a second frontier which also moved westward, two decades or so behind the first, and it followed in the wake of railroad building. Its main characteristics were the founding of towns and cities and the establishment of the major industries needed to exploit the natural resources taken from the land, the forests, and the mines. This second frontier brought in waves of population, filling the spaces between widely dispersed settlements. It also brought streams of immigrants who did not settle on the land but found industrial jobs in the towns and cities. They were content, for a time, to work for low wages, and the hours were long. They filled the poverty-level slums. The first frontier reached the Pacific about 1850, the second about thirty years later. The first began to die about 1890, while the spread of the second was being completed in 1920.

The first of these frontiers was one of amazing discovery, romantic adventure, and challenge to initiative. Timber and ranch lands were gobbled up and extensive mineral claims staked out. Men of imagination founded settlements which often became towns bearing their names. These westward waves usually found excitement and adventure but seldom wealth. The great majority worked for others. They worked and wandered, carrying their beds on their backs. They were the first hoboes. Their number multiplied when railroad building began and when other types of firm structuring were needed. They worked in places where no labor supply existed.

The true hobo was the in-between worker, willing to go anywhere to take a job and equally willing to move on later. His in-between role related to the two frontiers. He came on the scene after the trail blazer, and he went off the scene as the second frontier was closing. We can hardly overestimate the im-

portance of his interim role.   His kind of labor was
going out of demand at the time *The Hobo* was written.   Migratory workers were still needed, and still
are in agriculture, but they have been drawn from
other sources of supply.   They no longer belong to
Hobohemia.

With the moving of more people to the land, the
big ranches began to disappear.   The wide empire of
the migrating cowboy was broken into thousands of
fragments.   Mining camps depending on a mobile
labor force have since become mining towns with a
permanent labor supply within walking distance.
The same applies to the old-style lumber camps.
Certain kinds of seasonal work, like ice harvesting,
have been eliminated by technological change.   The
harvesting combine in the grain fields reduced the old
rush each summer to the harvest.   Extra workers
are still needed to move the crops, but the demands
are much less compelling than before.

While the hobo reflected the mobility tradition,
his occupation made mobility a virtue.   Distant
jobs were always calling to him, and if no job beck-
oned, he went looking for it.   Going from place to
place, he followed the railroads.   Highway travel
was too pedestrian.   If he had to walk, it was along
the railroad track, and only to the next water tank
where he waited for a freight train.   His kind of
mobility belonged to an era which was his own.
When the automobile came in, he began to disappear.   With the coming of the automobile, mobility
did not diminish, but it took another form, making
it possible for more people to become more mobile.
The migrating family is now as evident as the migra-

tory man once was; only the pattern of mobility has
become more complex.[2]

Americans are clearly the most mobile of Western
peoples. They are the most mobile residentially,
as they move from one house to another. They are
the most mobile in moving from place to place, between city and country, between city and suburb,
between city and city, and between region and region.
They are the most mobile professionally, changing
from one job to another or from one kind of work to
another. They are the most mobile socially, in
their movement upward or downward from one
social class to another. The hobo moved also in
keeping with this tradition of mobility and may have
contributed to it.

Once I attempted to list the reasons why the in-
habitants of Hobohemia were in that almost womanless section. I asked questions about several individuals: Who they were, what they did or had done,
the circumstances leading them to that area. I
tried to determine if there was logic in their arrival
and presence there. I tried to trace the road, the
chain of events that brought them there. I found
that each had arrived in Hobohemia by a different
route.

In each of these cases arrival in Hobohemia had
been preceded by a different series of events (defeats
and disappointments). For some it was an interim
station, for others the point of a new beginning, but
for many the end of the road. In the competitive,

<hr>

[2] See Nels Anderson, *Men on the Move* (University of Chicago Press,
1938). This is a study of the new migrancy, but it is not fully representative because its chief concern is the migration caused by the Great Depression.

complex way of modern life, Hobohemia served a different purpose for each of its habitants. Some have proposed abolishing Hobohemia as a slum, but the many roads that lead to such a place as Hobohemia would still have to terminate at a common point.

Hobohemia, as I tried to describe it, belonged to a great variety of types. After a fashion they could be classified, and I attempted to do that, but my attention was mainly on the hobo. He was still the important figure on the scene in 1921–22. Hobohemia then belonged more to him than to certain other types. He shared the area in a bigger way than they could. He did not make Hobohemia, but he brought to it a unique type of cosmopolitanism. While utilizing the area, he also brought color and life to it.

It is clear now, although it was not recognized fully at the time, that the hobo was on his way out. That was fully understood by Jacob S. Coxey, but what he said—"The old timers will not be here much longer"—as we once walked through Madison Street did not have as much meaning then. He had in mind the types who had made up his "army" three decades earlier.

Since the hobo has moved on, this Introduction is my tribute to him. Whatever his weaknesses, and I knew them full well, I present him as one of the heroic figures of the frontier. With his work and help the railroads were built, out-of-the-way mines were developed, and outpost towns were established.

EDITOR'S PREFACE

THE present volume is intended to be the first of a series of studies of the urban community and of city life. The old familiar problems of our communal and social life—poverty, crime, and vice—assume new and strange forms under the conditions of modern urban existence. Inherited custom, tradition, all our ancient social and political heritages—human nature itself—have changed and are changing under the influence of the modern urban environment.

The man whose restless disposition made him a pioneer on the frontier tends to become a "homeless man"—a hobo and a vagrant—in the modern city. From the point of view of their biological predispositions, the pioneer and the hobo are perhaps the same temperamental type; from the point of view of their socially acquired traits, they are something quite different.

The city, more than any other product of man's genius and labors, represents the effort of mankind to remake the world in accordance with its wishes, but the city, once made, compels man to conform to the structure and the purposes he himself has imposed upon it. If it is true that man made the city, it is quite as true that the city is now making man. That is certainly a part of what we mean when we speak of the "urban" as contrasted with the "rural" mind. In any case, it is true that within the circle of these two tendencies, man's disposition, on the one hand, to create a world in which he can live, and, on the other, to adapt himself to the world which he himself has created, all, or most all of the problems and the processes are included with which the student of society is positively concerned. These processes go on, and these problems arise everywhere that men, coming together in order to live, find themselves compelled to carry on a common and communal life. In cities, however, and particularly in great cities, where social life is more intense than elsewhere, the processes produce new and strange effects, and the problems are more poignant and pressing.

A changing population of from 30,000 to 75,000 homeless men in Chicago, living together within the area of thirty or forty city blocks, has created a milieu in which new and unusual personal types flourish and new and unsuspected problems have arisen.

If the city were to be identified, as it sometimes has been, with its mere physical structure, its buildings, streets, street railways, telephones, and other communal efficiencies; if the city were, in fact, a mere complex of mechanical and administrative devices for realizing certain clearly defined purposes, the problem of the city would be one of engineering and of administration merely. But this takes no account of human nature; it takes no account of what we have come to refer to in industry as the "problem of personnel." At least it seems to assume that the individual men and women for whom these organized agencies—economic, social, and political—exist, and by whom they are conducted, remain, in all their varied associations and

relations, practically the same. Recent observation, on the other hand, has led to the conclusion
that human nature, as we ordinarily understand it,
while it is based on certain fundamental but ꜜot
clearly definable human traits and predispositions,
is very largely a product of the environment, and
particularly the human environment in which the
individual happens to find himself. That means
that every community, through the very character of
the environment which it imposes upon the individuals that compose it, tends to determine the personal
traits as it does determine the language, the vocation,
social values, and, eventually, the personal opinions,
of the individuals who compose it.

It isthe purpose of this and the succeeding studies
in this series to describe the changes that are taking
place in the life of the city and its peoples, and to
investigate the city's problems in the light of these
changes, and conditions of life generally of urban
people.   For this reason, this study of the "homeless
man" has sought to see him, first of all, in his own
habitat; in the social milieu which he has created
for himself within the limits of the larger community by which he is surrounded, but from which
he is, in large part, an outcast.

It is interesting to notice that within the area of
his own social environment, the hobo has created, or
at least there has grown up in response to his needs, a
distinct and relatively independent local community,
with its own economic, social, and social-political
institutions.

It is assumed that the study here made of the
"Hobohemia" of Chicago, as well as the studies that
are being planned for other areas and aspects of

the city and its life, will at least be comparable with the natural areas and the problematic aspects of other American cities. It is, in fact, the purpose of these studies to emphasize not so much the particular and local as the generic and universal aspects of the city and its life, and so make these studies not merely a contribution to our information but to our permanent scientific knowledge of the city as a communal type.

ROBERT E. PARK

COMMITTEE'S PREFACE

THE Committee on Homeless Men was organized by the Executive Committee of the Chicago Council of Social Agencies on June 16, 1922, to study the problem of the migratory casual worker. Its members included men and women in contact with the problem of homeless men from different points of view.

Mr. Nels Anderson, a graduate student in sociology in the University of Chicago, was selected to make the study. Mr. Anderson was already thoroughly familiar with the life of the migratory casual worker. He had shared their experiences "on the road" and at work, and had visited the Hobohemian areas of many of the large western cities. In the summer of 1921, he made a study of 400 migrants. Early in 1922, through the generous assistance and encouragement of Dr. William A. Evans, Dr. Ben L. Reitman, and Joel D. Hunter, he began a study of homeless men in Chicago, in connection with a field-study course at the University of Chicago.

The assumption of this study by the Chicago Council of Social Agencies, in co-operation with the Juvenile Protective Association, enabled an enlargement of its scope.[1]

The object of this inquiry, from the standpoint of the Committee, was to secure those facts which would enable social agencies to deal intelligently with the problems created by the continuous ebb and flow,

[1] A part of the investigation relating to the effects upon the boy of association with tramps, especially made for the Juvenile Protective Association, is not included in this report, but will appear in an early number of the *Journal of the American Institute of Criminal Law and Criminology.*

out of and into Chicago, of tens of thousands of foot-loose and homeless men. Only through an understanding both of the human nature of the migratory casual worker, and of the economic and social forces which have shaped his personality, could there be devised any fundamental program for social agencies interested in his welfare.

Earlier studies of the migratory casual workers in the United States have been limited almost entirely to statistical investigation. In the present inquiry a more intensive study of cases was decided upon in preference to an extensive statistical survey. For the past twelve months Mr. Anderson lived in Hobohemia, and in a natural and informal way secured upward of sixty life-histories, and collected, in addition, a mass of documents and other materials which are listed in Appendix B. Mr. Anderson has had, in certain parts of the field work, the assistance of C. W. Allen, L. G. Brown, G. F. Davis, B. W. Bridgman, F. C. Frey, E. H. Koster, G. S. Sobel, H. D. Wolf, and R. N. Wood, students in sociology at the University of Chicago, and has utilized the results of past studies of this subject by students in the department.

The Committee on Homeless Men held many meetings which were devoted to outlining the plan of investigation, to reports upon the progress of field work, and to the drafting of the findings and recommendations which appear as Appendix A.

The Committee and the author are indebted to the social agencies and to the many persons who co-operated in furnishing data for this investigation. They desire also to express their appreciation to Professor Robert E. Park for the inclusion of this volume as the first of a series of studies on the urban community of which he is editor, and for his services in the preparation of the manuscript for publication.

ERNEST W. BURGESS, *Chairman*
University of Chicago

WILFRED S. REYNOLDS, *Secretary*
Director, Chicago Council of Social Agencies

BRIGADIER JOHN E. ATKINS
Salvation Army, Workingman's Palace

MISS JESSIE BINFORD
Juvenile Protective Association

MRS. JOSEPH T. BOWEN
Juvenile Protective Association

FREDERICK S. DEIBLER
Advisory Board, Illinois Free Employment Service

T. ARNOLD HILL
Chicago Urban League

JOEL D. HUNTER
United Charities of Chicago

M. J. KARPF
Jewish Social Service Bureau

GEORGE B. KILBEY
Chicago Christian Industrial League

REV. MOSES E. KILEY
Central Charity Bureau

BRIGADIER DAVID MILLER
Salvation Army

DR. BEN L. REITMAN
Chicago Department of Health

WILLOUGHBY G. WALLING
President, Chicago Council of Social Agencies

TABLE OF CONTENTS

PART I. HOBOHEMIA, THE HOME OF
THE HOMELESS MAN

LIST OF ILLUSTRATIONS xv

CHAPTER

I. HOBOHEMIA DEFINED 3
II. THE JUNGLES: THE HOMELESS MAN ABROAD . 16
III. THE LODGING-HOUSE: THE HOMELESS MAN AT
HOME 27
IV. "GETTING BY" IN HOBOHEMIA 40

PART II. TYPES OF HOBOS

CHAPTER

V. WHY DO MEN LEAVE HOME? 61
VI. THE HOBO AND THE TRAMP 87
VII. THE HOME GUARD AND THE BUM 96
VIII. WORK 107

PART III. THE HOBO PROBLEM

CHAPTER

IX. HEALTH 125
X. SEX LIFE OF THE HOMELESS MAN 137
XI. THE HOBO AS A CITIZEN 150

PART IV. HOW THE HOBO MEETS
HIS PROBLEM

CHAPTER

XII. PERSONALITIES OF HOBOHEMIA 171
XIII. THE INTELLECTUAL LIFE OF THE HOBO . . . 185
XIV. HOBO SONGS AND BALLADS 194
XV. THE SOAP BOX AND THE OPEN FORUM . . . 215
XVI. SOCIAL AND POLITICAL HOBO ORGANIZATION . . 230
XVII. MISSIONS AND WELFARE ORGANIZATIONS . . . 250

APPENDIXES

A. SUMMARY OF FINDINGS AND RECOMMENDATIONS . . 263
B. DOCUMENTS AND MATERIALS 278
C. BIBLIOGRAPHY 287

INDEX 293

LIST OF ILLUSTRATIONS

A Jungle Camp 10

Summer Resorting behind Field Museum, Chicago . 10

Hobo Institutions on One Street along the Main
Stem 15

A Dining-Room on the "Main Stem". 34

Employment Bureaus 34

Leaders in the Educational Movement. 35

A Popular Resort in Hobohemia 35

Dr. Ben L. Reitman 172

Members of the Jefferson Park Intelligentsia . . 173

The Hobo Reads Progressive Literature 173

The Soap-Box Orator—The Economic Argument . . 216

An Outdoor Mission Meeting—The Religious Plea . 216

James Eads How 217

A Free Lunch at a Mission 258

A Winter's Night in a Mission 258

PART I

HOBOHEMIA, THE HOME OF THE HOMELESS MAN

CHAPTER I
HOBOHEMIA DEFINED

All that Broadway is to the actors of America, West Madison is to its habitués—and more. Every institution of the Rialto is paralleled by one in West Madison. West Madison Street is the Rialto of the hobo.

The hobos, themselves, do not think of Madison Street as the Rialto; they call it "The Main Stem," a term borrowed from tramp jargon, and meaning the main street of the town. "The Main Stem" is a more fitting term, perhaps, than the Rialto, but still inadequate. West Madison Street is more than a mere Rialto, more than the principal hobo thoroughfare of Chicago. It is the Pennsylvania Avenue, the Wilhelmstrasse of the anarchy of Hobohemia.—From an unpublished paper on the hobo by Harry M. Beardsley, of the *Chicago Daily News*, March 20, 1917.

A SURVEY of the lodging-house and hotel population, supplemented by the census reports of the areas in which they live, indicates that the number of homeless men in Chicago ranges from 30,000 in good times to 75,000 in hard times.

We may say that approximately one-third of these are permanent residents of the city. The other two-thirds are here today and gone tomorrow. When work is plentiful they seldom linger in the city more than a week at a time. In winter when jobs are scarce, and it takes courage to face the inclement weather, the visits to town lengthen to three weeks and a month. From 300,000 to 500,000 of these migratory men pass through the city during the course of a normal year.

A still larger number are wanderers who have spent their days and their strength on the "long, gray road" and have fled to this haven for succor. They are Chicago's portion of the down-and-outs.

An investigation of 1,000 dependent, homeless men made in Chicago in 1911 indicated that 254, or more than one-fourth of the 1,000 examined, were either temporarily crippled or maimed. Some 89 of this 1,000, or 9 per cent, were manifestly either insane, feeble-minded, or epileptic. This did not include those large numbers of border-line cases in which vice or an overwhelming desire to wander had assumed the character of a mania.

Homeless men are largely single men. Something like 75 per cent of the cases examined were single, while only 9 per cent admitted they were married.

"MAIN STEMS"

Every large city has its district into which these homeless types gravitate. In the parlance of the "road" such a section is known as the "stem" or the "main drag." To the homeless man it is home, for there, no matter how sorry his lot, he can find those who will understand. The veteran of the road finds other veterans; the old man finds the aged; the chronic grouch finds fellowship; the radical, the optimist, the crook, the inebriate, all find others here to tune in with them. The wanderer finds friends here or enemies, but, and that is at once a characteristic and pathetic feature of Hobohemia, they are friends or enemies only for the day. They meet and pass on.

Hobohemia is divided into four parts—west, south, north, and east—and no part is more than five minutes from the heart of the Loop. They are all the "stem" as they are also Hobohemia. This four-part concept, Hobohemia, is Chicago to the down-and-out.

THE "SLAVE MARKET"

To the men of the road, West Madison Street is the "slave market." It is the slave market because here most of the employment agencies are located. Here men in search of work bargain for jobs in distant places with the "man catchers" from the agencies. Most of the men on West Madison Street are looking for work. If they are not seeking work they want jobs, at least; jobs that have long rides thrown in. Most of the men seen here are young, at any rate they are men under middle age; restless, seeking, they parade the streets and scan the signs chalked on the windows or smeared over colored posters. Eager to "ship" somewhere, they are generally interested in a job as a means to reach a destination. The result is that distant jobs are in demand while good, paying, local jobs usually go begging.

West Madison, being a port of homeless men, has its own characteristic institutions and professions. The bootlegger is at home here; the dope peddler hunts and finds here his victims; here the professional gambler plies his trade and the "jack roller," as he is commonly called, the man who robs his fellows, while they are drunk or asleep; these and others of their kind find in the anonymity of this changing population the freedom and security that only the crowded city offers.

The street has its share also of peddlers, beggars, cripples, and old, broken men; men worn out with the adventure and vicissitudes of life on the road. One of its most striking characteristics is the almost complete absence of women and children; it is the most completely womanless and childless of all the city areas. It is quite definitely a man's street.

West Madison Street, near the river, has always been a stronghold of the casual laborer. At one

time it was a rendezvous for the seamen, but of late
these have made South Chicago their haven. Even
before the coming of the factories, before family life
had wholly departed, this was an area of the homeless man. It will continue to be so, no doubt, until
big businesses or a new union depot crowds the hobo
out. Then he will move farther out into that area
of deteriorated property that inevitably grows up
just outside the business center of the city, where
property, which has been abandoned for residences,
has not yet been taken over by businesses, and where
land values are high but rents are low.

Jefferson Park, between Adams and Monroe and
west of Throop Street, is an appanage of the "slave
market." It is the favorite place for the "bos" to
sleep in summer or to enjoy their leisure, relating
their adventures and reading the papers. On the
"stem" it is known as "Bum Park," and men who
visit it daily know no other name for it. A certain
high spot of ground in the park is generally designated
as "Crumb Hill." It is especially dedicated to
"drunks." At any rate, the drunk and the drowsy
seem inevitably to drift to this rise of ground. In
fact, so many men visit the place that the grass
under the trees seems to be having a fierce struggle
to hold its own. It must be said, however, that the
men who go to "Bum Park" are for the most part
sober and well behaved. It is too far out for the
more confirmed Madison Street bums to walk. The
town folks of the neighborhood use the park, to a
certain extent, but the women and children of the
neighborhood are usually outnumbered by the men
of the road, who monopolize the benches and crowd
the shady places.

HOBOHEMIA'S PLAYGROUND

The thing that characterizes State Street south of the Loop is the burlesque show. It is here that the hobo, seeking entertainment, is cheered and gladdened by the "bathing beauties" and the oriental dancers. Here, also, he finds improvement at the hands of the lady barbers, who, it is reported, are using these men as a wedge to make their way into a profitable profession that up to the present time has belonged almost wholly to men.

South State Street differs from West Madison in many particulars. For one thing there are more women here, and there is nothing like so complete an absence of family life. The male population, likewise, is of a totally different complexion. The prevailing color is an urban pink, rather than the rural grime and bronze of the man on the road. There are not so many restless, seeking youngsters.

Men do not parade the streets in groups of threes and fours with their coats or bundles under their arms. There are no employment offices on this street. They are not needed. Nobody wants to go anywhere. When these men work they are content to take some short job in the city. Short local jobs are at a premium. Many of these men have petty jobs about the city where they work a few hours a day and are able to earn enough to live. In winter many men will be found in the cheap hotels on South State, Van Buren, or South Clark streets who have been able to save enough money during the summer to house themselves during the cold weather. State Street is the rendezvous of the vagabond who has settled and retired, the "home guard" as they are rather contemptuously referred to by the tribe of younger and more adventurous men who still choose to take the road.

The white man's end of the south section of Hobohemia does not extend south of Twelfth Street. From that point on to about Thirtieth Street there is an area that has been taken over by the colored population. Colored people go much farther south, but if there are any homeless men in the "Black' Belt," they are likely to be found along State Street, between Twenty-second and Thirtieth. The Douglas Hotel, in this region, is a colored man's lodging-house.

To the south and southwest are the railroad yards. In summer homeless men find these yards a convenient place to pass the night. For those who wish to leave the city, they are the more accessible than the yards on the north and west. The railroad yard is, in most places, one of the hobo's favorite holdouts. It is a good place to loaf. There are coal and wood and often vacant spaces where he can build fires and cook food or keep warm. This is not so easily done in Chicago where the tramp's most deadly enemy, the railroad police, are numerous and in closer co-operation with the civil authorities than in most cities. In spite of this, hobos hang about the yards.

"BUGHOUSE SQUARE"

On the north side of the river, Clark Street below Chicago Avenue is the "stem." Here a class of transients have drifted together, forming a group unlike any in either of the other areas of Hobohemia. This is the region of the hobo intellectuals. This area may be described as the rendezvous of the thinker, the dreamer, and the chronic agitator.

Many of its denizens are "home guards." Few
transients ever turn up here; they do not have time.
They alone come here who have time to think,
patience to listen, or courage to talk. Washington
Square is the center of the northern area. To the
"bos" it is "Bughouse Square." Many people do not
know any other name for it. This area is as near
to the so-called Latin Quarter as the hobo dare come.
"Bughouse Square" is, in fact, quite as much the
stronghold of the more or less vagabond poets,
artists, writers, revolutionists, of various types as of
the go-abouts. Among themselves this region is
known as the "village."

Bohemia and Hobohemia meet at "Bughouse
Square." On Sundays and holidays, any evening,
in fact, when the weather permits, it will be teeming
with life. At such times all the benches will be
occupied. On the grass in the shade of the trees
men sit about in little groups of a dozen or less.
The park, except a little corner to the southeast
where the women come to read, or knit, or gossip,
while the children play, is completely in possession
of men. A polyglot population swarms here.
Tramps, and hobos—yes, but they are only scat-
teringly represented. Pale-faced denizens of the
Russian tearooms, philosophers and enthusiasts
from the "Blue Fish," brush shoulders with kindred
types from the "Dill Pickle," the "Green Mask,"
the "Gray Cottage." Free-lance propagandists who
belong to no group and claim no following, non-
conformists, dreamers, fakers, beggars, bootleggers,
dope fiends—they are all here.

Around the edges of the Square the curbstone
orators gather their audiences. Religion, politics,

science, the economic struggle, these are the principal themes of discussion in this outdoor forum. Often there are three or four audiences gathered at the same time in different parts of the park, each carrying on a different discussion. One may be calling miserable sinners to repent, and the other denouncing all religion as superstition. Opposing speakers frequently follow each other, talking to the same audience. In this aggregation of minds the most striking thing is the variety and violence of the antipathies. There is, notwithstanding, a generous tolerance. It is probably a tolerance growing out of the fact, that, although everyone talks and argues, no one takes the other seriously. It helps to pass the time and that is why folks come to "Bughouse Square."

To the hobo who thinks, even though he does not think well, the lower North Side is a great source of comfort. On the North Side he finds people to whom he can talk and to whom he is willing to listen. Hobos do not generally go there to listen, however, but burning with a message of which they are bound to unburden themselves. They go to speak, perhaps to write. Many of them are there to get away from the sordidness of life in other areas of Hobohemia.

A "JUNGLE" ON THE LAKE FRONT

Grant Park, east of Michigan Avenue, is a loafing place for hobos with time on their hands. They gather here from all parts of Hobohemia to read the papers, to talk, and to kill time. For men who have not had a bed it is a good place to sleep when the sun is kind and the grass is warm. In the long

A JUNGLE CAMP—THE "BOS" HID FROM THE CAMERA

SUMMER RESORTING BEHIND FIELD MUSEUM, CHICAGO

summer evenings Grant Park is a favorite gathering place for men who like to get together to tell yarns and to frolic. It is a favorite rendezvous for the boy tramps.

The section of Grant Park facing the lake shore is no less popular. Along the shore from the Field Museum northward to Randolph Street the homeless men have access to the lake. They take advantage of the unimproved condition of the park and make of the place, between the railroad tracks and the lake, a retreat, a resort, a social center. Here they wash their clothes, bathe, sew, mend shoes.

Behind the Field Museum, on the section of the park that is still being used as a dump for rubbish, the hobos have established a series of camps or "jungles." Here, not more than five minutes from the Loop, are numerous improvised shacks in which men live. Many men visit these sections only for the day. To them it is a good place to come to fish and they spend hours gazing at the water and trying to keep the little fish from biting.

WHY MEN COME TO CHICAGO

The hobo has no social centers other than the "stem," and the "jungle." He either spends his leisure in the "jungles" or in town. The "jungle" ordinarily is a station on his way to town. Life revolves for him around his contacts on the "stem," and it is to town he hies himself whenever free to do so.

Few casuals can give any reason for the attraction that the city has for them. Few have ever considered it. The explanations they give, when pressed for reasons, are more or less matter of fact and center in their material interests. Other motives, motives of which they are only half conscious, undoubtedly influence them.

The city is the labor exchange for the migratory worker and even for the migratory non-worker who is often just as ambitious to travel. When he is tired of a job, or when the old job is finished, he goes to town to get another in some other part of the country. The labor exchanges facilitate this turnover of seasonal labor. They enable a man to leave the city "on the cushins." This is the lure that draws him to the city. Hobohemia brings the job-seeking man and the man-seeking job together. Migrants have always known that a larger variety of jobs and a better assortment of good "shipments" were to be had in Chicago than elsewhere.

Chicago is the greatest railway center in the United States. No one knows these facts better than the hobo. It is a fact that trains from all points of the compass are constantly entering. and leaving the city over its 39 different railways. According to the *Chicago City Manual*, there are 2,840 miles of steam railways within the city limits. The mileage of steam railroad track in Chicago is equal to the entire railroad mileage in Switzerland and Belgium, and is greater than the steam railroad mileage found in each of the kingdoms of Denmark, Holland, Norway, and Portugal. Twenty-five through package cars leave Chicago every day for 18,000 shipping points in 44 states.

The termination of the seasonal occupations brings men cityward. They come here for shelter during the winter, and not only for shelter but for inside winter work. This is the hobo's only alternative, provided he cannot go to California or to one of the southern states. The dull routine of the inside job, which seemed so unattractive in the springtime, looks better with the falling of the temperature.

We may add, also, that many of the men who are attracted to the city in winter are not particularly interested in work. There are, however, among the improvident tramp class, "wise virgins" who save in the summer in order to enjoy the life of a boarding-house during the winter.

The hobo often goes to town for medical attention. For the sick and injured of the floating fraternity Chicago is a haven of refuge because of the large number of opportunities found here for free treatment. The county hospital, the dispensaries, and the medical colleges are well known to these men. Many get well and go their way, others get no farther than the hospital—and then the morgue.

A man whose income is limited to a few hundred dollars a year can do more with it in the large city than in a small town. In no other American city will a dollar go farther than in Chicago. It is not uncommon to find men living in Hobohemia on less than a dollar a day. Large numbers make possible cheap service, and cheap service brings the men.

THE PROBLEM DEFINED IN TERMS OF NUMBERS

Not only the extent, but the nature of the problem of the homeless man is revealed by a study of his numbers. In Chicago all estimates are in substantial agreement that the population of Hobohemia never falls below 30,000 in summer, doubles this figure in winter, and has reached 75,000 and over in periods of unemployment.[1]

[1] Mrs. Solenberger's figures of more than a decade ago put the number of the various types of homeless men in this city at 40,000–60,000:

"No exact census of the total number of homeless men of various types in the lodging-house districts of Chicago has been taken, but 40,000 is considered a conservative estimate by several careful students of the question who are closely in touch with local conditions. This number is somewhat increased at

These numbers, while large, are only between 1
and 2½ per cent of Chicago's population of nearly
3,000,000. Homeless men, however, are not distributed evenly throughout the city; they are concentrated, segregated, as we have seen, in three
contiguous narrow areas close to the center of
transportation and trade.

This segregation of tens of thousands of foot-
loose, homeless, and not to say hopeless men is the
fact fundamental to an understanding of the problem. Their concentration has created an isolated
cultural area—Hobohemia. Here characteristic
institutions have arisen—cheap hotels, lodging-
houses, flops, eating joints, outfitting shops, employment agencies, missions, radical bookstores, welfare
agencies, economic and political institutions—to

---

election times and very greatly increased when word goes out, as it did during
the winter of 1907–8, that relief funds were being collected and free lodgings
and food would be furnished to the unemployed. In December, January,
February, and March of that winter all private lodging-houses were filled to
overflowing, and the Municipal Lodging House, its annex, and two other houses
which it operated gave a total of 79,411 lodgings to homeless men as compared
with 6,930 for the same months of the winter before, an increase of 72,481.
The Health Department, which took charge of the municipal lodging-houses
and made a careful study of local conditions during the winter of 1907–8, estimated the number of homeless men then in Chicago to be probably not less
than 60,000."—One Thousand Homeless Men, p. 9, n.

Nearly if not quite one-fifth of the 700 hotels in Chicago cater to the
migratory and casual worker. The 63 hotels visited by investigators in this
study had a total capacity for the accommodation of 15,000 men. On the basis
of these figures, it seems safe to put the total capacity of the hotels in Hobohemian
areas at 25,000–30,000. A like number of men are probably provided for in
nearby boarding- and lodging-houses. Thousands of other men sleep at the
docks, in engine rooms, in vacant houses, in flophouses, or in summer in the parks.

The returns of the 1920 United States census show that in the three wards
of the city in which Hobohemian areas are located there are 28,105 more male
than female residents. This figure indicates that the so-called "home guard"
numbers about 30,000, the summer population of Hobohemia.

The Jewish Bureau of Social Service estimates that the number of homeless men in Chicago at any one time in the winter of 1921–22 was 120,000.
This figure, which seems high when compared with estimates arrived at by other
methods of calculation, assumes that the proportion of homeless men for the
city is the same as that for the Jewish community.

minister to the needs, physical and spiritual, of the homeless man. This massing of detached and migratory men upon a small area has created an environment in which gamblers, dope vendors, boot-leggers, and pickpockets can live and thrive.

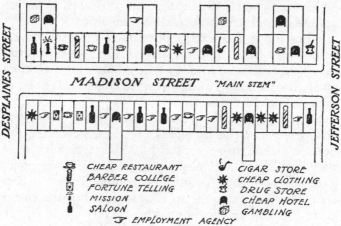

HOBO INSTITUTIONS ON ONE STREET ALONG "MAIN STEM"

The mobility of the migratory worker complicates the problem of the missions, police, and welfare agencies. The mission measures its success not only in numbers of converts but in the numbers of men fed and lodged. The police department, on the contrary, alarmed by the influx of hobos and tramps in response to free meals and free flops, has adopted a policy of severity and repression for the protection of the community. Welfare agencies, opposing alike the demoralizing results of indiscriminate feeding and lodging, and the negative policy of the police, favor a program of organized effort based upon an investigation of the needs of each individual case.

CHAPTER II
THE JUNGLES: THE HOMELESS MAN ABROAD

IN THE city, under ordinary circumstances, the homeless man gathers with his kind. Even so he is very much alone and his contacts with his fellows are relatively formal and distant.

City life is interesting but full of danger. Even in a world where the conditions of life are so elementary, prudence dictates a certain amount of reserve and hence formality and convention in the relations of men. The flophouse and the cheap hotel compel promiscuity, but do not encourage intimacy or neighborliness. On the outskirts of cities, however, the homeless men have established social centers that they call "jungles," places where the hobos congregate to pass their leisure time outside the urban centers. The jungle is to the tramp what the camp ground is to the vagabond who travels by auto. It has for the hobo, perhaps, greater significance, since it becomes a necessary part of his daily life. The evening camp fire for the tourist, on the contrary, is a novelty merely, an experience but not a necessity.

LOCATION AND TYPES OF JUNGLES

Jungles are usually located in close proximity to a railroad division point, where the trains are made up or where trains stop to change crews and engines. Sometimes they are located near a "tank town," where occasional stops are made for water or fuel. Not infrequently they are near the intersection of railroad lines. In the South, and on the West Coast, jungles are often located along the highways. This is due to the fact that many men go South in winter not to work but to escape the rigors of the northern climate. The railroad for the time being has no attraction for them and they are content to stroll abroad, seeing the country. In the West, where men frequently carry bedding and cooking equipment, they can camp anywhere. It is easier for them, therefore, to leave the railroad and venture along the highways.

Accessibility to a railroad is only one of the requirements of a good jungle. It should be located in a dry and shady place that permits sleeping on the ground. There should be plenty of water for cooking and bathing and wood enough to keep the pot boiling. If there is a general store near by where bread, meat, and vegetables may be had, so much the better. For those who have no money, but enough courage to "bum lumps," it is well that the jungles be not too far from a town, though far enough to escape the attention of the natives and officials, the town "clowns."

Jungle camps may be divided into two classes— the temporary and the permanent, or continuous. Temporary jungles are merely stop-over or relay stations inhabited intermittently by the men of the road. Men temporarily stranded in a town usually seek a secluded spot at the edge of a village, not too far from the railroad, where they may while away the time without being molested. Men on the road look for places where other men preceding them have camped. There they are likely to find pots and kettles in which to cook food or wash clothes. At points where trains stop frequently, making it possible for men to get away at any time, the population of a temporary jungle is likely to be larger and more permanent.

The continuous or permanent jungles are seldom deserted, at least in summer. There is usually some-one there to keep the fire burning and usually there are men or boys occupied at various tasks—cooking, washing or boiling clothes, shaving, sewing, bathing, and reading.

Women are often found in the areas of the cities where the homeless men congregate but not in the jungles. Here is an institution where the hobo is his own housewife. He not only cooks his own food, but has even invented dishes that are peculiar to jungle life. Chief among these is "mulligan" stew. "Mulligan," or "combination," is a "throw together" of vegetables and meat. There are certain ideal mixtures of vegetables and meat, but the tramp makes "mulligan" from anything that is at hand. Onions, potatoes, and beef are the prime essentials. Some men become adept at frying and roasting over camp fires.

The hobo who lives in the jungles has proved that he can become domesticated without the aid of women. He has established the habit of keeping his clothes and person clean. It is not difficult to select from a group of transients the men who have just come from the jungles. Their clothes will be clean and even bear evidence of jungle sewing. Overalls that have seen service will be bleached almost white from numerous washings. The hobo learns here the housewife's art of keeping pots clean and the camp in order. The man who cannot, or will not, learn these few elementary principles of housekeeping is likely to fare ill in the jungle.

If it is a warm day some men will be sleeping. They may have been riding trains all night or have found the night too cold for sleep. A daily paper from an adjoining town may be going the rounds. There may be newspapers from different cities brought in by men traveling different directions. Travelers meeting this way have much of common interest to talk about and conversation is enlivened with discussions of questions of concern to "bos." The jungle is always astir with life and movement, and the hobo enters into this life as he does no other. Here he turns his back on the world and faces his fellows, and is at ease.

Absolute democracy reigns in the jungle. The color line has been drawn in some camps, but it is the general custom, and especially in the North, for Negroes, Mexicans, and whites to share the same jungle. The jungle is the melting pot of trampdom.

The average man of the road has had a variety of experience and not a little adventure. In the jungles there is always an audience for anyone who wants to talk, whether of his thoughts, his experiences, or his observations. There is plenty of opportunity to tell stories. The art of telling a story is diligently cultivated by the "bos" in the assemblies about the fire. This vagabond existence tends to enrich the personality and long practice has developed in some of these men an art of personal narrative that has greatly declined elsewhere. Many of them develop into fascinating *raconteurs* in the literal as well as the literary sense of the term. Talk in the jungle is of the open road and the day to come, and in that there is sufficient matter to occupy them.

Jungle populations are ever changing. Every hour new faces appear to take the place of those that have passed on. They come and go without cere-

mony, with scarcely a greeting or "fare-you-well."
Every new member is of interest for the news he
brings or the rumors that he spreads. Each is
interested in the other so far as he has something to
tell about the road over which he has come, the work
conditions, the behavior of the police, or other significant details. But with all the discussion there is
seldom any effort to discuss personal relations and
connections. Here is one place where every man's
past is his own secret.

Only in the case of very young boys or sick men
and sometimes old men is there any effort to learn
something of the individual's past. Men will brush
elbows in the jungles for days and even weeks without ever learning one another's names. They live
closed lives and grant others the same privilege.

THE LAWS OF THE JUNGLE

In every permanent camp there is likely to be a
permanent group that makes the camp its headquarters. Sometimes these groups are able to take
possession and exploit the transient guests. The
I.W.W. has at times been able to exclude everyone
who did not carry the red card of that organization.
As a rule, however, the jungle is extremely hospitable
and democratic.

The freedom of the jungles is, however, limited by
a code of etiquette. Jungle laws are unwritten, but
strictly adhered to. The breaking of these rules, if
intentional, leads to expulsion, forced labor, or physical punishment.

Jungle crimes include (1) making fire by night in jungles
subject to raids; (2) "hi-jacking" or robbing men at night
when sleeping in the jungles; "buzzing," or making the jungle

a permanent hangout for jungle "buzzards" who subsist on
the leavings of meals; (4) wasting food or destroying it after
eating is a serious crime; (5) leaving pots and other utensils
dirty after using; (6) cooking without first hustling fuel; (7)
destroying jungle equipment. In addition to these fixed offenses
are other crimes which are dealt with as they arise. Men are
supposed to use cooking cans for cooking only, "boiling up"
cans for washing clothing, coffee cans to cook coffee, etc. After
using, guests are expected to clean utensils, dry them, and
leave them turned bottom side up so that they will not fill with
rainwater and rust. They are expected to keep the camp clean.
To enforce such common-sense rules, self-appointed committees
come into existence.[1]

Exclusive camps are usually the result of the
efforts of the older residents to enforce discipline.
Most "jungle buzzards," men who linger in the
jungles from season to season, take an interest in
the running of things. For the most part they are
parasitic, begging food from others, but they are
generally on the alert to keep the place clean and
orderly.

The following description of a day in the jungles
was written by a migratory worker, a man who knows
the life from years of experience. His narrative presents a faithful picture of an average day in an
average jungle.

A Day in the Jungles

1.[2] This jungle is on the edge of a strip of timber. A stream
fed from a spring runs into the lake near by. The empty box

---

[1] It is interesting here to note that there is a striking parallel between the
rules of the jungles and the rules of cow camps and other camps of the hills. It
is the custom of the cow men of the west to maintain camps in the hills which
are stocked with provisions and equipped with utensils and furnishings. These
camps are usually left open and anyone who passes is welcome to spend the
night, provided he puts the place in order when he leaves.

[2] The documents from which extracts have been taken are numbered
consecutively in the text. For complete list of documents used in each chapter
see pp. 281–88.

cars on the railroad siding close by offer protection against rain
and a place to sleep. Half a mile away is the junction of two
railroads where all trains stop, and a mile and a half further on
is a small town.

At one o'clock in the morning a few men step off a freight
train. One speaks up: "Does anyone know if there is a jungle
in this place?" "Yes," someone answers, "The jungle is up
in that direction," pointing towards a woods, "but what's the
use in going over there now? You can't build a fire at this time
of night. I am going to hunt up a box car for a flop."

After a moment of silence someone else asks, "Any town
close by?" "Yes, there it is," replies another, pointing to
some lights showing in the distance. The men form groups
according to acquaintance and talk in a low tone. "Come on,
let us hunt up a place to flop till daylight." The different
groups start off. One starts out for the town, one goes towards
the box cars, and one makes for the jungles. I was with the
group bound for the jungles.

A hundred feet from the railroad right-of-way under the
darkness of big trees we see three or four dying camp fires.
Around one fire we can see the shadows of men. Some are
sitting on the butts of logs, smoking or dozing; others are
stretched out on the ground sound asleep.

The new arrivals walk up to the fire, look over the bunch to
find, perhaps, some old acquaintances. Then some of us find
seats or lie down; others, with as little noise as possible, hunt
up cans which they fill with water and place over the glowing
coals. The men take ground coffee from packages in their
pockets and pour it into boiling water. The feed is open to
everybody. Bread and sausage are brought out; even sugar
is passed around as long as it lasts. The men eat in silence.
Each one takes the utensils he used and walks to the creek to
wash them. Nearly all of the men then lie down, but some
leave. Nobody asks anyone about himself and nobody says
"hello" or "goodbye."

Daylight comes. The breaking of sticks for firewood is
heard. Fires are started, cooking utensils are chosen. The law
of the jungle is that no one can call a vessel his except at the
time he uses it. Packages and receptacles are opened revealing
food of all kinds. Eating commences. If any man with more
than enough for himself sees someone else not eating, it is

etiquette to offer to share with his neighbor. If the other man accepts the offer, he thereby takes upon himself the responsibility of cleaning the dishes.

At any time men will be seen leaving the jungles to hustle food, or to get wood, or to catch trains. Anytime is eating time in the jungles and someone is always bringing in "chuck" that he has bought or "bummed." Talking goes on as long as the daylight lasts. Heated arguments often develop. Papers and pamphlets are distributed, union cards are taken out; business meetings are held to decide policies and actions, how to get the next meal or how to win the battle between labor and capital.

About ten o'clock in the morning two townsmen displaying stars come into the jungle. One of them tells the men that they will have to clean out because people are kicking. A holdup has been committed in town the night before and they intend to prevent any more from being committed, "So you fellers have to leave."

One man in the jungles speaks up and tells the officers that we are not holdup men, that we are getting ourselves something to eat, and that we have got to have some place to do that. "We have paid for everything. What would you do if you was in our place; go into town and get pulled and let the town feed us?"

The officer looks nonplussed, but curtly replies, "Well, I am going by orders." After that he walks away. The timid men leave the jungle. The others reply by roundly cursing indiscriminately all their enemies. They are town clowns, sky pilots, Bible ranters, bulls, politicians, home guards, hicks, stool pigeons, systems, scissor bills, and capitalists. Incidentally they advocate strikes, rebellion, mass action, complete revolution of the political system, abolishment of the wage system.

It is close to twelve o'clock. Fires are replenished, cans, pots and pans are put into service. Plans are being made in anticipation of a coming raid by the police. At two o'clock, someone suggests a song. After a fiery song of the class struggle, a speech follows advising the men to organize.

By three o'clock only about fifteen or twenty are left in the jungle. The officer followed by townsmen armed with guns return. Some of the hobos retreat into the woods. Those remaining are ordered to hold up their hands with "You damn bums" added to the command. Some comply, others refuse.

One even has the courage to shout, "Go ahead and shoot, you damn cowards." This starts a general shooting into every pot, pan and can in sight. The men scatter.

After the invaders leave, an inventory is immediately made to assess the damage. Since the utensils in best condition had been hidden in the brush, no serious loss to the jungle has resulted.

By four o'clock the story of the raid has traveled and men come in from all directions. The decision of the majority is to remain in the jungle over night. Food is brought in and preparations for supper begin. The men are doubling up to cook together. Those belonging to certain unions have as many as eight or ten in a bunch. There are from thirty to forty angry men in camp by now and more are coming in. There is some talk of revenge.

By six o'clock supper is well under way. Several fires are burning. Containers of every description are used to cook in; broken shovels and tie plates are used to fry on, empty tobacco tins are used as cups, and tomato cans serve as fry pans, soup kettles and soap dishes. Potatoes are roasted on the coals, wires are bent upon which to broil meat. All are still talking excitedly of the clash with the police.

While some of the men are busily engaged in cooking, others are sewing and mending their clothes or shoes, and still others are shaving. Now and then as at breakfast someone will shout, asking if anybody wants some spuds or a piece of punk or a piece of "gut" (sausage); and usually there is an affirmative answer. After supper, pans and cans are cleaned out, the paper is read and passes the rounds. Already it is growing dark, and the hunt begins for dry sleeping places.

Suddenly a commotion is started; a man is roughly rushed into the open. He is a hi-jack caught in the act of robbing a fellow who was sleeping, a greater crime in the jungle than an open hold up. Cries of "Burn the ——" and "Let us hang him!" are heard from all sides. A council is hurriedly called, a chairman is selected, motions are made with amendments and substitutes. After a short discussion a vote is taken to give him a whipping. The man is tied to a tree facing toward it. His back is bared, and men are called for to apply punishment. No one steps forward; everybody declines to apply the strap or stick.

Another council is called but before they get started a young
fellow has declared his willingness to fight the hi-jack to a
finish because he knew him and didn't like him anyway. The
proposition is accepted. The hi-jack is more than ten pounds
heavier than the challenger; but whether from fear or not, for
he knows that the challenger has the crowd back of him to a
man, the hi-jack is slow to start. Perhaps he feels that the
crowd will give him a beating whether he wins or not. He soon
loosens up but he does not show the goods. The "bo" is more
than a match for him but the hi-jack does not give up easily.
He displays some courage but the "bo" fights like a madman
and strikes the hi-jack blow after blow. The fight lasts more
than ten minutes before the hi-jack is completely knocked out.

After he gets to his feet he is given a chance to wash his face
and stick paper on the cuts; then he is "frisked," that is, ordered
to donate all but one dollar to the jungle. Then he is sent out
of camp with orders not to show up in any of the diggings along
the line for it would be murder if anyone should spot him.

By eleven o'clock the excitement is over. Different men
announce that they were headed for so and so and that the
freight starts at such a time. To this someone replies that he
is going that way too so they start off together. Others walk
back among the trees to the places where they have prepared
to sleep. Others who have insufficient clothes to stand the
night chill bunch up around the glowing camp fires. Soon
everything is quiet except for an occasional sound out of the
darkness of men mumbling in conversation. Occasionally the
sound of groans and snores or sighs, or curses are heard. These
betray the dreams of men living like hunted animals.

I look at my watch and note that it is near midnight and
that all is over for the night, so I curl up on some papers beside
a bed of coals.[1]

THE MELTING POT OF TRAMPDOM

The part played by the jungles as an agency of
discipline for the men of the road cannot be over-
estimated. Here hobo tradition and law are formu-
lated and transmitted. It is the nursery of tramp

[1] Written by A. W. Dragstedt, secretary in 1922 of the "Hobo College" of
Chicago.

lore. Here the fledgling learns to behave like an
old-timer. In the jungles the slang of the road and
the cant of the tramp class is coined and circulated.
It may originate elsewhere but here it gets recognition. The stories and songs current among the men
of the road, the sentiments, the attitudes, and the
philosophy of the migratory laborer are all given due
airing. In short, every idea and ideal that finds
lodgment in the tramp's fancy may be expressed here
in the wayside forum where anyone who thinks may
speak, whether he be a jester or a sage.

Suspicion and hostility are the universal attitudes
of the town or small city to the hobo and the tramp.
Accordingly, the so-called "floater" custom of passing vagrants on to other communities is widespread.[1]
The net effect of this policy is to intensify the anti-
social attitude of the homeless man and to release
and accentuate criminal tendencies. The small town
is helpless to cope with the situation. As things
are, its action perhaps cannot be different. Agriculture, as it becomes organized upon a capitalistic
basis, is increasingly dependent upon seasonal labor,
in harvesting crops for example. The report of the
Commission on Industrial Relations states:

> The attempts to regulate movements of migratory workers
> by local organizations have, without exception, proved failures.
> This must necessarily be true no matter how well planned or
> well managed such local organizations may be. The problem
> cannot be handled except on a national scale and by methods
> and machinery which are proportioned to the enormous size
> and complexity of the problem.[2]

[1] For a discussion of the practice of "floating" with reference to the treatment of misdemeanants, see Stuart A. Queen, *The Passing of the County Jail.*

[2] *Final Report*, p. 158.

CHAPTER III
THE LODGING-HOUSE:
THE HOMELESS MAN AT HOME

HOBOHEMIA is a lodging-house area. The accommodations it offers the homeless man range from a bed in a single room for fifty cents to location on the floor of an empty loft for a dime. Lodging-house keepers take thin profits but they serve large numbers. There are usually more men than there are beds, particularly in winter. An estimate indicates that all hotels are full from December to May. During the rest of the year they are likely to be filled to two-thirds of their capacity.

Chicago has known three types of cheap hotels: the so-called "barrel-house," the welfare institution, and the business enterprise. The first, the barrel-house, was a rooming-house, saloon, and house of prostitution, all in one. Men with money usually spent it in the barrel-houses. There they found warmth and companionship. They would join the circle at the bar, buy drinks for the crowd, and have a good time. Men who were afraid of being robbed placed their money with the bartender and charged against it the drinks purchased. As soon as they were overcome by drink they would be taken upstairs to bed. The following day the program would be repeated. A three- or four-hundred-dollar stake at this rate usually lasted a week. Not infrequently the barrel-house added to its other attractions the opportunity for gambling.

The barrel-house is a thing of the past. Its place has been taken in part by hotels like the Working-

men's Palace; the Reliance; the New Century, owned
and operated by the Salvation Army; the Rufus F.
Dawes, owned and maintained by General C. G.
Dawes; the Popular Hotel, owned and maintained
by the Chicago Christian Industrial League. In
places of this sort, charges are small, usually not
enough to cover operating expenses.

The Rufus F. Dawes and the Workingmen's
Palace are both large, fire-proof structures, clean and
modern, constructed originally for other purposes.
Like all paternalistic, quasi-charitable institutions,
however, they are not popular, although the charges
for a room and bed are hardly sufficient to cover the
operating expenses. This is the second type of
lodging-house.

The pioneers in the cheap hotel business in Chicago operated on a commercial basis were Harvey and
McGuire, the founders of the well-known Harvey-
McGuire hotel system. Harvey, an evangelist, in his
work with the "down-and-outs" had learned the
evils of barrel-houses. He went into a partnership
with McGuire, a man acquainted with the rough
side of life. After a number of years the Harvey-
McGuire system went out of existence. McGuire
went into the hotel business for himself and now owns
a number of cheap lodging-houses. Harvey sold his
interests to his nephew and went back to evangelistic
work. The nephew went into partnership with Mr.
Dammarell. There are eight hotels in the present
Harvey-Dammarell system with a combined capacity
for lodging 3,000 men. The Ideal opened in 1884,
probably the oldest men's hotel in the city, originally
known as the Collonade, at 509 West Madison Street,
is an example of the type. The Mohawk, the most

modern men's hotel, is also the property of the Harvey-Dammarell system.

The men who run these hotels do not claim to be philanthropists. Mr. Harvey has defined the situation. He says:

We are in the hotel business to make a living. We give the men the best service they can pay for. We give nothing away and we ask nothing. Consequently, we do not lay ourselves open to criticism. We insist on order and sobriety and we usually get it. We hold that the men have a right to criticize us and come to us if they are not satisfied with the service we give. That is business. The man who pays seventy-five cents for a bed has a right to seventy-five cents' worth of service. If a man can only pay twenty-five cents for a bed he is entitled to all that he pays for and is entitled to kick if he doesn't get it.

Different types of hotels attract different types of men. The better class of workingmen who patronize the Mohawk, where the prices range from forty to seventy cents, wear collars and creased trousers. The hotel provides stationery and desks. Hotels where the prices range from twenty-five cents to forty cents are patronized by a shabbier group of men. Few of them are shaven. Some of them read, but most of them sit alone with their thoughts. In some second-class places a man is employed to go the rounds and arouse the sleepers.

In the twenty-five-cent hotels, the patrons not only are content to sit unshaven, but they are often dirty. Many of them have the faces of beaten men; many of them are cripples and old men. The exceptions are the Popular and the Rufus F. Dawes, where the price is twenty cents or less to be sure, but the guests are more select. Since these places are semi-charitable, they can force certain requirements upon their patrons.

The term "room" is a misnomer when applied to a sleeping apartment in a cheap hotel. These rooms have been aptly termed "cubicles," and among the patrons they are known as "cages." A cubicle is usually from 6 to 8 feet in width and from 8 to 12 feet in length. The thin walls, composed of steel or matched lumber, are usually about 8 feet in height. A wire netting over the top admits air and prevents the guests climbing from one cubicle to another. The furnishings are simple; sometimes only a bed, sometimes a bed and a chair, and in more expensive places a stand. They are not constructed either for comfort or convenience; lighting and ventilation are usually bad. But they are all they were intended to be: places for men to sleep with a limited degree of privacy.

A canvass of the Hobohemian hotels has been made with a view to learning the approximate mobility of the hotel population. Few of these hotels are prepared to make any but general statements, though some of them have made an effort to get the facts. The consensus of opinion of hotel clerks is that the greatest turnover is in the cheapest hotels. Better-class places like the Acme, the Ironsides, and the Workingmen's Palace have a large proportion of permanent guests. The permanent guests, those who remain two or three months or more, range from a third to a half of the total number of roomers. Many of the older hotels have permanent patrons who are seasonal but regular. Others never leave the city.

THE "FLOPHOUSE"

"Flophouses" are nearly all alike. Guests sleep on the floor or in bare, wooden bunks. The only

privilege they buy is the privilege to lie down somewhere in a warm room.

2. "Hogan's Flop" is known from coast to coast among
hobos. A tramp who has been in Chicago long enough to learn
of Lynch's place, the Workingmen's Palace, Hinky Dink's, or to
eat doughnuts in missions has heard of Hogan's.

The first "Hogan's Flop" was located on South State Street.
Later it moved to the West Side and for some time was on Meridian Street. Since it left Meridian Street it has been located in
several places. The original Hogan, who was a Spanish-
American War veteran, has passed to his reward. Only his name
remains. Every winter, however, someone starts a "flop" and
it invariably inherits the name and fame of Hogan. Hogan is
now a myth, a sort of eponymous hero. A tramp discussing this
matter said: "Hogan may be dead but the bugs that were in
business with him are still on the job. They follow this joint
wherever it goes. You know when they moved from Meridian
Street it wasn't three days before the bugs got the new address
and followed us."

The following account is adapted from a description of a night spent in "Hogan's Flop":

3. I spent the evening at the Bible Rescue Mission where
sincere folks were pleading with men of the road to come forward
and make things right with the Master. Two came forward
and it was a time of rejoicing. They prayed and sang and fed
us rolls and coffee, and to those who had no bed for the night they
gave tickets to "Hogan's." They offered me a ticket but I
thanked them and assured them that I still had a little money.

You have to know where "Hogan's" is to find it. In the
spring of 1922, it occupied the second and third floors of a building at 16 South Desplaines Street. A narrow, shaky stairs, a
squeaky door, a feebly lighted entrance, a night clerk who demands a dime and you are within. You may take your choice of
sleeping on this floor or go on up to the third. There is no difference in the price. I chose the second floor. It was less crowded.
The fire, from a large heater in the center of the room, was
warmer.

The men around the stove had evidently been exposed to the
elements. One was drying his shoes for it had rained all day.

Another was drying his shirt. Two were engaged in listless conversation. Others were silent. The air was stuffy, the light dim.
I walked around the room looking for a place to lie down. Dozens
of men were sleeping on the floor with their heads to the wall.
Some were lying on paper, others on the bare floor. Some were
partly covered by their overcoats; some had no overcoats. It
is an art to curl up under an overcoat. One man of fifty years
or more had removed his shirt and trousers and was using the
latter for a pillow. He had tied his shoes to his trousers which is
evidence that he knew "flop" house ethics. When men sleep in
box cars they sometimes use their shoes for pillows but this is not
necessary in "Hogan's." A planking around the walls affords
a resting place for weary heads.

A number of the faces here I had seen a great many times on
the "stem." Two were old men in their seventies who had been
in the city several years and were mendicants most of the time.
There was a one-legged man whom I had seen chumming with
another one-legged man on the streets. Both peddled lead
pencils and shoestrings. On the only cot on the floor, two young
fellows were lying. They were sleeping with their heads at
opposite ends of the narrow bed and their bodies were entangled
to prevent their falling off.

I found a vacant place on the floor where I could have about
two feet between myself and my nearest neighbor so I spread my
papers and lay down. I had more paper than I needed so I gave
half to another man who was just circling about for a place to go
to bed. I asked the man nearest me if the bugs bothered much.
He answered in the richest of Irish brogues that Hogan's bugs
were sure efficient. Another man chimed in. He said they were
better organized than the German army. How well organized
they were I can't say but I was not long in learning that they
were enterprising.

Two men near me engaged in a discussion about the economic
conference at Genoa. One man had very positive, orderly ideas
of how things should go. The other interrupted occasionally
only to agree. Someone wanted to know why he didn't hire a
hall. Then there was silence, except for snores. I never heard
such a variety of snores but none of them seemed to suggest
peaceful slumbers or pleasant dreaming. Once the snores were
broken into by some man bawling out, "Hey, you; quit spittin'
over this way; you're gettin' it on my paper." "Well, dammit;

How much room do you want to take up?" His neighbor retorted, "It's none of your —— business how much room I take. You lay off'n that spittin', see."

More snores. A man got up, stretched, rubbed his legs, came to the center of the room to the stove. More snores. Some men came in, paid their dimes and looked for an opening on the floor. A man ran to the toilet to vomit. A wag called to him to "heave it up."

After an hour or so I felt something on my hand. I crushed it. There were others to be seen on the white papers. I lay down to try to sleep again. A second attack brought me suddenly to my feet. I lay down resolved a third time not to be disturbed. My companions seemed to be suffering more from the hard floor than anything else; and the floor was hard. I turned my thoughts to the hardness of the floor at "Hogan's."

How long I dozed I can't say but I awoke marveling at the endurance of the man of the road. While I pondered thus a man jumped to his feet and hastened out. He was cursing the bugs and saying that he knew an engine room that had this "place beat all hollow." I felt better. Someone else had weakened first. I got up and started home. It was two-thirty.

RESTAURANTS AND LUNCHROOMS

Hobohemian restaurants serve meals for a half or a third of the prices current in the Loop. In some of these lunchrooms the charges are so low that one marvels. However, the food is coarse and poor and the service rough and ready.

The homeless man is as casual in his eating as he is in his work. He usually gives all the restaurants a trial. If he has any money when meal time comes he generally does a little "window shopping." He meanders up and down the street reading the bills of fare in the windows. The Hobohemian restaurants know this and accordingly use window displays to attract the roaming patron. Food is placed in the windows, cooking is done within sight of the street, but the chief means of attraction are the menus

chalked on the windows. The whole window is
sometimes lettered up with special entrées of the day.
Some of these bills of fare are interesting.

Gus's place on South Halsted Street near the
Academy Theater, July 28, 1922, displayed the
following:

Pig's Snouts and Cabbage or Kraut......	15c	Pig's Feet and Potato Salad.............	15c
Corn Beef Hash......	10c	Beef Stew and Kraut..	15c
Hamburger Roast....	10c	Sausage and Mashed Potatoes...........	15c
Liver and Onions.....	15c	Roast Beef...........	20c
Hungarian Goulash...	20c	Roast Pork..........	25c
Pig's Shank and Cabbage..............	15c	T-Bone Steak........	30c
Spare Ribs and Cabbage	20c		

The same day the James Restaurant on Madison
Street near Desplaines advertised the following under
the caption, "A Full Meal for Ten Cents":

Veal Loaf............	10c	Sausage and Mashed Potatoes..........	10c
Sardines and Potato Salad.............	10c	Brown Hash and One Egg...............	10c
Hamburger and One Egg...............	10c	Liver and Brown Gravy.............	10c
Baked Beans.........	10c	Salt Pork Plain.......	10c
Liver and Onions.....	10c	Salmon and Potato Salad.............	10c
Corn Beef Plain......	10c		
Macaroni Italian.....	10c		
Three Eggs any Style	15c	Corn Flakes and Milk	5c
Kidney Stew........	10c	Four Eggs any Style..	20c

One eating-house on West Madison Street is
"The Home Restaurant, Meals Fifteen Cents and
Up." This is a popular appeal. Restaurants fre-
quently advertise "Home Cooking," "Home Made
Bread," "Home Made Coffee," "Doughnuts Like
Mother Used to Make."

A DINING-ROOM ON THE "MAIN STEM"

EMPLOYMENT BUREAUS OFFER OPPORTUNITY FOR
TRAVEL

LEADERS IN THE EDUCATIONAL MOVEMENT AMONG
THE HOBOS

A POPULAR RESORT IN HOBOHEMIA

At meal time, especially at noon, scores of men flock into these eating-houses. The men, a noisy and turbulent crowd, call out their orders, which are shouted by the waiters to the cooks who set out without ceremony the desired dishes. Four or five waiters are able to attend to the wants of a hundred or more men during the course of an hour. The waiters work like madmen during the rush hours, speeding in with orders, out with dirty dishes. During the course of this hour a waiter becomes literally plastered with splashes of coffee, gravy, and soup. The uncleanliness is revolting and the waiters are no less shocking than the cooks and dishwashers. In the kitchens uncleanliness reaches its limit.

But what is the opinion of the patron? They know that the hamburger is generally mixed with bread and potatoes, that the bread is usually stale, that the milk is frequently sour. There are few who do not abhor the odors of the cheap restaurant, but a steady patron reasons thus: "I don't allow myself to see things, and as long as the eyes don't see the heart grieves not."

OUTFITTING STORES AND CLOTHING EXCHANGES

The hobo seldom dresses up. If he does it is evidence that he is making an effort to get out of his class. When he does buy clothing, either rough clothing or a good "front," he finds his way to places where new clothes are on sale at astonishingly low prices. The seasonal laborer's outfitters handle a very cheap grade of goods. Much of it is out of date and either shopworn or soiled. Cheap clothing stores are not peculiar to Hobohemia, but here they cater to the wants of the homeless man.

Clothing exchanges, which is a polite term for second-hand clothing stores, are numerous in Hobohemia.   There are many of them along North Clark Street and west of Clark on Chicago Avenue.   These establishments make a specialty of buying slightly worn clothing, sample suits and overcoats from broken lots, which they sell at remarkably low prices.

Second-hand clothing stores are not entirely monopolized by the hobo trade, but the veteran hobo knows of their existence and he knows how to drive a bargain.

The cobbler who deals in shoes, both second-hand and new, as a sideline, gets his share of the Hobohemian trade.   Coming off the road with a roll, the hobo is likely to invest in a whole outfit—shoes, suit, and overcoat—only to sell them again in a few days when he is broke.   The second-hand dealer meets him both ways, coming and going.

PAWN SHOPS

Pawn shops are not typical of Hobohemia.   They are usually located in that region just outside the limits of the lodging-houses, a sort of border land between respectability and the down-and-outs.   Not that the hobo is unwilling, when he is broke, to put anything valuable he happens to have in "hock," but usually he does not happen to have anything valuable.   Still there are men who make a practice of carrying a watch or a ring upon which, in case of need, they can raise a few dollars.

Pawn shops are, to a limited extent, clothing exchanges.   They are places where the hobo does much of his buying and selling of tools, fire arms, leather goods, jewelry, and like articles of that sort.

MOVIES AND BURLESQUES

Commercialized entertainment has had difficulty in getting a foothold in Hobohemia. The movie has firmly established itself on the border land, where it may be patronized by both the transient and the resident population. The movies put the admission fee at ten cents. As a matter of fact, there is one on South Halsted Street which charges only a nickel. The pictures shown in these houses have usually passed from the first-class theaters through the various grades of cheaper houses until finally they arrive here much out of date, badly scarred, and so scratched that they irritate the eyes.

Vaudeville and burlesque have become fully established on the South Side. Certain of these theaters cater to "men only." Advertisements of "classy girls," "bathing beauties," or "fancy dancing" have a strange attraction for the homeless and lonely men.

Many men in the Hobohemian population do not patronize either the movie or the burlesque. Those who do are sometimes merely looking for an opportunity to sit down in quiet for an hour. Some theaters, in recognition of this fact, extend an invitation to the audience to "Stay as Long as You Like." This draws a great many men, especially in cold weather.

BARBER COLLEGES AND BARBERS

Chicago has several barber colleges in close proximity to the "stem." Four of them are located on West Madison Street and most of them are so situated that they can attract men who are willing to submit to the inexperienced efforts of students.

Students must have practice, and here are men, who as they themselves say, can stand it.

The cheap rooming-houses do not always offer facilities for shaving, so they are willing to sacrifice themselves in the interest of education and art. If they are fortunate they may be served by a Senior, but they always are in danger of falling into the hands of a Freshman. Hair cuts cost ten or fifteen cents. This is governed by the law of supply and demand. The colleges must have patrons to keep the students busy. The lady barber flourishes in Hobohemia. The hobo, at least, seems to have no prejudice against a razor being wielded by feminine hands.

BOOKSTORES

Hobohemia has its bookstores where new and second-hand books are sold. The "Hobo Bookstore," sometimes called the "Proletariat," located at 1237 West Madison Street, is the best known. This place makes a specialty of periodicals of a radical nature which are extensively read by the "bos." A large line of books on many subjects are sold, but they are chiefly the paper-bound volumes that the transient can afford. The "Radical Book Shop," located on North Clark Street, is popular among the intellectuals who pass their time in "Bughouse Square."

SALOONS AND SOFT DRINK STANDS

The saloon still lives in Hobohemia, though with waning prestige. The five-cent schooner and the free lunch of pre-war days have passed, but the saloons are far from being dead. One can still get a "kick" out of stuff that is sold across the bar, but the crowds do not gather as before prohibition. Formerly, men who got drunk were kept inside, today they are hustled outside or at least kept out of sight. As the saloon has lost its prestige, the bootlegger has gained, and the "drunks" for which he is responsible parade the streets or litter the alleys.

Fruit and soft drink stands and ice-cream cone peddlers are in evidence since prohibition. Enthusiastic and persistent bootblacks swarm in the streets and Gypsy fortune-tellers who hail every passer-by for the privilege of "reading" his mind, and, perhaps, in order to turn a trick at his expense.

THE HOUSING PROBLEM

Standards of living are low in Hobohemia. Flops are unwholesome and unsanitary. Efforts have been made to improve these conditions, but they have not been wholly successful. The Salvation Army and the Dawes hotels have improved the lodging-houses. But the municipal free lodging-house has been opposed by the police on the ground that it was already too popular among casual and migratory workers. The same may be said of any other effort to deal with the problem from the point of view of philanthropy.

The only other alternative would seem to be to encourage the migratory workers to organize to help themselves. This is difficult but not impossible, but the history of these efforts is another chapter in the story of Hobohemia.

CHAPTER IV
"GETTING BY" IN HOBOHEMIA

A MAN who is conservative can live in Hobo-hemia on a dollar a day. If he is not too fastidious he can live for sixty cents, including a bed every night. Sleeping in a ten-cent "flop" and sticking to coffee and rolls, he can get along for fifty cents. Old men who do not move around much will live a long time on "coffee-an'," which they can get at the average restaurant for a nickel. The man who is reduced to "coffee-an'," however, has touched bedrock.

An old beggar who lingers about the Olive Branch Mission on South Desplaines Street claims that if he were guaranteed forty cents a day he could get on nicely. This would give him a bed every night and, as he says, a good bed is sometimes better than a meal.

The daily routine of this old man's life rarely takes him beyond the limits of a single block. On the south side of Madison Street, between 62 Desplaines Street and the Transedes Hotel, he is at home. All else is, for him, the open sea. When he ventures beyond the limits of this area into outlying territory he plans the trip the day before.

There are perhaps a hundred old men on South State and West Madison streets whose interests and ambitions have shrunk to the same unvarying routine and the same narrow limits.[1]

Every man who enters Hobohemia is struggling to live above the "coffee-an'" level, and the various devices that are employed in accomplishing this are often ingenious. This business of wringing from chance source enough money each day to supply one's insistent wants is known on the "stem" as "getting by." "Getting by" may mean anything from putting in a few hours a day at the most casual

[1] See Document 18.

labor to picking a pocket or purloining an overcoat. It includes working at odd jobs, peddling small articles, street faking, "putting over" old and new forms of grafts, "working" the folks at home, "white collar" begging, stealing, and "jack rolling."

WORKING AT ODD JOBS

In spite of all that has been said to the contrary, the hobo is a worker. He is not a steady worker but he earns most of the money he spends. There are migratory casual workers, who spend three or four months each year in a Chicago lodging-house, who never look to the public for assistance. They know how much money they will need to tide them over the winter, and they have learned to spread it thin to make it reach. Casual in their work, they are conservative in their spending.

There are others who are never able to save anything. No matter how much they bring to town they soon spend it. For these the odd job is the likeliest means of livelihood. In a city like Chicago there are almost always opportunities for men who are content to take small jobs. Every restaurant must have dishwashers and waiters. Every hotel needs porters; every saloon or pool hall employs men to do odd jobs. Petty as these jobs are and little as they pay, men not only take but seek them. One man who has been twenty years on West Madison Street is working as night clerk in a lodging-house; another does janitor work at nights and loafs daytime; still another has been for some time a potato peeler in a Madison Street restaurant.

Men who spurn steady jobs in favor of petty ones with pay every night sometimes do so because they

hate to leave the street.   Often it is because they are
not properly clad or have no money to pay their way.

PEDDLING A DEVICE FOR "GETTING BY"

In the eyes of the law, peddling in Chicago, at
least, is not begging.[1]   Nevertheless much of the
peddling in the streets is merely legalized begging.
Usually the articles offered for sale are cheap wares
which are disposed of for whatever "you care to
give."   Not infrequently the buyer gives four times
what the article is worth.   There are hundreds of
cripples in Chicago who gain a livelihood by selling
pencils or shoestrings.   Many of these are homeless men.   Pencils bought for thirty-five cents a
dozen retail for a dime, or whatever the purchaser
cares to tax himself.   A peddler's license is a protection against the police and serves as a moral prop to
the beggar.

A peddler of shoestrings and pencils usually
measures his success by the number of sales made
in which no change is asked.   He expects to be
overpaid.   Sometimes he persuades himself he is
entitled to be overpaid.   The business of "getting
by" by "touching hearts" is usually spoken of as
"work."   A peddler who works the North Side
will say: "I didn't work yesterday; the day before
I made three dollars and eighty-five cents."   This
man considers himself a *real* cripple, because he has
locomotor ataxia.   He is incensed when he meets a
one-armed peddler, because a man with one arm is
not a real cripple.   Real cripples should have first
consideration.   An able-bodied man who begs when

[1] The mayor's office issued about 6,000 free permits in 1922 to peddle
from house to house (not from wagon or cart), from basket or other receptacle,
only for a period of sixty days.

broke is beneath contempt. That is "panhandling" and an able-bodied "panhandler" is always considered despicable.

Many peddlers live in Hobohemian hotels, and spend their leisure on the "stem." When they go to "work" they take a car. Some of them have regular stands. Not infrequently a peddler will assume to monopolize a position in front of a church or near the entrance of a factory where girls go and come. Beggars have a liberal fund of knowledge about pay days. They know the factories where the workers, when they have money, are "good."

STREET FAKING

The chief difference between peddling and street faking is one of method. The peddler appeals to the individual; the faker appeals to the crowd. The faker is a salesman. He "pulls" a stunt or makes a speech to attract the crowd. The peddler is more than often a beggar. It requires considerably more initiative and force to play the rôle of a street faker than to peddle.

Almost any time of the day at some street corner of the "stem" one may see a faker with a crowd around him. His wares consist perhaps of combination sets of cuff buttons and collar buttons, or some other such "line." Success depends upon the novelty of the article offered. A new line of goods is much sought after and a good street faker changes his line from time to time. Many fakers are homeless men. Numbers of the citizens of Hobohemia have tried their hand at some time or other at this kind of salesmanship. Those who are able to "put it over" generally stay with the work.

Peddling jewelry is one old device for getting money, but it is not too old to succeed. There are men who carry with them cheap rings or watches which they sell by approaching the prospective buyers individually. Sometimes they gather a crowd around them but that rarely succeeds as well as when they work quietly. A faker may sit beside a man in a park or approach him on the street and proffer a ring or watch or pair of eyeglasses for sale cheap, on the grounds that he is broke. Sometimes he will pretend that he found the article and would like to get a little money for it. Often he will tell of some sentiment connected with an article that he is trying to dispose of. A man may have a ring that his mother gave him and he will only part with it on condition that he might have the privilege of redeeming it later. If he thought he could not redeem it he would rather starve than part with it, etc. Hobos are often the victims as well as the perpetrators of these fakes.

GRAFTS OLD AND NEW

Few of these tricks are new but none of them are so old that they do not yield some return. They probably owe their long life to the proverbial identity of fundamental human nature wherever it is found.

One of the most ancient and universal forms of deception is the fake disease. In Hobohemia a pretended affliction is called "jiggers" or "bugs."

4. L. J. appealed to the Jewish Charities with a letter signed by a doctor in a hospital in Hot Springs saying that he had treated L. J. who was suffering from syphilis and that his eyes were affected and he would "undoubtedly go blind." It was learned later that this letter was a forgery as were other credentials that the man carried. He had been in a hospital and had

been treated for a venereal disease. While there he familiarized himself enough with the terminology of the disease so that he could talk with some intelligence about his case. He would say with conviction, "I know I'm going blind before long." It further developed that he had been exploiting charity organizations in several cities. Before his entry upon this deception it was learned that he had earned a prison record.

An ancient ruse is to feign to be deaf and dumb. A man who played "deaf-and-dumb" worked restaurants, drug stores, groceries, and other places of business. He would enter the places and stand with cap in hand. Never would he change the expression of his face, regardless of what was said or done. When spoken to he would point to his ears and mouth until he received some money, and then he would bow. If there was a chance of getting something, he would never leave a place unless he was in danger of being thrown out. An investigator followed him for two hours before he learned he was neither deaf nor dumb. Three months later he met the same man working the same graft in another part of the city.

"The hat trick," as it is sometimes called, is a popular means of "getting by." On a Sunday, a holiday, or indeed any evening, the streets of Hobohemia are likely to be enlivened by men who have a message, haranguing the crowds. They may be selling papers or books on the proletarian movement. In any case, most of them terminate their speeches by passing the hat. Few speakers spend their eloquence on the audiences of Hobohemia without asking something in return. It must not be assumed that these men are all insincere. Many of them are, but most of them are in the "game" for the money it yields. One of these orators is conspicuous because his stock

in trade is a confession that he is not like the other
speakers. He admits that he is out for bed and
board. He will talk on any subject, will permit himself to be laughed at, and jollied by the crowd, but
when he passes the hat he usually gets enough for
another day's board.

The missions attract men who are religious primarily for profit. Many who are really sincere find
it more profitable to be on the Lord's side. Nearly
every mission has a corps of men who perform the
"hat trick" by going from house to house begging
old clothes or cash or whatever the people care to
give. The collector's conscience is the only check on
the amount of money taken in. Some missions
divide all cash collections with the solicitors. Sometimes the collector gets as much as fifty cents on the
dollar.

The exploitation of children is as old as the history
of vagrancy. Even the tramp has learned that on
the road boys may be used to get money. A boy
can beg better than an older man, and frequently
men will chum with boys for the advantages such
companionships give them. Boys who are new on
the road are often willing to be exploited by a veteran in exchange for the things they can learn from
him.

"WORKING THE FOLKS"

There is a type of tramp who lives on his bad
reputation. He may have been sent away for the
sake of the family, or have fled for safety, or he may
have gone voluntarily to start life anew. Seldom
does he succeed, but family pride stands between
him and his return. He capitalizes the fact that his
family does not want him to return.

Such a man resides on South State Street. He comes from a good family but his relatives do not care to have him about. He is fat and greasy and dirty; he seems to have no opinions of his own; is always getting into people's way and making himself disagreeable by his effort to be sociable. His relatives pay him four dollars a week to stay in Chicago. On that amount, with what he can earn, he is able to live.[1]

Another man raises funds now and then when he is broke by writing or telegraphing that he is thinking about returning home. His return means trouble. His requests for assistance are a kind of blackmail levied on the family.[2]

"WHITE COLLAR" BEGGING

Most interesting among the beggars is the man, the well-dressed and able-bodied individual, who begs on the strength of his affiliations. These are the men who make a specialty of exploiting their membership in fraterorgannal izations. Labor unions are very much imposed upon by men who carry paid-up cards but who are temporarily "down." The organizations as such are not appealed to as much as individual members. It is hard for a union man who is working to turn away a brother who shows that he is in good standing with the organization.

Of late the "ex-service-man" story has been a good means of getting consideration, and the American Legion buttons have been worked to the limit. Most of the men who wear parts of a uniform or other insignia indicative of military service have

[1] Unpublished Document 111.

[2] Unpublished Document 112.

really seen service and many have seen action, but a great many of them have heard more than they have seen.

There are men who make a specialty of "working" the charity organizations. Some of them are so adept that they know beforehand what they will be asked and have a stereotyped response for every stereotyped question. These men know a surprising amount about the inside workings of the charitable agencies and they generously hand on their information to their successor. They usually know, for example, what material aid may be had from each organization. A typical case is that of Brown.

5. Brown had not been in Chicago an hour until he had located the chief organizations to which he might go for help. He knew that he could check his bag at the Y.M.C.A. He learned where to go for a bath, where to get clean clothes, how to get a shave and haircut and he actually succeeded in getting some money from the United Charities. He was able to "flop" in a bed even though he came to town without money late in the afternoon; whereas many other men in the same position would have been forced to "carry the banner." He knew about the charity organizations in all the cities he had visited from the Atlantic to the Pacific. After his case was traced it was learned that he told about the same story wherever he went and that he was known in organizations in all the cities to which he referred. He is 27 years old and has been living for the most part in institutions or at the expense of organizations since he was 13.

6. Another case is that of P. S., a Jewish boy who made his way between New York and Chicago three times and received accommodation at the Jewish charity associations in nearly every big city on his road between here and New York. He is a mental case and goes to the Charities because of a sense of helplessness. Since the last contact with him that the Chicago Jewish charities have had he has learned to get over the country with a little more confidence but he never fails to hunt up the welfare organization as soon as he comes to town. He was last heard of in California.

BORROWING AND BEGGING

Nearly every homeless man "goes broke" at times. Some of them do not feel that a trip to town has been a success if they return to the job with money in their pockets. On the other hand, they do not feel that they have had their money's worth unless they remain in town a week or two after they have "blown in." As they linger they face the problem of living. They may have friends but that is unusual. The homeless man used to get advances from the saloon keeper with whom he spent his money. Such loans were often faithfully made good, but they were just as often "beat." Prohibition has put an end to that kind of philanthropy.

Many of the men who visit the city intermittently loaf and work by turns. These men often beg but they do not remain at it long, perhaps a day or so, or until disgust seizes them. Often when they beg they are drunk or "rum-dum." As soon as they are sober they quit. Sometimes they succeed in attaching themselves to a friend who has just arrived with a "roll." But living at the expense of another migrant quickly palls. Soon they will be found scanning the "boards" for free shipment to another job. They disappear from the streets for a season. As soon as they get a "stake," however, they will be seen again treating the boys and swapping stories on the "main stem"; if not in Chicago, then in some other city. It is the life.

The more interesting types are those who live continuously in the city and are broke most of the time. Some of them have reduced the problem of "getting by" to an art. The tramp who only occasionally goes "broke" may try to imitate these

types but he soon tires of the game and goes to work.
The chief classes of beggars are the "panhandlers"
and the "moochers."

The "panhandler" can sometimes extract from
the pockets of others what amounts to large sums of
money. Some "panhandlers" are able to beg from
ten to twenty dollars a day. The "panhandler" is
a beggar who knows how to beg without loss of
dignity. He is not docile and fawning. He appeals
in a frank, open manner and usually "comes away
with the goods." The "moocher" begs for nickels
and dimes. He is an amateur. He goes to the back
door of a house or hotel and asks for a sandwich.
His appeal is to pity.

The antagonisms between beggars and peddlers are
very keen. The man who carries a permit to peddle
has no respect for the individual who merely begs.
Nevertheless, some peddlers, when business is slow,
themselves turn beggars. On the other hand, the
man who begs professes to consider himself far more
respectable than the peddler who uses his license as
an excuse to get money. This is the language and
opinion of a professional: "Good begging is far more
honorable than bad peddling and most of this shoe-
string and lead pencil peddling is bad. I am not
going to beat around the bush. I am not going to do
any of this petty grafting to get enough to live on."[1]
These antagonisms are evidence of a struggle for
status. When a peddler denounces the beggars he
is trying to justify himself. His philosophy, like
most philosophies, is an attempt to justify his vocation. The same is true of plain beggars. Most of
them are able to justify their means of "getting by."

[1] Unpublished Document 113.

STEALING

Hobos are not clever enough to be first-class crooks nor daring enough to be classed as criminals. Yet most of them will steal something to eat. There are men who are peculiarly expert at stealing food from back-door steps—pies or cakes that have been set out to cool, for example. There are men who wander about the residential areas, in order to steal from back doors. Some men follow the milkman as he goes from door to door delivering milk and cream, in order to steal a bottle when the opportunity offers. A quart of milk makes an excellent breakfast.

Stealing becomes serious when men break into stores and box cars. It is not what they take but what they spoil that does the damage. This is the chief complaint of the railroad against the tramp. In the country the tramp is often destructive to the orchards he visits. He will shake down more fruit than he can possibly use and dig up a dozen hills of potatoes to get enough for a "mulligan."

"JACK ROLLING"

"Jack rolling" may be anything from picking a man's pocket in a crowd to robbing him while he is drunk or asleep. On every "stem" there are a goodly number of men who occasionally or continually "roll" their fellow-tramps. Nearly every migrant who makes periodical trips to the city after having saved his earnings for three or four months can tell of at least one encounter with the "jack roller." Scarcely a day goes by on Madison Street but some man is relieved of a "stake" by some "jack" who will, perhaps, come around later and join in denouncing men who will rob a workingman.

The average hobo is often indiscreet with his money, and especially so when he is drunk. He often displays it, even scatters it at times. This is a great temptation to men who have been living "close to their bellies" for months. As unpopular as the "jack roller" is among the tramps there are few who would overlook an opportunity to take a few dollars from a "drunk," seeing that he was in possession of money that someone else was bound to take sooner or later.

7. An investigator became acquainted with two men who were jack rollers who operated on Madison Street west of Halsted. They were well dressed for the "street" though not so well groomed as to be conspicuous. The investigator pretended to them that he had just spent ninety days in the jail in Salt Lake City for "rolling" a drunk. They had no sympathy for a man who would get drunk and wallow in the gutter. "He's not entitled to have any money." Neither of these men drank but they "chased women" and one of them played the races. Neither had any scruples against taking money from a drunken or sleeping man. They were able to justify themselves as easily as the peddlers and beggars do. Said one of them, "Everybody is eating on everybody he can get at, and they don't care where they bite. Believe me, as long as I can play safe I'm going to get mine."

"GETTING BY" IN WINTER

During the cold winter months the problem of "getting by" becomes serious. In the spring, summer, and fall hobos can sleep in the parks, in vacant houses, on the docks, in box cars, or in any other place where they may curl up and pass a few hours in slumber without fear of disturbance. But finding "flops" in winter usually engages the best effort a "bo" can muster. Besides food and shelter, the hobo must manage in some way to secure winter clothing. Above all he needs shelter, and shelter for the man without money is not easy to find in the city.

The best scouting qualities the average man can command are needed to get along in winter. There are many places to sleep and loaf during the day, but the good places are invariably crowded. For sleeping quarters police stations, railroad depots, doorways, mission floors, and even poolrooms are pressed into service. It is not uncommon for men who cannot find a warm place to sleep to walk the streets all night. This practice of walking the streets all night, snatching a wink of sleep here and a little rest there, is termed, in the parlance of the road, "carrying the banner." He who "carries the banner" during the night usually tries to snatch a bit of sleep during the day in places he does not have access to in the night time. He may go into the missions, but in cold weather the missions are crowded. They are crowded with men who sit for hours in a stupor between sleeping and waking. In almost every mission on the "stem" there are attendants known as "bouncers," whose duties during the meetings are to shake and harass men who have lost themselves in slumber.

Lodging-houses are also imposed upon by men who have no money to pay for a bed but who loaf in the lobbies during the day. Most lodging-houses make an effort to keep men out who are not guests. Fear is instilled into their hearts by occasionally calling the police to clear the lobbies of loafers. All who dare spend their leisure time in the public library, but the average tramp, unkempt and unclean from a night on the street, cannot muster sufficient courage to enter a public library.

The missions and other charity organizations play an important part in supplying the cold-weather wants of the tramp. They usually make it a point to get on hand at the beginning of winter a large supply of overcoats, or "bennies," and other clothes that are either sold at moderate prices or are given away. Such clothes are usually solicited from the public, and the men on the "stem" believe that they are entitled to them. Hence each man makes an effort to get what he feels is coming to him. When winter comes they begin to bestir themselves and concoct schemes for securing the desired amount of clothing to keep out the cold. During the winter time many of these men will submit to being "converted" in order to get food and shelter.

Competition between homeless men in winter is keen. Food is scarce, jobs are less plentiful, people are less generous, and there are more men begging. Many of the short-job men become beggars and a large number of those who are able to peddle during the summer likewise enter the ranks of the beggars. As beggars multiply, the housewife is less generous with the man at the back door, the man on the street also hardens his heart, and the police are called on for protection.

8. "Fat" is a very efficient "panhandler." He does not always "panhandle" but works when the opportunities present and the weather permits. He gets his money from men on the street, but he does most of his begging in winter when he cannot get the courage to leave town. He can beg for three or four hours and obtain about three dollars in that time. He only "panhandles" when his money is gone. He has a good personality and appeals for help in a frank, open manner giving no hard-

luck story. He says that he is a workingman temporarily down and that he is trying to get some money to leave town. He does not work the same street every day. He keeps sober.

He has no moral scruples against begging, nor against work. He works and works well when circumstances force him to it. He doesn't feel mean when out begging or "stemming." He looks upon it as a legitimate business and better than stealing, and so long as the situation is such he might as well make the best of it. He seldom "panhandles" in summer.

He has an interesting philosophy. He calculates that according to the law of averages out of each hundred persons he begs, a certain number will turn him down, a certain number will "bawl him out," a certain number will give him advice, and a certain number will give him something, and his earnings will average about three dollars. So he goes at the job with vigor each time in order to get it over as soon as possible. "You get to expect about so much police interference and so much opposition from the people, and you get more of this in winter than in summer, but that is the case in whatever line you go into."

"Fat" works and begs as the notion strikes him but he does less begging in summer and less work in winter. If he doesn't like one city he goes to another. Last winter (1921–22) he was in Chicago, not because he likes Chicago but because he happened to be here.

THE GAME OF "GETTING BY"

"Getting by" is a game not without its elements of fascination. The man who "panhandles" is getting a compensation that is not wholly measured by the nickels and dimes he accumulates. Even the peddler of shoestrings likes to think of "good days" when he is able to surpass himself. It matters not by what means "the down-and-out" gets his living; he manages to find a certain satisfaction in the game. The necessity of "putting it over" has its own compensations.

No group in Hobohemia is wholly without status. In every group there are classes. In jail grand

larceny is a distinction as against petit larceny. In
Hobohemia men are judged by the methods they use
to "get by." Begging, faking, and the various other
devices for gaining a livelihood serve to classify these
men among themselves. It matters not where a
man belongs, somewhere he has a place and that
place defines him to himself and to his group. No
matter what means an individual employs to get a
living he struggles to retain some shred of self-respect.
Even the outcast from home and society places a high
value upon his family name.

9. S. R. is an Englishman fifteen years in this country.
When he came to the United States to earn a "stake" he left his
wife in England. His intention was to save enough money to
send for her. He came here partly to overcome his love for
alcohol but he found as much drink here and it was as accessible.
He earned "big money" as a bricklayer but he never saved any.
He became ashamed of himself after a year or two and ceased to
write to his wife. That is, he had other interests here.

Today he is a physical wreck. He is paralyzed on one side
and he is also suffering from tuberculosis brought on by injudicious exposure and drink. He told his story but asked that his
real name, which he told, should not be used. For, he said, "I am
the only one who has ever disgraced that name."

Several old men on West Madison Street are living on mere pittances but are too proud to go to the
poorhouse. They much prefer to take their chances
with other mendicants. They want to play the game
to the end. As long as they are able to totter about
the street and hold out their hands they feel that they
are holding their own. To go to an institution
would mean that they had given up. Dependent as
they are and as pitiful as they look, they still have
enough self-respect to resent the thought of complete
surrender.

In the game of "getting by" the homeless man is practically sure sooner or later to lose his economic independence. At any time (except perhaps in periods of prolonged unemployment), only a small proportion of homeless men are grafters, beggars, fakers, or petty criminals. Yet, all the time, the migratory casual workers are living from hand to mouth, always perilously near the margin of dependence. Consequently, few homeless men have not been temporary dependents, and great numbers of them must in time become permanent dependents.

This process of personal degradation of the migratory casual worker from economic independence to pauperism is only an aspect of the play of economic forces in modern industrial society. Seasonal industries, business cycles, alternate periods of employment and of unemployment, the casualization of industry, have created this great industrial reserve army of homeless, foot-loose men which concentrates in periods of slack employment, as winter, in strategic centers of transportation, our largest cities. They must live; the majority of them are indispensable in the present competitive organization of industry; agencies and persons moved by religious and philanthropic impulses will continue to alleviate their condition; and yet their concentration in increasing numbers in winter in certain areas of our large cities cannot be regarded otherwise than as a menace. The policy of allowing the migratory casual laborer to "get by" is, however, easier and cheaper at the moment, even if the prevention of the economic deterioration and personal degradation of the homeless men would, in the long run, make for social efficiency and national economy.

PART II
TYPES OF HOBOS

CHAPTER V
WHY DO MEN LEAVE HOME?

WHY are there tramps and hobos? What are the conditions and motives that make migratory workers, vagrants, homeless men? Attempts to answer these questions have invariably raised other questions even more difficult to answer. Homeless men themselves are not always agreed in regard to the matter. The younger men put the blame upon circumstance and external conditions. The older men, who know life better, are humbler. They are disposed to go to the other extreme and put all the blame on themselves.

> 10. "My old man tried his d—dest to get me to go to school; but no, I couldn't learn anything in school. I could make my own way. I could get along without the old man or his advice. Well, when I woke up I was forty years old, of course it was too late. I couldn't go back. That's what's the matter with half of these d—d kids on the road. No one can tell them anything. They're burning up to learn something on their own hook; and they'll learn it, too."

From the records and observations of a great many men the reasons why men leave home seem to fall under several heads: (*a*) seasonal work and unemployment, (*b*) industrial inadequacy, (*c*) defects of personality, (*d*) crises in the life of the person, (*e*) racial or national discrimination, and (*f*) wanderlust.

SEASONAL WORK AND UNEMPLOYMENT

Chief among the economic causes why men leave home are (1) seasonal occupations, (2) local changes in industry, (3) seasonal fluctuations in the demand for labor, and (4) periods of unemployment. The cases of homeless men studied in Chicago show how these conditions of work tend to require and to create the migratory worker.

1) The industrial attractions of seasonal work often make a powerful appeal to the foot-loose man and boy. A new railroad that is building, a mining camp just opening up, an oil boom widely advertised, a bumper crop to be harvested in Kansas or the Dakotas fire the imagination and bring thousands of recruits each year into the army of seasonal and migratory workers.

11. Fifty-eight years old and born in Belgium. He came to this country with his parents in 1882. His family moved to a farm in northern Wisconsin where they remained several years. The boy worked during his spare time in the woods. His father soon became tired of farming and decided he could do better in the coal camps of southern Illinois, for he had been a miner in Belgium. After the family moved, the boy grew restless in the mining town and decided to return to his old home town in Wisconsin where he could get a job in the woods which was more to his liking. For several years he divided his time between the northern woods in winter and the mines at his Illinois home in summer. But he never liked coal mining and later began to go to the harvest fields for his summer employment. Sometimes he worked on railroad construction or at other seasonal work. He has spent several winters in Chicago, and usually (he says) he has been able to pay his way. However this year, 1921–22, he has been eating some at the missions.

This case shows the steps by which a stationary seasonal worker becomes a migratory worker. It indicates how easily and naturally the migrant may sink still lower in the economic scale until he spends his winters in Hobohemia "feeding at the missions."

2) Local changes in industry dislocate the routine of work of the wage-earner. The timber in certain regions gives out, mines close down when the ore is

exhausted or when prices drop, or in the reorganization of an industry a branch factory may be abandoned. Under these circumstances, certain workers are compelled to look elsewhere for employment. Those who are free to move naturally migrate. The following case is that of a migratory worker who with the passing of the West finds it difficult to make the necessary adjustment.

12. A. is the pioneer type of hobo. He came to Chicago because he was pressed eastward by the closing down of the mines in the West. He is about fifty years old. He was born in southern Illinois but grew restless on the farm. He left home in his teens to drive a team on the railroad grades. He moved West with the railroad building. He got into the mining game at Cripple Creek, and then turned prospector. He spent a couple of years in the mines of Alaska. He has never been able to attach himself to an old established camp. He has worked in the mines of northern Michigan but did not like it there. He regrets that he came East. He says that he was never so hopelessly down in the West. He plans to go back where he knows people and where he can go out and get some kind of a job when he feels like going to work.

This man always carried a bundle in the West. He laments that he found it necessary to throw his bed away when he came East. He claims that a man with a bed and a desire to work can get along better in the West than he has seen anyone get along here. Out there he only went to town four or five times a year. The rest of the time he was out in the hills. Out there he could always find work (until this recent industrial depression), but here he has not seen any jobs he cares for.

3) Seasonal fluctuations in the demand for labor accompanied by the seasonal rise and fall in wages have greatly affected the ebb and flow of workers.

Industrial fluctuations may be classed as cyclical and seasonal. Cyclical fluctuations result from business depressions and at times double the amount of loss of time during a year, which is illustrated by the fact that the railroads employed 236,000 fewer

men in 1908 than in 1907. Seasonal fluctuations may either be
inappreciable, as in municipal utilities, or may displace nearly
the entire labor force. The seasonal fluctuations in the canning
industry in California, for example, involve nearly nine-tenths
of all the workers; in logging camps, which depend upon the
snow, operations are practically suspended in summer; while in
the brick and tile industry only 36.5 per cent of the total number
of employees are retained during the dull season. Irregularities
in the conduct of industry and in the method of employing labor
are evident in dock work, in the unskilled work in iron and steel,
and in slaughtering and meat packing; in the competitive conditions in industries which force employers to cut labor cost down
to the utmost and to close down in order to save operating
expenses; in speculative practices which result in the piling up
of orders and alternate periods of rush production and inactivity;
in loss of time due to inefficient management within plants. In
some cases it has been charged, although without definite proof,
that irregularity of employment is due to a deliberate policy of
employers in order to lessen the chance of organized movement,
as well as to keep the level of wages down in unskilled occupations
by continually hiring new individuals.[1]

4) Periods of unemployment throw hundreds of
thousands of men out of work. But the effects of
unemployment are not ended with the passing of the
period of business depression. The majority of men,
it is true, return to work with their economic efficiency little if any impaired by the stress and strain
of uncertainty and deprivation. But upon thousands of men the enforced period of idleness has had
a disorganizing effect.[2] The demoralizing effect of
being out of work is particularly marked upon the
unskilled laborer. His regular routine of work has
been interrupted; habits of loafing are easily acquired.

---

[1] *Final Report of the Commission on Industrial Relations* (1915), pp. 163–64.

[2] B. Seebohm Rountree, *Unemployment; A Social Study.* London, 1911.
See especially chap. vii, "Detailed Descriptions of Selected Families," where
the demoralizing effects of unemployment upon the laborer are clearly indicated.

The path of personal degradation may lead to the "bread line" at the mission, and from there to panhandling in the Loop.

An increasingly large number of laborers go downward instead of upward. Young men, full of ambition and high hopes for the future start their life as workers, but meeting failure after failure in establishing themselves in some trade or calling, their ambitions and hopes go to pieces, and they gradually sink into the ranks of migratory and casual workers. Continuing their existence in these ranks they begin to lose self-respect and become "hobos." Afterwards, acquiring certain negative habits, as those of drinking, begging, and losing all self-control, self-respect, and desire to work, they become "down-and-outs"—tramps, bums, vagabonds, gamblers, pickpockets, yeggmen, and other petty criminals—in short, public parasites, the number of whom seems to be growing faster than the general population.[1]

THE INDUSTRIALLY INADEQUATE

Every year thousands of men fail in the struggle for existence. For one reason or another, they cannot, or at least they do not, keep the pace set by modern large-scale industry. These men are "misfits," industrially inadequate.

The majority of individuals, commonly regarded as industrially inadequate, are probably feebleminded or restless types like the emotionally unstable and the egocentric and fall into the group of defective personalities to be considered later. Other causes of industrial incompetency are (1) physical handicaps due to accidents, sickness, or occupational diseases; (2) alcoholism and drug addiction; and (3) old age.

1) The workers in certain industries are exposed to dangerous dusts and gases. The printers have learned the risks of their trade and endeavor to cope with them. Other industries have taken steps to

[1] *Final Report of the Commission on Industrial Relations* (1915), p. 157.

eliminate industrial hazards. Many transients are miners who go from one job to another exposing themselves to different dangers.

13. O. O. is fifty-three years old and he has been a migrant for many years. He has been a lumber-jack and a harvest hand. He has tried his hand at various casual jobs but most of his time has been spent in the mines. He used to work in the most dangerous mines because they generally pay the most money. Three years ago (about 1919) while working in the copper mines in Butte, Montana, he contracted miner's "con," which is some sort of lung trouble. He had no place to go, could not hold a job, and has wandered about the country ever since. He has no hope of regaining his health and is too proud to return to his people who live in Ohio.

Other industries also have their victims.

14. G. T. came from the New England states. He was wandering about the country in hope of regaining his health. He was a textile worker and claims that the dyes and dust were the cause of his condition. There was no means at hand of proving his story but the fact that he was in ill health, very much underweight, and he was not able to do heavy work. Numerous times he was rebuked because he asked for light work.

Many men in Hobohemia have limbs or parts of limbs missing, or bent and twisted bodies. These are victims of industrial or non-industrial accidents.

15. Red begs and sometimes peddles pencils along Halsted Street. He lost his leg several years ago while working in the coal mines. In his sober moments he claims that his own carelessness was partly to blame for his loss, but he also holds that the company was negligent. His leg at first had only been bruised and he went back to work in a damp, cold place, and inflammation set in. He has since become accommodated to a life of begging and peddling.

2) Alcoholism decreases the economic efficiency of the worker and so tends to depress him into the group of homeless men. Before prohibition the

saloon had no better patron than the homeless man. In Chicago today bootleggers and blind pigs in the vicinity of the "stem" thrive upon the homeless man's love for liquor.

16. E. J. loafs on West Madison Street and South State Street. He drinks and does not care who knows it. He has been a drinking man for years. "Booze put me on the bum. Now, I'm here and I'm too old to be good for anything, so why not keep it up? You're goin' t' die when your time comes anyway; so why not keep it up?" His philosophy helps him to live and he lives as well as he can by begging a little, working when any jobs come his way. He used to be a carpenter but has lost his efficiency at that trade. He threw up his membership in the union several years ago.

Drinking is responsible for keeping many men on the road. One man said that he left home because he had too many drinking friends. He has been on the road for several years but wherever he goes he finds other drinking friends. An old man refuses to live with his children in the country because he cannot get his "morning's morning" while with them. They have written him time and again but he does not answer.

Drug addiction likewise decreases the industrial efficiency of its victims. Drug addicts among homeless men seldom are transient. Those who are transient are often cocaine users who are able to do without the drug for considerable periods of time. Not infrequently "coke heads" or "snow-birds" are found among the hobo workers. When on out-of-town jobs, they are prone to go to town occasionally to indulge in a cocaine spree much as a "booze-hoister" indulges in a liquor spree. When their money is gone they return to work and do not touch the "snow" for weeks or months. Users of heroin or morphine are not able to separate themselves from the source of supply for so long a time.

Because of the secret nature of the practice, the extent of drug addiction among homeless men is unknown. Men who use drugs are loath to disclose the fact to anyone but drug users. The drug addict employs every scheme to keep his practice a secret whereas the drinking man strives to share his joy with others. The fear of being discovered drives many addicts from the circle of their family and friends and many of them drift into the homeless man areas where they enjoy the maximum seclusion.

17. The investigator was accosted by a beggar in the Loop. He was impressed by the fervor and the hurry with which the man begged him and was away. He followed the man for several blocks and watched him accost more than a hundred persons, all men. The only men from whom he failed to solicit were those accompanied by women. If two men were standing two or three yards apart he accosted each one individually. Only one or two men gave him anything. Most of them looked with suspicion at him, and not without reason, for although he was fairly well dressed he was very dirty and his clothes looked as if he had been sleeping out. He had a pallid, leaden complexion, and he had a ten days' growth of beard. He had a wild, hunted expression and impressed the investigator as being a drug addict. He continued to follow the man and engaged him in conversation. He learned that he had just beat his way from Boston. He had ridden passenger trains all the way and had come in less than three days. His only difficulty was in Buffalo where he says that a policeman pulled him off the train and beat him. Why he left Boston he would not say. He denied being a "dope" then and it was not till three days later when he was seen in Grant Park that he admitted the fact. He came to Chicago because he knew more people here and was certain of getting morphine.

Drug users need as much as three or four dollars a day, and even more, to supply their wants. As a rule they are physically unfit to earn a living. They cannot live as the hobos do because the average hobo does not have money enough to buy drugs. They may be forced to live in cheap hotels and to eat in cheap restaurants but only to save money to satisfy the craving for "dope." Drug addicts wander very little except to make rapid trips from city to city. The drug addict tends to become a criminal rather than a migratory worker. Their natural habitat is the great city.

3) Many old men in the tramp class are not able to work and are too independent to go to the almshouse. Some of them have spent their lives on the road. These old, homeless men usually find their way to the larger cities. Unlike the younger men they have no dreams and no longer burn with the desire to travel. Many have been self-supporting until they were overtaken by senility. It is pitiable to see an old man tottering along the streets living a hand-to-mouth existence.

18. J. is an old man who lives in a cheap hotel on South Desplaines Street, where a few cents a day will house him. He is seventy-two, very bent and gray. Once he was picked up on the street in winter and sent to the hospital where he remained a day or two and was transferred to the poor house at Oak Forest. He ran away from the poor house two years ago and has managed to live. He seldom gets more than a block or two from his lodging. Even today (1923) he may be seen on a cold day shivering without an overcoat on Madison Street. He is a good beggar and manages to get from fifty cents to a dollar a day from the "boys" on the "stem." Sometimes during the warm weather he makes excursions of three to five blocks away on begging tours. He is exceedingly feeble and walking that distance is hard work for him. Work is out of the question. There are very few jobs that he could manage.

This case is typical. During the summer time, when it is possible to sit outdoors in comfort, numbers of old men may be found in groups on the pavements or in the parks. In winter they are too much occupied seeking food and shelter.

The physically handicapped and industrially inefficient individuals are numerous among the homeless men. The handicap is, in part at least, the reason of their presence in that class. Competition with able-bodied workers forces them into the scrap heap.

DEFECTS OF PERSONALITY

Psychological and sociological studies of vagabondage in France, Italy, and Germany have led to the conclusion that the vagabond is primarily a psychopathic type.[1] The findings of European psychopathologists are, of course, the result of case-studies of beggars and wanderers in these countries and cannot without reservation be accepted for the United States. Undoubtedly there are large numbers of individuals with defects of personalities among American hobos and tramps, but there are also large numbers of normal individuals. The American tradition of pioneering, wanderlust, seasonal employment, attract into the group of wanderers and migratory workers a great many energetic and venturesome normal boys and young men.

William Healy, for several years director of the Psychopathic Institute of Chicago, sums up the relation of mental deficiency to vagabondage in these words:

We have seen vagabondage in connection with feeble-mindedness, epilepsy, dementia precox, but we have also seen the same behavior in normal boys who had conceived a grudge, with or without good reasons, against home conditions. Again, we

[1] See Bibliography, p. 287.

have seen normal lads who have been seeking larger experiences in this way.[1]

Dr. Healy's observations were made primarily with juveniles, but he adds cautiously a conclusion as to the explanation of adult vagabondage:

When vagabondage is continued beyond the unstable years of adolescence, generalizations on the character of the individuals are more likely to be correct. But even here the only chance of adequate conception of the relationship between the behavior and the type of individual who engages in it is to be found in a personal study of him.

The proportion of feeble-minded is popularly supposed to be higher among the migratory and casual laborer than in the general population. In the earlier studies, only the most obvious cases of mental defect were noted. Mrs. Solenberger by common-sense observation or medical examinations found only eighty-nine of the one thousand men she examined to be feeble-minded, epileptic, or insane.[2]

In recent years mental tests have been given to small groups of unemployed men, in which the types of the hobo, tramp, and bum were well represented. Knollin found 20 per cent of the 150 hobos he tested feeble-minded.[3] Pintner and Toops examined two groups of applicants at Ohio free employment agencies by standardized tests other than the Stanford revision of the Binet-Simon. Of the 94 men taking the tests at Columbus, 28.7 per cent were diagnosed as feeble-minded. Of the 40 unemployed men examined at Dayton 7.5 per cent were assigned to the feeble-

[1] *The Individual Delinquent*, pp. 776–79.

[2] *One Thousand Homeless Men*, pp. 88–89.

[3] L. M. Terman, *The Measurement of Intelligence*, p. 18.

minded class.[1] Glenn R. Johnson gave the Stanford revision of the Binet-Simon tests to 107 men
out of work in Portland, and found 18 per cent
feeble-minded, i.e., under twelve years mental age.[2]
As he had expected, he found the proportion of infe-
rior intelligence lower than that of the 62 business
men and high-school students upon which Terman
had standardized his tests for adults, but he also
found among hobos a higher percentage of superior
adults. He found also that the higher the intelligence of the individual the shorter the period of
holding a job among the unemployed. The testing
of an unselected group of 653 men in the army by
the Stanford revision of the Binet-Simon tests affords
an interesting opportunity for a comparison with the
results of the Portland study.

This comparison would indicate that the intelligence of the unemployed is not lower, but, if anything, higher than that of the adult males tested in
army camps. Apparently other factors than intelligence are decisive in determining whether an individual is employable or unemployable, or whether
he makes or fails to make an adequate adjustment in
the normal routine of industrial organization.

The defects in personality commonly found in the
cases of homeless men studied in Chicago are those
noted by the students of vagabondage and unemployment, namely, feeble-mindedness, constitutional
inferiority, emotional instability, and egocentricity.
In a survey of 100 cases of unemployment which had

[1] Rudolph Pintner and H. A. Toops, "Mental Tests of Unemployed Men,"
Journal of Applied Psychology, I (1917), 325-41; II (1918), 15-25.

[2] "Unemployment and Feeble-mindedness," *Journal of Delinquency*, II
(1917), 59-73.

been received as patients in the Boston Psychopathic Hospital, Dr. Herman M. Adler found that 43 fell into the class of *paranoid personality* (egocentricity). The next largest group of 35 cases was assigned to the class of *inadequate personality* (mentally defective

MENTAL CAPACITY OF ARMY GROUP AND OF PORT-
LAND UNEMPLOYED AS MEASURED BY
STANFORD-BINET

MENTAL AGE	ARMY GROUP	PORTLAND UNEMPLOYED
	653 Cases	105 Cases
	Per Cent	Per Cent
5	0.2	....
6	0.3	....
7	0.2	1.9
8	3.4	1.9
9	9.5	3.8
10	10.1	6.7
11	10.6	5.7
12	12.4	8.6
13	10.6	16.2
14	11.8	18.1
15	9.6	11.4
16	8.3	9.5
17	7.2	7.6
18	5.2	7.6
19	0.8	2.9

or feeble-minded).   The remaining cases, 22 in number, were diagnosed as *emotionally unstable personality*.   An analysis of the months employed per case showed that the emotionally unstable group averages 50 months to each job; the inadequate group 24.7 months to each job; and the paranoid group 20.6 months to each job.[1]

Many individuals not feeble-minded find their way into the group of casual and migratory workers

[1] Herman M. Adler, "Unemployment and Personality—A Study of Psychopathic Cases," *Mental Hygiene*, I (January, 1917), 16-24.

by reason of other defects of personality, for example, emotional instability and egocentricity. Among transient laborers the very great turnover cannot be entirely accounted for by industrial conditions. Much of their shifting from scene to scene is indicative of their emotional instability and restlessness.

19. W. E. was born in a little village in Kentucky. His first job away from home was on the section. When he learned that it was the meanest job on the railroad he decided to change. He got a job on an extra-gang where he moved about considerably, worked in several towns during the summer. Later got a steady job on a farm but he soon tired of "eating at the same table day after day" and he went to Kansas City where he worked in a box factory. He became expert at it but soon tired of using the same tools, and working as fast as possible day after day, and he changed. He worked in several factories making boxes but there was no difference. Then with his meager experience with tools he got in the maintenance of way work of a railroad. Here he had some variety and remained a year. Decided he wanted to work in the mines and he got a job timbering. Later he tried his hand at millwright work but he soon quit that and went back to the bridge gang. He still goes to town every month or two to spend his money and each time he goes out to some different job.

In hard times when work is scarce and wages are low, voluntary quitting of jobs is much less than in good times. Hobos are easily piqued and they will "walk off" the job on the slightest pretext, even when they have the best jobs and living conditions are relatively good. Hobo philosophy is disposed to represent the man who is a long time on the job as a piker. He ought to leave a job once in a while simply to assert his independence and to learn something else about other jobs. The following case shows the relation of instability and egocentricity to labor turnover:

20. Yes, Pete had had plenty of good jobs, but something had always gone against him. At one place not long ago they wanted him to continue work in spite of the dust which was blowing everywhere. Another rude employer never spoke to him (or any other of the employees) politely.

No one should work for a man like that. Upon another occasion the boss suggested reform of a certain habit—as if he had any right to tell an American citizen what he ought to do.

He had worked at almost everything, but it went against his very nature to do one thing very long. He would, in two or three weeks, quit and look for a different occupation. Why he quit, I am sure he didn't know. "Independence," "Justice," and "American Equality" furnished the material for his excuses, but they were only excuses.

A survey of the so-called "intellectuals" of Hobohemia reveals a group of egocentric and rebellious natures who decry most things that are. Intellectuals, just because they are highly organized and specialized, are very likely to become misfits outside of the environment to which they artificially are adapted. When, added to this handicap, they lack the discipline which a regular occupation affords they are likely to become quite impossible.

21. H. has a great chart that he uses to preach evolution to the curb-stone audiences. He has learned a few scientific terms from one or two books he has read. He has no use for the modern scientists. He considers them heretic. He is a student of Darwin "and those old timers." When pinned down he is not able to discuss clearly what contributions the old-timers made or what they believed.

22. D. H. is a student of economics according to Karl Marx. He has no room in his thinking for any contribution of any other man. Indeed, he does not think that anyone has made any contribution since Marx. One of his stock phrases is "Now get this into your heads. I am making it simple so that you can understand it."

23. B. is writing a novel. He has been working on it for several years. He also writes songs, popular songs. But he has

never sold a song nor has he ever been able to interest a publisher
in his novel.   He calls the publishers a lot of grafters and claims
that they are in league to keep the poor writers down.

24. L. is a soap-box orator.   He has one hobby.   He is a
single-taxer.   He is a great believer in Lincoln, Washington,
Jefferson.   To him there is only one problem, to find out who is
exploiting the people, and there is only one remedy and that the
single tax.   He will entertain no argument against the single tax.
Anyone who does not share his opinion is to be pitied.

The intellectuals are frequently egocentric.   They
are obsessed by some peculiar point of view.   As
egocentrics they are in conflict with the rest of the
world.   Their cry is often a lament and just as often
a justification or defense.

A study of individual cases seems to indicate that
there is a large proportion of inadequate personalities
among homeless men.   The following cases indicate
the variety of ways in which personal defects lead
to a migratory existence which lands them eventually at the bottom of the social scale.

25. D. is a man who could not get along at home.   He was
continually into difficulty with his father.   He always had ideas
and schemes that his father thought foolish and he was never
permitted to carry any of them out.   He still has the habit of
working up schemes and programs.   One week he will be writing
a play.   Again he will be inventing some mechanical device.   He
has tried several different courses in mechanical engineering but
has not completed any of them.

26. F. has an idea that he can become a singer but he refuses
to spend his time in the rigid and arduous training that would be
required.   He buys cheap books on voice culture.   When he gets
money enough ahead to take lessons he forgets his musical ambition and drinks or gambles.

27. L. was the "simple Simon" in his home town.   During the
war he was rejected for military service so he decided to go to
the city to work.   Here he earned fair money, more than at home.
The people at home used to tease him but at first he got by fairly

well in Minneapolis. Later he went to Detroit because the fellows where he worked in Minneapolis used "to run him." They used to tease him in Detroit and he left two jobs there on that account. He is the type of person that invites teasing. He puts himself in the way of it but resents it if it reaches a certain extent. With the slack season in industry in 1921–22 he had a hard time to get along but he would not return home.

28. H. is a man who thinks that he is getting the worst of every deal he has with others. He says that at home he was imposed on by his people so he left. He is always on the lookout for plots directed against him. If he is working along with others on a job and a bad piece of work falls his way he concludes that it happened purposely. However, he is ready to gloat over favors. His best efforts are made to ingratiate himself with others. Whenever he leaves a place, he does so with bitterness in his heart. He usually keeps his grudge to himself.

29. M. is a good worker but a transient. He behaves well when sober but he becomes quarrelsome when drunk. If he is not discharged because of a drunken scene he usually quits voluntarily because he feels ashamed of himself. He argues a great deal when sober but he has the ability to control himself. His periods of drunkenness last from a week to ten days and are staged whenever his finances will permit. Not infrequently he is arrested while drunk.

CRISES IN THE LIFE OF THE PERSON

Crises in the life of the person, as family conflict, for example, the feeling of failure, disgrace or embarrassment, the fear of punishment for the commission of an offense may cause a man to desert home and community. With the severance of family and social ties the man or boy is all the more likely to drift aimlessly from place to place, and at last perhaps find himself permanently in the group of migratory and casual laborers.

Conflict at home forces many men and boys into the group of homeless men. Not infrequently boys run away from home because of difficulties with their

people.   One youth says that his father tried to tell
him "where to head in at," and he "wouldn't stand
for it."   Another boy could not get along with his
brothers who were older than he.   They tried to
"boss" him.

Many men in Hobohemia manifest no inclination
to wander but are as completely cut off from their
home associations as are the migrants.   These men
of the "home guard" types may have had trouble
with their parents or with their wives.

30. H. claims that he was married and that he held a job as
traveling salesman.   He maintained an apartment on the South
Side where he left his wife while he was away on trips through the
Southwest.   His story is that his wife was untrue to him and he
divorced her.   This experience "broke him up" so that he quit
his job and went West where he remained a year.   Today he
loafs on West Madison Street and blames his wife for his failure
in life.   The divorced wife's story learned from other sources
lays considerable of the responsibility at his feet.   This much of
his story is true: he was not in the tramp class before he married.
The circumstances surrounding his home trouble were unfortu-
nate and were partly due to the shortcomings of both.

31. G. lays the blame for his condition upon family trouble.
He has not lived with his wife for nine years.   They are not
divorced because he and his wife are both Catholic and do not
believe in it.   He worked most of the time before their separation
and claims that he owned his own home which is now in the possession of his wife.   What his wife is doing now he does not know
nor does he know anything about their child.   He is content
where he is; doing just enough work to pay expenses.

Deaths in a family will sometimes turn a person
out into the world and he may drift into the hobo and
tramp group.

32. M.'s father died when he was about six years old.   Five
years later his mother died.   Kindly neighbors took him in
charge by turns.   It seemed to him that wherever he was the
people would parade the fact that they were taking "care of"

someone else's child. It was charity. He stayed with several different families. Some of them he liked and others he didn't. Some sent him to school and others didn't seem to care what became of him. More than one family tried to pass him on to others on the ground that it was too much of an expense. When he began to be old enough to work then they all wanted him. He hated it all so he left the country. He came through Chicago on his way to Texas. (A sixteen-year-old boy and small for his age.) He said he had a brother in the cavalry who was stationed in Texas. The brother tried to persuade him to wait till he had saved enough money to pay his fare but he preferred to take his "chances," so he was "beating his way."

Embarrassing situations often make it easier to leave home than to remain and face the criticism or sympathy of the public. On the road, a man is more or less immune to attacks upon his self-consciousness and self-respect, for his relations to other persons are loose and transient and he has no status to maintain. The opposite is true in his home town where his every act is known.

33. One man who works in and near Chicago claims that he was put on the "bum" by a woman. He was to have been married to this girl and prepared for the wedding in good faith. A few days before the ceremony she ran away with another man. He was laughed at by his friends and rather than remain and for a long time be the butt of the joke, he packed his things and has not been back since. His home is in a country town in southern Illinois, and although he has been near the place several times during the past ten years he has never returned.

34. F. is another case of injured pride. For some boyish prank he had been sent to the reformatory for three years. Upon his release he was given transportation home and started in high glee. His people met him at the station and took him home. Although he was treated well he felt uncomfortable. "They treated me good because I happened to be a part of the family. I felt like I didn't belong there, so as soon as it got dark I skinned out. They write to me to come back and maybe I will after a while." He is an average man of the migratory worker type.

He comes to Chicago when he has money and when he is "broke" he goes out on some job and is not seen for two or three months or until he has another stake. He gets arrested now and then but only on petty offenses that he commits while drunk.

The following case shows that a sense of failure and fear of ridicule may force a boy to leave his home community:

35. This lad was working in a grocery store at the age of twelve. He became dissatisfied with the job and asked for a raise which was denied. He was somewhat embarrassed at being set back and lest he be laughed at for staying on after making a demand he quit. Someone asked him what he would do since there was no other job to be had. This was really another challenge and he met it with the reply that Podunk was not the only place to work. He left home to make his bluff good.

He met with many reverses. He was small and no one wanted to hire him. So he begged and he "managed." Sometimes he did odd jobs, but he didn't go home. Other people had left home and come back beaten and had to take the "horse laugh" and he did not admire any of them. He couldn't think of going back unless he had more money than when he left and better clothes, so he went on. He ·learned to like the road and he traveled over the country for about two years before he went back. When he did return he was in a position to talk. He had some money to spend, he had seen the country. He had been East and West, and he had been to sea. He had something to talk about. But he only remained in his home town long enough to stir up admiration and envy and he was off again. He is still under twenty-one and is still traveling in response to the same urge.

Other individuals began their migratory career by fleeing from the consequences of some offense. If the offense is of such gravity that the consequences seem to outweigh the advantages of remaining in the community, then flight is the natural course.

36. A. states that he left home to avoid the wrath of his father. He had been to town with the horse and buggy. On the

way home the horse became excited, left the road, ran into a post, and broke the buggy. His father was absent for the day and he and his brothers tried to repair the buggy so that the parent would not suspect. It could not be fixed and they all knew what the consequences would be. The brothers helped him pack up and he ran away. He did not return for three years; then it was only to remain for a short time.

37. Red left home because he feared the consequences of an affair with a woman. He claims that the woman had relations with another man and that he was not sure that the child would be his. The other man was a Mexican and Red says that he has heard since that the child is a dark-skinned little fellow and that eases his conscience.

38. O. could not get along with his wife. They were divorced and he was ordered by the court to pay her thirty dollars a month. He paid it faithfully for a couple of months and then failed for a month or two. She had him arrested and he agreed to make good. As soon as he was released, he fled the country. He has been living in and about Chicago the past year. It has been two or three years since he left home. He has not communicated with his home because he fears arrest. His alimony bill has mounted to terrifying proportions. He hopes that his wife is married again.

RACIAL AND NATIONAL DISCRIMINATION

In certain situations racial or national traits cause discrimination in employment and so result in a descent from regular to casual work. So far as selection for employment is adverse to the Negroes they tend to recruit the ranks of homeless men. During the war, a much higher proportion of foreign-born of German origin was observed on West Madison Street than had previously been reported. Interviews with certain Russians on the "main stem" in the spring of 1922 suggest that the public disapproval of Bolshevism had reacted unfavorably on the chances for employment of this nationality in the United States.

WANDERLUST

Wanderlust is a longing for new experience. It is the yearning to see new places, to feel the thrill of new sensations, to encounter new situations, and to know the freedom and the exhilaration of being a stranger.

In its pure form the desire for new experience results in motion, change, danger, instability, social irresponsibility. It is to be seen in simple form in the prowling and meddling activities of the child, and the love of adventure and travel in the boy and man. It ranges in moral quality from the pursuit of game and the pursuit of pleasure to the pursuit of knowledge and the pursuit of ideals. It is found equally in the vagabond and the scientific explorer.[1]

Even those of us who seem to have settled down quite comfortably to exacting routine are sometimes intolerably stirred by the wanderlust. It comes upon us unaware; and often we cut away and go. There are automobiles, railway cars, steamships, airplanes—serving little other purpose, really, than the gratification of wander tendencies. Usually we do not say it so openly of course; we make good reasons for travelling, for not "staying put." Many a business man has developed a perfect technique for escaping from his rut; many a laborer has invented a physical inability to work steadily that lets him out into the drifting current when monotony sets in on the job. Life is full of these moral side doors; but we need not view man's rationalizing power cynically, merely understandingly. The escapes he contrives are a damaging critique of the modern mode of life. We may infer from them the superior adjustments we strive so blindly toward.[2]

Wanderlust is a wish of the person. Its expression in the form of tramping, "making" the harvest field, roughing it, pioneering, is a social pattern of American life. The fascination of the life of the road is, in part, disclosed in the following case-study.

[1] R. E. Park and H. A. Miller, *Old World Traits Transplanted*, p. 27.

[2] Rexford Tugwell, "The Gypsy Strain," *Pacific Review*, pp. 177–78.

39. S. who is 19 years old has been a wanderer for nearly four years. He does not know why he travels except that he gets thrills out of it. He says that there is nothing that he likes better than to catch trains out of a town where the police are rather strict. When he can outwit the "bulls" he gets a "kick" out of it. He would rather ride the passenger trains than the freights because he can "get there" quicker, and then, they are watched closer. He likes to tell of making "big jumps" on passenger trains as from the coast to Chicago in five days, or from Chicago to Kansas City or Omaha in one day. He only works long enough in one place to get a "grubstake," or enough money to live on for a few days.

He says that he knows that he would be better off if he would settle down at some steady job. He has tried it a few times but the monotony of it made him so restless that he had to leave. He thinks that he might be able to stay in a city if he had a steady job and he agreed to take such a job if he could get it. Jobs were scarce and the investigator promised to take him to the United Charities to help him get placed.

The following morning the lad came to the office with another boy with whom he had become acquainted that morning. He had changed his mind about that job but wanted to thank everyone who had taken an interest in him. He and his "buddy" were going to "make the Harvest."

The longing to see the world is often stimulated in a boy by reason of the experiences of some relative or friend whom he admires. One boy went on the road because of the influence his uncle had upon him. The uncle did not advise him to leave home, in fact, he did not know very much about the boy. But the uncle had been to war, and had traveled in China, Alaska, and South America. The boy had to go on the road to become disillusioned. He now knows that his uncle is a plain tramp and that he himself has become a hobo.

40. W. left home when he was sixteen. He was the oldest of a family of five boys and three girls. His father owned a farm in Michigan and was usually hard pressed for means. He

needed help at home and so W. was kept out of school a great deal. When he did go to school it was hard for him to learn. When the father saw that the younger boys were passing W. in school he decided that it was time wasted to send W. to school. W. was big for his age and the father imposed more work on him than on the other boys who were smaller. W. felt that he was not getting a square deal so he ran away.

He remained away a year before he dared to write. One reason he did not write sooner was because he was not earning much money, and the other reason was that he feared his father would hunt him down and force him to return. When he felt secure he wrote more frequently and most of his letters were boastful. He told of prospering and he moved from place to place often to show the other children at home that he could go and come as he pleased. He traveled in different parts of the country and from each part he would write painting his experiences in a rosy hue.

He succeeded in stirring up unrest in the hearts of the other boys who left home one by one. In about two years N. followed W. L. soon began to feel that he too could make "his way" so he left. All five of the boys left home before they were sixteen. Each felt that he was wasting his time about home while the other boys were seeing the country and making good money. Only one of the five boys returned home. The others roamed the country following migratory work. One married but only lived with his wife a year and then deserted her.

The father always blamed W. for leading the boys away. W. used to send presents to the other members of the family. He used to send the mother money now and then. He was the idol of the rest of the children and they left home to follow in his footsteps.

A visit to the "jungles" at the junction of any railroad or at the outskirts of any large city or even small town reveals the extent to which the tramp is consciously and enthusiastically imitated. Around the camp fire watching the coffee pot boil or the "mulligan" cook, the boys are often found mingling with the tramps and listening in on their stories of adventure.

To boys the tramp is not a problem, but a human being, and an interesting one at that. He has no cares nor burdens to hold him down. All he is concerned with is to live and seek adventure, and in this he personifies the heroes in the stories the boys have read. Tramp life is an invitation to a career of varied experiences and adventures. All this is a promise and a challenge. A promise that all the wishes that disturb him shall be fulfilled and a challenge to leave the work-a-day world that he is bound to.

THE MULTIPLE EXPLANATION

No single cause can be found to explain how a man may be reduced to the status of a homeless, migratory, and casual laborer. In any given case all of the factors analyzed above may have entered into the process of economic and social degradation. Indeed, the conjunction of several of these causes is necessary to explain the extent and the nature of the casualization and mobility of labor in this country. Unemployment and seasonal work disorganize the routine of life of the individual worker and destroy regular habits of work but at the same time thousands of boys and men moved by wanderlust are eager to escape the monotony of stable and settled existence. No matter how perfect a social and economic order may yet be devised there will always remain certain "misfits," the industrially inadequate, the unstable and egocentric, who will ever tend to conflict with constituted authority in industry, society, and government.

The description, however, of these causes of vagabondage—(a) unemployment and seasonal work, (*b*) industrial inadequacy, (*c*) defects of personality, (*d*) crises in the life of the person, (*e*) racial or national discrimination, (*f*) wanderlust—is a necessary condition to any solution of the problem of the homeless man. A program is remedial and not preventive that does not grapple with the fundamental causes here revealed. These causes have roots at the very core of our American life, in our industrial system, in education, cultural and vocational, in family relations, in the problems of racial and immigrant adjustment, and in the opportunity offered or denied by society for the expression of the wishes of the person.

CHAPTER VI
THE HOBO AND THE TRAMP

THE term "homeless man" was used by Mrs. Alice W. Solenberger in her study of 1,000 cases in Chicago to include all types of unattached men, tramps, hobos, bums, and the other nameless varieties of the "go-abouts."

Almost all "tramps" are "homeless men" but by no means are all homeless men tramps. The homeless man may be an able-bodied workman without a family; he may be a runaway boy, a consumptive temporarily stranded on his way to a health resort, an irresponsible, feeble-minded, or insane man, but unless he is also a professional wanderer he is not a "tramp."[1]

There is no better term at hand than "homeless men" by which the men who inhabit Hobohemia may be characterized. Dr. Ben L. Reitman, who has himself traveled as a tramp, in the sense in which he uses the word, has defined the three principal types of the hobo. He says:

There are three types of the genus vagrant: the hobo, the tramp, and the bum. The hobo works and wanders, the tramp dreams and wanders and the bum drinks and wanders.

St. John Tucker, formerly the president of the "Hobo College" in Chicago, gives the same classification with a slightly different definition:

A hobo is a migratory worker. A tramp is a migratory non-worker. A bum is a stationary non-worker. Upon the labor of the *migratory worker* all the basic industries depend. He goes forth from the crowded slavemarkets to hew the forests, build and repair the railroads, tunnel mountains and build ravines. His is the labor that harvests the wheat in the fall and cuts the ice in the winter. All of these are hobos.

[1] *One Thousand Homeless Men*, p. 209.

M. Kuhn, of St. Louis (and elsewhere), a migrant, a writer, and, according to his own definition, a hobo, in a pamphlet entitled "The Hobo Problem" gives a fairly representative statement of the homeless man's explanation of his lot.

The hobo is a seasonal, transient, migratory worker of either sex. Being a seasonal worker he is necessarily idle much of the time; being transient, he is necessarily homeless. He is detached from the soil and the fireside. By the nature of his work and not by his own will, he is precluded from establishing a home and rearing a family. Sex, poverty, habits and degree of skill have nothing whatever to do with classifying individuals as hobos; the character of his work does that.

There are individuals not hobos who pose as such. They are enabled to do this for two reasons: first, hobos have no organization by which they can expose the impostor; second, the frauds are encouraged and made possible by organized and private charity. The hobo class, therefore, is unable to rid itself of this extremely undesirable element. With organization it can and will be done even if charity, which is strongly opposed by the hobo class, is not abolished.

Nicholas Klein, president of the "Hobo College" and attorney and adviser to James Eads How, the so-called hobo millionaire, who finances the "Hobo College," says:

A hobo is one who travels in search of work, the migratory worker who must go about to find employment. Workers of that sort pick our berries, fruit, hops, and help to harvest the crops on the western farms. They follow the seasons around giving their time to farms in spring, summer, and autumn, and ending up in the ice fields in winter. We could not get in our crops without them for the hobo is the boy who does the work. The name originated from the words "hoe-boy" plainly derived from work on the farm. A tramp is one who travels but does not work, and a bum is a man who stays in one place and does not work. Between these grades there is a great gulf of social distinction. Don't get tramps and hobos mixed. They are quite different in many respects. The chief difference being that the hobo will work and the tramp will not, preferring to live on what he can pick up at back doors as he makes his way through the country.[1]

Roger Payne, A.B. and LL.B., who has taken upon himself the title "hobo philosopher," sees only one type of the wanderer and that is the hobo. The hobo to him is a migratory worker. If he works but does not migrate, or if he migrates but does not work, he is not a hobo. All others are either tramps or bums. He makes no distinction between them. The hobo, foot-loose and care-free, leads, Mr. Payne thinks, the ideal life.

Although we cannot draw lines closely, it seems clear that there are at least five types of homeless men: (a) the seasonal worker,[2] (b) the transient or occasional worker or hobo, (c) the tramp who "dreams and wanders" and works only when it is convenient, (d) the bum who seldom wanders and seldom works, and (e) the home guard who lives in Hobohemia and does not leave town.[3]

THE SEASONAL WORKER

Seasonal workers are men who have definite occupations in different seasons. The yearly circuit of their labors takes them about the country, often into several different states. These men may work in the clothing industries during cold weather but in summer are employed at odd jobs; or they may have steady work in summer and do odd jobs in

---

[1] *Dearborn Independent*, March 18, 1922.

[2] The seasonal worker may be regarded also as the upper-class hobo.

[3] The first three types of homeless men are described in this chapter; the last two types are considered in chapter vii.

winter. One man picks fruit in summer and works
as a machinist in winter. He does not spend his
summers in the same state nor his winters in the
same city but follows those two occupations throughout the year.

41. Bill S. is a Scotchman and a seasonal worker. During
the winter he is usually in Chicago. He works as a practical
nurse. He is efficient and well liked by his patients and a
steady worker during the winter. In summer he quits and goes
to the harvest fields or works on a construction job. Since leaving his winter job (March to October, 1922) he has had several
jobs out of Chicago none of which lasted more than a week or
two. Between times he loafs on West Madison Street. He
does not drink. He is well behaved. Seldom dresses up. When
last heard of he was in Kansas City, Missouri, where he thought
he would spend the winter.

42. Jack M. works on the lake boats during the sailing season.
When the boats tie up for the winter he tries to get into the
factories, or he goes to the woods. Sometimes during the tie-up
he takes a notion to travel and goes West or South to while away
the time. He has just returned from a trip East and South
where he has been "seeking work" and "killing time" a week or
so before the season opened. He has already signed up for the
summer. He is loafing and lodging in the meanwhile on West
Madison and South State streets.

The seasonal worker has a particular kind of work
that he follows somewhere at least part of the year.
The hotels of Hobohemia are a winter resort for
many of these seasonal workers whose schedule is
relatively fixed and habitudinal. Some of these who
return to the city regularly every winter come with
money. In that case, they do not work until next
season. Others return without money. They have
some kind of work which they follow in the winter.
The hobo, proper, is a transient worker without a
program.

THE HOBO

A hobo is a migratory worker in the strict sense of the word. He works at whatever is convenient in the mills, the shops, the mines, the harvests, or any of the numerous jobs that come his way without regard for the times or the seasons. The range of his activities is nation wide and with many hobos it is international. He may cross a continent between jobs. He may be able in one year to function in several industries. He may have a trade or even a profession. He may even be reduced to begging between jobs, but his living is primarily gained by work and that puts him in the hobo class.

43. E. J. is a carpenter. He was at one time a good workman but due to drink and dissipation he has lost his ability to do fine work and has been reduced to the status of a rough carpenter. At present he follows bridge work and concrete form work. Sometimes he tries his hand at plain house carpentry but due to the fact that he moves about so much, he has lost or disposed of many of his tools. A spree lasts about three weeks and he has about three or four a year. Sometimes he travels without his kit and does not work at his trade. He never drinks while working. It is only when he goes to town to spend his vacations that he gets drunk. He is restless and uncomfortable and does not know how to occupy his mind when he is in town and sober. He is fifty-six years old. He never married and never has had a home since he was a boy.

44. M. P. is interesting because he has a trade but does not follow it seasonally. He is a plasterer and he seems to be a good one. In his youth he learned the trade of stone mason. He came to this country from England in his twenties and he is past fifty now. He married in Pennsylvania where his wife died and where a daughter still lives. He became a wanderer and for many years did not work at his trade. He did various kinds of work as the notion came to him. As he is getting older he is less inclined to wander and he makes fewer excursions into other lines of work outside his trade. During the past year he has not

left Chicago and he has done little other than to work as a plasterer. He lives in the Hobohemian areas and is able to get along two or three weeks on a few days' work. He seldom works more than a week at a time. He takes a lively interest in the hobo movement of the city and has been actively engaged in the "Hobo College." Recently he won a lot in a raffle. It is located in the suburbs of the city. During the summer (1922) he had a camp out there and he and his friends from Madison Street spent considerable time in his private "jungle."

The hobo group comprises the bulk of the migratory workers, in fact, nearly all migrants in transit are hobos of one sort or other. Hobos have a romantic place in our history. From the beginning they have been numbered among the pioneers. They have played an important rôle in reclaiming the desert and in subduing the trackless forests. They have contributed more to the open, frank, and adventurous spirit of the Old West than we are always willing to admit. They are, as it were, belated frontiersmen. Their presence in the migrant group has been the chief factor in making the American vagabond class different from that of any other country.

It is difficult to classify the numerous types of hobos. The habits, type of work, the routes of travel, etc., seem to differ with each individual. Some live more parasitic lives than others. Some never beg or get drunk, while others never come to town without getting intoxicated and being robbed or arrested, and perhaps beaten. One common characteristic of the hobo, however, is that he works. He usually has horny hands and a worker's mien. He aims to live by his labor.

As there are different types of homeless men, so different varieties of this particular brand, the hobo, may be differentiated. A part of the hobo group known as "harvest hands" follows the harvest and other agricultural occupations of seasonal nature. Another segment of the group works in the lumber woods and are known as "lumber jacks" or "timber beasts." A third group is employed in construction and maintenance work. A "gandy dancer" is a man who works on the railroad track tamping ties. If he works on the section he may be called a "snipe" or a "jerry."

A "skinner" is a man who drives horses or mules.

A "mucker" or a "shovel stiff" is a man who does manual labor on construction jobs.

A "rust eater" usually works on extra-gangs or track-laying jobs; handles steel.

A "dino" is a man who works with and handles dynamite.

A "splinter-belly" is a man who does rough carpenter work or bridge work.

A "cotton glaumer" picks cotton, an "apple knocker" picks apples and other fruit.

A "beach comber" is a plain sailor, of all men the most transient.

For every vocation that is open to the migratory worker there is some such characteristic name. In the West the hobo usually carries a bundle in which he has a bed, some extra clothes, and a little food. The man who carries such a bundle is usually known as a "bundle stiff" or "bundle bum." The modern hobo does not carry a bundle because it hinders him when he wishes to travel fast. It is the old man who went West "to grow up with the country" who still clings to his blanket roll.

THE TRAMP

While the word "tramp" is often used as a blanket term applied to all classes of homeless and potentially vagrant or transient types, it is here used in a stricter sense to designate a smaller group. He is usually thought of, by those familiar with his natural history, as an able-bodied individual who has the romantic passion to see the country and to gain new experience without work. He is a specialist at "getting by." He is the type that Josiah Flynt had in mind when he wrote his book, *Tramping with Tramps*. He is typically neither a drunkard nor a bum, but an easy-going individual who lives from hand to mouth for the mere joy of living.

45. X. began life as a half orphan. Later he was adopted and taken from Ohio to South Dakota. In his early teens he grew restive at home and left. But for brief seasons he has been away ever since and he is now past forty-five. He has traveled far and wide since but has worked little. He makes his living by selling joke books and song books. Sometimes he tries his hand at selling little articles from door to door. A few years ago he wrote a booklet on an economic subject and sold several thousand copies. During the winter of 1921–22 he sold the *Hobo News* each month. He is able to make a living this way. Any extra money he has he loses at the gambling tables. He spends his leisure time attempting to write songs or poetry. He knows a great deal about publishers but it is all information that has come in his efforts to sell his songs. He claims that he has been working for several years on a novel. He offered his work for inspection. He tries to lead the hero through all the places that he has visited and the hero comes in contact with many of the things he has seen or experienced in many cities but nowhere does his hero work. He enjoys life just as X. endeavors to do now. During the summer (1922) he has taken several "vacations" in the country for a week or more at the time.

46. C. is twenty-five years old. His home is in New York but he has not been home for more than ten years. He introduced himself to the "Hobo College" early in the spring of 1922 as "B-2." This name he assumed upon the conviction that he is the successor of "A-1," the famous tramp. He said that he had read "A-1's" books and although he did not agree in every respect, yet he thought that "A-1" was the greatest of tramp

writers. "B-2" claimed that he had ridden on every railroad in the United States. His evidence of travel was a book of post-office stamps. When he comes to a town he goes to the post-office and requests the postmaster to stamp his book much as letters are stamped. Another hobby he has is to go to the leading newspapers and endeavor to sell a write-up. He carries an accumulation of clippings. He has an assortment of flashy stories that take well with newspaper men. He claims that he has been pursued by bloodhounds in the South, that he has been arrested many times for vagrancy, that he is the only man who has beat his way on the Pikes Peak Railroad. He always carries a blanket and many other things that class him among wanderers as an individualist. He has been in the Army, saw action and was in the Army of Occupation. He does not seek work. He says his leisure time can be better spent. He carries a vest pocket kodak. He says that the pictures and notes he takes will some day be published.

The distinctions between the seasonal worker, the hobo, and the tramp, while important, are not hard and fast. The seasonal worker may descend into the ranks of the hobos, and a hobo may sink to the level of the tramp. But the knowledge of this tendency to pass from one migratory group to another is significant for any program that attempts to deal with the homeless man. Significant, also, but not sufficiently recognized, is the difference between these migratory types and the stationary types of homeless men, the "home guard" and the "bum."

CHAPTER VII
THE HOME GUARD AND THE BUM

THE seasonal worker, the hobo, and the tramp are migratory types; the home guard and the bum are relatively stationary. The home guard, like the hobo, is a casual laborer, but he works, often only by the day, now at one and again at another of the multitude of unskilled jobs in the city. The bum, like the tramp, is unwilling to work and lives by begging and petty thieving.

THE HOME GUARD

Nearly if not quite one-half of the homeless men in Hobohemia are stationary casual laborers. These men, contemptuously termed "home guards" by the hobo and the tramp, work regularly or irregularly at unskilled work, day labor, and odd jobs. They live or at least spend their leisure time on the "main stem," but seldom come to the attention of the charities or the police, or ask alms on the street. Many of them have lived in Chicago for years. Others after a migratory career as hobos or tramps "settle down" to a stationary existence. This group includes remittance men, often the "black sheep" of families of standing in far-off communities who send them a small regular allowance to remain away from home.

47. L. E. was born on the West Side and at present his family lives in Logan Square. He is twenty-three years old and has been away from home a year. He claims that after his mother's death he and his father could not agree. He immediately found his way to West Madison Street where he has lived since. During the winter (1921–22) he was converted in the Bible Rescue Mission but later he got drunk and would not

try again. However, he used to visit the mission after that when he had no bed and was hungry. He is a teamster and works regularly though he saves no money. He has no decent clothing and cares for none. He cares only to spend his Sundays and leisure time on West Madison Street, where he has a few acquaintances. He usually returns to work Monday morning after such visits, sick from the moonshine whisky. His health is not good. Most of his teeth are decayed but he will not save money to get dental work done. If he has any money to spend aside from that wanted for booze he goes to the movies and loafs the time away. He also attends the Haymarket or the Star and Garter theaters. He left his job two or three times during the summer. While he was not working he slept in stables. He doesn't go home nor communicate with his people.

The tendency for the casual worker to sink to the level of the bum is illustrated by the case of "Shorty":

48. "Shorty" claims that he has lived in the Hobohemian areas on South State and West Madison streets for thirty-nine years. He has never lived anywhere else. He doesn't care to go anywhere else. He tried married life a while but failed because of drink and returned to the "street." Drink is still getting him into trouble. He has dropped down the economic scale from an occasional worker to the status of a bum. This summer (1922) he has been arrested several times, and he has served two terms at the House of Correction. All the arrests were for drunkenness and disorder. He is developing into a professional panhandler or beggar. During the summer he has had two or three jobs. Once he was at the stockyards where he claims to have worked steadily in the early days. Being well known on the "streets" he is able to get odd jobs now and then that give him money enough to "get by." He has not been divorced from his wife. She won't live with him and he does not care. He has a child twelve or thirteen years old but he has not seen her for several years. He does not know where she is. He is not interested. He spends his leisure time on Madison Street near Desplaines where he may be found almost every day standing on the corner or sitting on the curb talking to some other "bo."

THE BUM

In every city there are ne'er-do-wells—men who are wholly or partially dependent and frequently delinquent as well. The most hopeless and the most helpless of all the homeless men is the bum, including in this type the inveterate drunkard and drug addicts. Old, helpless, and unemployable, these are the most pitiable and the most repulsive types of the down-and-outs. From this class are recruited the so-called "mission stiffs" who are so unpopular among the Hobohemian population.

49. L. D., forty-five years old, is a typical so-called "mission bum." He has not been known to work for eight months. During winter he is always present in some mission. Once he permitted himself to be led forward and knelt in prayer but was put out of the same mission later for being drunk. He claims that he was a prize fighter in his youth. He has traveled a great deal but he has always been a drinking man. When he is sober he is morose and quiet. As soon as spring permitted him to sleep out he ceased to visit the missions.

He has spent most of the summer on the docks along the river where he sleeps nights and where he has been getting work now and then unloading the fruit boats that ply between Chicago and Michigan. During the eight months he has been observed he has bought no new clothes. Not once during the summer has he left the city. He says that he has been in town for three years. The future seems to mean nothing to him. He does not worry about the coming winter.

50. A. B. is an habitual drunkard. He migrates a great deal but it seems that his migrations are to escape tedium and monotony rather than to work. He is a little, hollow-chested, undersized man and he claims to be thirty-two. He says that his health has not been good. He has a work history, it seems, but it is a record of light jobs. He picked berries, washed dishes, peddled, but he was also a successful beggar. His success in begging seems to lie in the ability to look pitiful. He has been in but four or five states of the Middle West but has been in most

of the large cities.   He does not patronize the missions because
he says he can do better begging.

OTHER TYPES OF HOMELESS MEN

Many of the terms which are epithets picturesquely
describe special types of homeless men.   The popular
names for the various types of tramps and hobos are
current terms that have been picked up on the street
as they pass from mouth to mouth.   Some of them
are new, others are old, while all of them are in
flux.   Names of types are coined by the men themselves.   They serve a while and then pass out, giving
place to new and more catchy terms.   Change is
characteristic of tramp terminology and tramp
jargon.   Words assume a different meaning as they
are extensively used, or they become too general in
their use and newer terms are invented.   Many of
the names by which types are designated were at
first terms of derision, but terms seem to lose their
stigma by continued use.[1]

Among tramps who seldom if ever work are those
who peddle some kind of wares or sell some kind of
service.

The Mushfaker is a man who sells his services.   He may be
a tinker, a glazier, an umbrella mender, or he may repair sewing
machines or typewriters.   Some mushfakers even pose as piano
tuners.   The mushfaker usually follows some occupation which
permits him to sit in the shade while he works.   Often the trade
or art he plies is one that he has learned in a penal institution.

The Scissor Bill is a man who carries with him tools to
sharpen saws, knives, razors, etc.   Often he pushes a grindstone
along the street.

Beggars among tramps are usually named with reference to
the methods they employ.

[1] The term "punk" is an instance; it had a special meaning at one time
but is beginning to have a milder and more general use and the term "lamb" is
taking its place.

The following classification is taken from a narrative work by "A No. 1, The Famous Tramp," who claims to have traveled 500,000 miles for $7.61. His books are more or less sensational and are not popular among many tramps, because they say the incidents he relates are overdrawn.[1]

The Rating of the Tramps by "A No. 1"

1. Pillinger..............Solicited alms at stores, offices, and residences
2. Moocher..............Accosted passers-by in the street
3. Flopper...............Squatted on sidewalk in business thoroughfares
4. Stiffy.................Simulated paralysis
5. Dummy...............Pretends to be deaf and dumb
6. Wires.................Peddling articles made of stolen telegraph wires
7. Mush Faker }
8. Mush Rigger }........Umbrella mender who learned trade in penal institution
9. Wangy................Disguised begging by selling shoestrings
10. Stickers...............Disguised begging by selling court plaster
11. Timbers...............Disguised begging by selling lead pencils
12. Sticks.................Train rider who lost a leg
13. Peg...................Train rider who lost a foot
14. Fingy or Fingers.......Train rider who lost one or more fingers
15. Blinky................Train rider who lost one or both eyes
16. Wingy................Train rider who lost one or both arms
17. Mitts.................Train rider who lost one or both hands
18. Righty................Train rider who lost right arm and leg
19. Lefty.................Train rider who lost left arm and leg

[1] *Mother Delcassee of the Hobos*, pp. 43–44.

20. Halfy..................Train rider who lost both legs below knee
21. Straight Crip...........Actually crippled or otherwise afflicted
22. Phoney Crip............Self-mutilated or simulating a deformity
23. Pokey Stiff.............Subsisting on handouts solely
24. Phoney Stiff............Disposing of fraudulent jewelry
25. Proper Stiff............Considered manual toil the acme of disgrace
26. Gink or Gandy Stiff.....Occasionally labored, a day or two at the most
27. Alkee Stiff }
28. White Line Stiff } ....Confirmed consumers of alcohol
29. Rummy Stiff...........Deranged intellect by habitual use of raw rum
30. Bundle Stiff }
31. Blanket Stiff } ....carried bedding
32. Chronicker.............Hoboed with cooking utensils
33. Stew Bum ⎫
34. Ding Bat ⎪
35. Fuzzy Tail ⎬ ....The dregs of vagrantdom
36. Grease Tail ⎪
37. Jungle Buzzard ⎭
38. Shine or Dingy.........Colored vagabond
39. Gay Cat...............Employed as scout by criminal tramps
40. Dino or Dynamiter......Sponged food of fellow hobos
41. Yegg..................Roving desperado
42. Gun Moll..............A dangerous woman tramp
43. Hay Bag...............A female stew bum
44. Jocker................Taught minors to beg and crook
45. Road Kid or Preshun....Boy held in bondage by jocker
46. Punk..................Boy discarded by jocker
47. Gonsil................Youth not yet adopted by jocker

The beggar is one who stands in one place. He supplicates help by appealing to the pity of the passers-by. The moocher is an individual who is somewhat more mobile than the beggar. He moves about, going to the houses and asking for food, cloth-

ing, and even money, if he can get it. The panhandler is a beggar of a more courageous type. He
hails men on the street and asks for money. He does
not fawn nor whine nor strive to arouse pity. Dr.
Reitman says: "The only difference between a
moocher and a panhandler is that the moocher
goes to the back door while the panhandler goes to
the front door."

The beggar types may also be divided into the
able-bodied and the non-able-bodied. The non-able-
bodied beggars are more numerous in the cities. They
are forced, because of their handicaps, to remain
where the greatest number of people are. Some
handicapped beggars, however, are able to travel
with marvelous speed over the country. These non-
able-bodied types go by different names according
to their afflictions.

Peggy is a one-legged man. Stumpy is a legless man.
Wingy is a man with one or both arms off. Blinky is a man with
one or both eyes defected. A Dummy is a man who is dumb or
deaf and dumb. Some of these types do not beg. They make
a livelihood by peddling or working at odd jobs. A Nut is a
man who is apparently mentally deranged.

The Hop Head is an interesting type. He is
usually in a pitiful condition, for he has small chance,
living as he does, in the tramp class, to get money to
buy "dope." Frequently he resorts to clever and
even desperate means to secure it. One type of
dope fiend is the Junkie. He uses a "gun" or needle
to inject morphine or heroin. A Sniffer is one who
sniffs cocaine. More frequent than the drug habit
is the drink habit.

The tramp class has different types of predatory
individuals and petty or even major offenders:

The Gun is a man who might be termed a first-class crook. He is usually a man who is living in the tramp class to avoid apprehension. He may be a robber or a burglar.

¶ The Jack Roller is a tramp who robs a fellow-tramp while he is drunk or asleep. There is a type of "Jack" who operates among the men going to and from the harvests. He may hold them up in a box car with a gun or in some dark alley. He is usually called a Hi-Jack.

Among other types of tramps are:

The Mission Stiff who preys upon the missions. He will often submit to being converted for his bed and board.

The Grafter is frequently a man who is able to exploit the private and public charity organizations, or the fraternal organizations.

The Bad Actor is a man who has become a nuisance to his people and they pay him money provided he does not show himself in his home town.

The Jungle Buzzard is a tramp who lives in the jungles from what he can beg. He will wash the pots and kettles for the privilege of eating what is left in them.

From the point of view of abnormal sex relations there are several types of tramps:

A Punk is a boy who travels about the country with a man known as a jocker.

A jocker is a man who exploits boys; that is, he either exploits their sex or he has them steal or beg for him or both. The term "wolf" is often used synonymously with jocker.

Fairies or Fags are men or boys who exploit sex for profit.

From the economic standpoint, migratory workers are employables and unemployables. Between the extremes there are individuals of every shade of employability. The ability of a man to support himself is presumed to be related to his ability and to his opportunity to work. The tramp problem has been interpreted first of all as an unemployment problem, but this does not take account of the unemployables.

First of all, there are the physically handicapped, the crippled, the blind, the deaf, and the aged, and many who are too fat or too puny or too sickly to do heavy manual work. Perhaps a half of the whole group in a city like Chicago are physically handicapped to a greater or less extent.

Second, the psychopathic types include many irresponsible and undependable persons found in the population of Hobohemia. These either cannot hold a job, or do not care to; they have other ideals. They could, no doubt, do some sort of work but most of them would have to be supervised.

To what degree homeless men are employable, to what degree some of them are partially employable, and to what extent the whole group is unemployable is a question that cannot be finally answered.[1]

The problem of the homeless men is variously interpreted. The courts and the police are interested in them as offenders. As offenders, they are generally recidivists; to the social worker and the missionary they represent a body of men who have no purpose or direction.

One mission worker says:

A few of them can hold their own. They manage to work most of the time and pay their way, but most of them are "broke" some of the time and some of them are without money all the time. They are always making resolutions and never keeping them. They don't seem to have any stiffening in their backbone.

However we may classify this group, the fact remains that we have here a great body of persons,

---

[1] The unemployables are a more or less permanent class and do not come and go with the seasons as do the employables. Able-bodied employables are an effect of economic depression.

probably more than a million in the United States,[1] and that they furnish a problem that seems to be ever present. It is, as we shall see later, a great heterogeneous group, unorganized and incapable of being organized. They have been gathered from every walk of life and for a thousand different reasons find themselves in this class. There are restless and normal boys and young men who are out in the world for adventure and whose stay in the class is more or less temporary; there are able-bodied men of more mature age who are either wholly self-supporting or are self-supporting most of the time; and there are old men who are too aged and infirm to work and too proud to surrender themselves to an institution. There are the physically incapacitated and the mentally inadequate who are more or less dependent and are likely to continue so, and there are many types of persons who are the victims of lingering diseases or who are addicted to drink or drugs and are not able to hold their own. All these are making the best struggle that their wits, their strength, and their opportunities permit to get a living. Some of them are in the group by choice and have their minds clearly made up to climb out, others hope to get out and strive to but never will, and yet others never have any such visions.

RELATIVE NUMBERS OF DIFFERENT TYPES

An estimate has already been made that the number of homeless men in Chicago range from 30,000 in the summer to 60,000 in the winter, reach-

---

[1] Estimates vary; Lescohier (Commons, *Trade Unionism and Labor Problems*, 133) gives the number as "more than half a million men," while Speek (*Annals of the American Academy*, 1917) refers to estimates that go as high as five million.

ing 75,000 in periods of unemployment. Any attempt to state the numbers of the different types of homeless men can be little more than a guess. The difficulty is the greater because individuals are continually passing from one group into another group. One man in his lifetime may perchance have been, in turn, seasonal laborer, hobo, tramp, home guard, and bum.

The public generally fails to distinguish between these types. The group of bums, beggars, and petty thieves, often mistakenly thought of as representative of the homeless men's group, probably does not exceed in Chicago a total number of 2,500. The number of the home-guard type, the stationary casual worker, has been placed at 30,000, the summer population of Hobohemia on the basis of the number of permanent guests at lodging-house and hotel, and the number of registered voters among the homeless men.[1] The number of tramps who visit Chicago each year can only be roughly estimated at 150,000,[2] or an average of perhaps 5,000 at any given time. The migratory worker, including both the seasonal laborer and the hobo, number on the average around 10,000 and reach a total of 300,000 or more persons who come to Chicago for the winter or to secure a shipment to work outside the city. In periods of economic depression the numbers of homeless men in Hobohemia are swollen with men out of work, the majority of whom for the first time have been turned adrift on the "main stem."

[1] See p. 14 n.

[2] These numbers indicate the number of visits rather than the number of separate individuals since a certain proportion of men visit Chicago two or more times during the year.

CHAPTER VIII
WORK

THE occupations that select out of the foot-loose males in our population the most restless types are:

1. *Agriculture or crop moving.*—When the crops are ready to be garnered labor must be imported at any cost. The leading crops in these seasonal demands are grain harvesting, corn shucking, fruit picking, potato digging, beet topping, cotton picking, hop picking, etc. If a man follows the wheat harvest, he may be occupied from the middle of June when the crop is ready in Oklahoma until November or December when the season ends with threshing in North Dakota and Canada. Workers who pick fruit may remain in one locality and have some kind of fruit always coming on.

2. *Building and construction work.*—Next to crop moving the building trades and construction jobs make the heaviest seasonal demands upon the labor market. Railroad construction, ditch digging, and similar occupations are generally discontinued during the winter. Carpentry, masonry, brick and concrete work are only carried on with reduced numbers of men through the cold months.

3. *Fishing.*—Salmon fishing on the Pacific Coast and oyster fishing on the Atlantic Coast are also seasonal industries. In the fishing industry, as in other seasonal occupations, there is a demand for experienced workers that cannot always be had when most needed.

4. *Sheep shearing.*—Sheep shearing is a skilled trade. Thousands of men are needed to harvest the

wool crop each year and these men are forced to become migratory. The shearing season, like the harvest, moves from border to border during a period of three or four months. In the Southwest the sheep are sometimes clipped twice a year. The shearing jobs are usually short but lucrative.

5. *Ice harvesting.*—Formerly the ice harvest furnished employment to an army of men for two months or more during the winter. Ice-manufacturing plants have diminished the demand for natural ice, though ice cutting still furnishes winter jobs for many men.

6. *Lumbering.*—Working in the lumber woods and in the saw mills is not now so much of a seasonal job as it was when the industry centered around the Great Lakes. The industry has gone West or over the border into Canada, where, with the longer winter season and improved facilities, it operates almost all year. It is not necessary in Washington, Oregon, and California to wait for the snow to begin work in the woods as in Michigan and Wisconsin in the early days.

Certain occupations not essentially seasonal have a tendency to contribute to migrancy. In many metal mines a man's health will not permit him to work long. He leaves and goes into some other mine in the same or a different district where the danger is not present. A miner tends to become a migrant for the sake of his health. There are other industries in which hazards exist that force workers to become transient.

The American hobo has been a great pioneer. New mining camps, oil booms, the building of a town in a few weeks, or any mushroom development utilizes a great many transient workers. After a flood, a fire, or an earthquake, there is a great demand for labor. The migratory worker is always ready to respond. It is his life, in which he finds variety and experience and, last but not least, something to talk about.

JOB HUNTING AMONG THE CASUAL WORKERS

In seasonal and casual work, as in all types of industry, a process of selection takes place. Great numbers of men are attracted into seasonal occupations because of the good wages offered. But only those remain who are content to migrate from one locality to another in response to the demands for labor. The average man soon realizes that in the course of a year seasonal work does not pay even if fabulous wages are received for short-lived jobs. The man who continues as a migratory worker is likely, therefore, to be a person who is either unable to find or unable to hold a permanent job. Some workers become restless after a few weeks or months in one place. Seasonal and casual work seems to have selected out these restless types and made hobos of them.

Migratory workers have a certain body of traditions: they know how to get work; what kind of work to look for; when to look for certain kinds of work, and where certain work may be found. They fall in with the seasonal migration of workers and drift into certain localities to do certain jobs; to the potato fields, the fruit picking, the wheat harvest.

The hobo worker finds his way to out-of-town jobs more often than to city work. Upon leaving an out-of-town job he is likely to return to the city in

order to locate another job out of the city or even out
of the state. This tendency of the foot-loose worker
to drift into the city has turned the attention of the
employer to the city whenever he needed help. Both
the worker and the employer have been attracted to
the city in an effort to solve their labor difficulties.
Intermediate agencies spring up to bring together the
jobless man and the man with jobs to offer. Employment agents, congregating in the Hobohemian sections of the city, convert those areas into labor
markets.

Chicago is probably the greatest labor exchange
for the migratory worker in the United States, if
not in the world. Probably no other city furnishes
more men for railroad work. In days past, when so
many new railroads were being built, there were
great demands for men in the West, and it was not
uncommon to get a 1,000-mile shipment any time
in the year. One is still able to secure free shipments of from 400 to 600 miles.

There are more than 200 private employment agencies in Chicago. There were, on August 14, 1922, 39
licensed private agencies of the type patronized by
the homeless man. Eighteen of these were on Canal
Street, thirteen were on West Madison Street, and
the rest in close proximity to that area. In addition
to these there are many agencies not operating on a
commission basis which hire men for a private corporation and are maintained by that corporation.
As such they are not licensed nor does the law affect
them.

No figures are at hand to show how many men
these private agencies place during the year. Their
records are not merely inadequate; they are a joke.

In fact, few of them keep records that list all applicants, all men placed, jobs registered, etc., though the state law definitely declares that this must be done.

The inclusion of the non-fee-collecting agencies will raise the number from 39 to over 50. If each agency sends out, at a low estimate, 10 men a day, and if each operates 300 days a year, a total of 150,000 men are placed in jobs annually. Over 57,000 men in 1921–22 were placed by the free employment agency. Many of these homeless men have access to other private agencies than those situated on the "stem," and often they prefer to go to such agencies. If 100 of these agencies furnished jobs to 2 homeless men a day for 300 days a year, we would have an additional 60,000. About 250,000 homeless men pass through the Chicago employment agencies every year.

Employment agencies fall into two classes—the public, or those operated by the federal government, the state, or the municipality and those conducted under private management. The private agency is the pioneer. It was not only the outgrowth of a certain condition in the labor market but it was the reason for the creation of the public employment bureau.

PRIVATE EMPLOYMENT AGENCIES

The idea is becoming general that employment offices have a social responsibility. They have duties to the applicants, to the employers, and to the public that are more than economic; more than a business of selling jobs to jobless men. It is a responsibility that is not imposed upon the ordinary business man and that has no prominent place in the code of business ethics.

The private employment agencies that cater to
the homeless men are chiefly located on the West
Side. The 1919–20 *Report of the Illinois Department
of Labor*[1] shows that during that period there were
295 licensed private employment agencies in Chicago.
As we noted above, about fifty of these serve the
homeless men. Most of these fifty agencies are
located along Canal Street opposite the Union
Depot, or along Madison Street between the Chicago
River and Halsted Street. Some of these operate
the year round, while others come and go with the
seasons, opening up in prosperous times and going
out of existence when the demand for labor falls.

A few of the private agencies are fairly well
equipped; that is, they have desks, counters, telephone, chairs or benches, and a waiting-room which
in cold weather is kept warm for the patrons.
Others, the majority, have very little equipment,
perhaps a chair and a table in a single, bare room.
They keep no books other than what they carry in
their pockets. For the average small labor agent an
office is only used as a place to hang the license. He
gets his patrons by standing on the street and soliciting. The other private agents are playing the rôle
of man catcher, and he must do the same if he would
succeed.

There are two types of private labor agencies—
the commission agencies, and the boarding or commissary agencies. The commission agency is the
pioneer job-selling institution which survives by
charging a fee to the employer who seeks workers, or
by charging a fee to the applicants, or by charging
both. Usually they charge both the applicant and

[1] P. 51.

the employer, and formerly their prices were governed by the demand for jobs, on the one hand, and for workers, on the other. (If the competition is for workers they can raise the price charged the employer. If jobs are scarce they can raise the price charged the applicant.) The boarding and commissary agency charge no fee for the job. Their profit is made in keeping the boarding-house for the men they hire.

In the past it was proverbial that better shipments could be had from the private agencies in Chicago than from any other city. A few years ago the Chicago agencies were shipping men to all the big jobs within a radius of from 500 to 1,000 miles, and men would come to Chicago from 500 to 1,000 miles in one direction to be sent by the agencies to work on some job equally as far in another direction. These long-distance interstate shipments have been the chief factor in the prosperity of the private agencies. High prices were charged for the long shipments but the men were willing to pay them whether the job was good or not in order to secure free transportation west or south or east. The long shipments are not so numerous at present and the high fees are no longer permitted.

The charge sometimes made that the private agencies are gruff and discourteous would seem well founded if one failed to consider the behavior of homeless men on the street. These men would not pass the same judgment. They are used to speaking roughly to each other. They take and give hard blows in their dealings with the "labor shark." Many men can get along much better with the blunt and unceremonious private agent than with the sleek, precise, courteous, and business-like officials in the public agencies. Their preference for the private agent is not for his gruffness or the ease with which they **may** approach him. It is mainly because he serves them better. They hate him for his fees but he gets the jobs they want.

The migratory worker resents the idea of being obliged to pay for the privilege of securing work. In every program that the hobo has advocated to change society he has made reference to the "labor shark." The hobo worker is never disappointed to find that the job has been misrepresented by the agency. Nor is the agency surprised if the applicant does not go to work when he arrives on the job.

PUBLIC EMPLOYMENT AGENCIES

The state has been forced into the employment business because of the problems presented by private agencies. The public employment agency in Chicago has not displaced or even seriously affected the private employment agency. It is still only in the experimental stage, a laboratory in which the employment problem may be studied.

There are three public free employment offices in Chicago: one at 116 North Dearborn for skilled workers, one at 105 South Jefferson Street for unskilled workers, and one at 344 East Thirty-fifth Street, chiefly for Negro workers. The homeless man is chiefly interested in the Federal and State Labor Exchange located at 105 South Jefferson Street. However, the central office on Dearborn Street, which specializes in skilled and permanent employment, attracts two or three hundred homeless men a day, mainly from South State Street. This office is careful not to send out on jobs "dead line men."

By "dead line men" are meant men who live on Madison west of Canal Street. Men "living" on Clark, State, and Dearborn streets are more reliable and stand a better chance

than the "dead line men" to get jobs. The firms that place
their demand for help with the Dearborn Street bureau generally
want references, showing place of residence and name of former
employer. Such firms will not consider a West Madison Street
man. The clerks sometimes advise an applicant to change his
address to that of some relative in case the applicant makes a
favorable impression with the clerk. If a man looks and speaks
intelligently but is too ragged and dirty to send out on a job, the
suggestion is sometimes made to clean up and spruce up a bit.
The transformation in some cases is astonishing.[1]

Probably four or five times as many men are
placed by the private as by the public employment
agencies. It seems paradoxical that the migratory
worker should patronize the private labor agent
whom he regards as an exploiter and a parasite rather
than the free employment office, yet there are good
reasons for his behavior.

In the first place, the office of the public agency,
although little more than a block away, is not on the
"main stem." Strangers in the city find their way
to the "slave market" without difficulty but may
never become aware of the existence of the free
employment office. A migratory worker likes to do
a little "window shopping" before he takes a job.
He likes to go along the streets reading the red or
blue or yellow placards announcing jobs and shipments until he has made up his mind. The signs and
scribbled windows of the private agency are maneu-
vers of salesmanship. The public agency has no
such signs on the outside. The men must go inside
to see the blackboard upon which the jobs are written.

Further, the public agency is in duty bound, as
the private agency is not, to keep records and to get
certain information from the workers who apply for

[1] Koster, unpublished manuscript, pp. 17-18.

jobs, and from the employers as well. The men who patronize these agencies dislike the "red tape" of the public agency; they are often unwilling to be catalogued and given a number, or go through the other formalities so necessary for efficiency. The decisive reason why the migratory worker patronizes the private agency is because it carries a better class of jobs. Jobs involving interstate shipments are usually given to the private agencies, partly because it is customary, and partly because they know how to solicit such contracts for labor. It is difficult for a man to get an out-of-state job in the public agency since it is more or less local in its jurisdiction. The private agencies attract the hobos also because they make no effort to see that he goes to work after he has been sent. Indeed, it is to their advantage if he does not go to work, for then they have the chance to send another man. The public agency makes an effort to "follow up" the applicants and to "keep tab" on them. The hobo worker shies from such solicitous treatment.

Mr. J. J. Kenna, chief inspector of private employment agencies, believes that the private agencies should be obliged to do likewise. He wrote in his report to the State Department of Labor in 1920:

Another question that might be given consideration is the subject of public information pertaining to the business of private employment agencies for the instruction of those interested in labor problems and legislation, namely:

A law compelling the agencies to furnish the State Department of Labor with a monthly report of the number of all applicants applying for positions, their ages, etc., and also the number of persons brought into the State and sent out of the State and to where sent, the kind of employment for which they were engaged, etc.[1]

[1] *Third Annual Report of the Department of Labor* (1920), p. 50.

Nothing would do more for efficiency in the employment office business than to compel the private agencies to keep as efficient records as the public bureau. The spirit of competition so prevalent in the private agencies is not present in the public labor bureau. The public agency stands complacently on the side, never entering the struggle to get jobs and men together. It is too much of an office and too little of an agency.

The public and private agencies operate upon diametrically opposing assumptions. The assumption of the public agency is that the man once placed will remain so long as the job lasts, and a large proportion of their jobs, especially in the Dearborn Street office, are for "long stake" men. A man's record, his qualifications, are taken and he is sent out to the job with the notion that he will work steady. The private agencies, on the contrary, assume that few of these men will remain long on the job; that they may stay ten days or two weeks and seldom longer than three months. The public agency with an eye to permanency may be expected to move slowly in placing men on jobs, whereas the private agency will send anyone to any job that he says he can do and that he is willing to pay for.

THE CASUALIZATION OF LABOR

The casualization of labor, in spite of its concern to place men permanently, has a tendency to attract "home guards," i.e., men who do not care to leave the city and yet do not want steady work. They may work from a day to a week, then they return for another job.

The following are a few of the names taken at
random from a list of men who had been given ten or
more jobs by the Federal and State Labor Exchange
between March 1, 1922, and August 15, 1922 (five
and one-half months):

	Number	Jobs
Wm. Mitchell	1,735	20
Jas. Perry	5,878	10
Tony Felk	1,195	10
Jas. Griffin	5,811	12
F. Mullen	5,069	21
Ed. Moorhead	635	20
Fred Wagoner	5,334	15
Jas. Purl	682	16
F. A. Murlin	5,390	13
W. Galvin	628	18
A. Myers	3,700	17
W. Slavis	2,202	19
P. Myshowi	2,408	15
C. Carroll	4,742	16
Jas. Lewis	3,872	16

The records show hundreds of similar instances.
Some men have been sent to as many as forty or
fifty jobs during a period of six months and few
stayed with a job more than a month or two.

John M. secured 26 jobs from the Free Employment Bureau
in less than three months between May 4 and July 26. The
following is the list of employers with the dates of employment:[1]

1. Morris and Co. ....May 4
2. Ravina Nursery ....May 6
3. Edison Co. ....May 10
4. Ed Katzinger ....May 18
5. New Era Coal Co. ....May 24
6. Ravina Nursery ....May 26

[1] E. H. Koster, unpublished notes, pp. 42–43.

7. Home Fuel Co............... May 27
8. Morris and Co.............. .May 31
9. Ill. Bell Telephone Co........ June 8
10. Flazman Iron Co............ June 12
11. Greenpoint Beef Co......... June 13
12. Astrid Rosing Co. .... June 14
13. Armstrong Paint Co......... June 21
14. Const. Mattress Co.......... June 22
15. Armour Co. .... June 26
16. Oxweld Acetylene Co........ June 27
17. Oxweld Acetylene Co........ June 29
18. Wisconsin Lime Co.......... June 30
19. American Express Co....... July 1
20. Wisconsin Lime Co.......... July 5
21. Oxweld Acetylene Co........ July 10
22. Oxweld Acetylene Co........ July 11
23. Edison Co.................. July 15
24. Low Pipe Co............... July 24
25. International Har. Co....... July 25
26. J. A. Ross................. July 26

John M. is a casual laborer.   He is one of a type
that works by the day, is paid by the day, and lives
by the day.   Don. D. Lescohier has described the
characteristics of the casual workers:

A man becomes a casual when he acquires the casual state of
mind.   The extreme type of casual never seeks more than a
day's work.   He lives strictly to the rule, one day at a time.
If you ask him why he does not take a steady job, he will tell
you that he would like to, but that he hasn't money enough to
enable him to live until pay-day, and no one will give him credit.
If you offer to advance his board until pay-day, he will accept
your offer and accept the job you offer him, but he will not show
up on the job, or else will quit at the end of the first day.   He has
acquired a standard or scale of work and life that makes it
almost impossible for him to restore himself to steady employment.   He lacks the desire, the will-power, self-control, ambition,
and habits of industry which are essential to it.[1]

[1] Lescohier, *The Labor Market*, p. 264.

The demoralizing effect of a period of unemployment upon the migratory and casual worker is indicated in an interview given to the investigator by Mr. Charles J. Boyd, general superintendent of the Illinois Free Employment Offices in Chicago.

Depending on one's point of view, the homeless man, owing to the serious industrial depression during the winter of 1921–1922 had remarkable success in begging or panhandling. The spirit of the public during the depression was to help the unemployed man and advantage of this situation was not lost sight of by the hobo who worked on the sympathy of the public. With the approach of summer and improved industrial conditions, the hobo continued to make a living in other ways than by working for it. There seems to be an understanding among this class of men not to work for less than 50c an hour, and they are loath to accept steady employment at 35c to 37½c hour when they can do temporary work, and work at a different job every day, or any day one pleases, at 45c to 50c an hour. The hobo is reluctant to work in foundries or steel mills. He likes the open and when winter is past, the hobo, with few exceptions, refuses inside work.

The hobos of today are made up of young men, ranging in ages from 18 to 35 years. They form in groups of six or seven, camp in the "brush" and send a different one of their group out each day to panhandle in the town or village near which they may be camping. Then too, these men have very decided views on the Volstead law, before the enactment of which the hobo felt he had some inducement to work, for he liked his beer, if it was only 1½ per cent, and he did not know it. But since prohibition, his attitude seems to be "Why should I work any more than I really have to?" or in other words, more than to get enough for food and a place to sleep.[1]

The hobo is not unfamiliar with strike jobs. Corporations, when forced to the wall in a labor crisis, often come to the "stem" for their strikebreakers. By offering alluring wages and the assur-

[1] From the unpublished notes of an interview by E. H. Koster.

ance of security, they are able to attract from ranks
of even the casual workers enough men to keep the
plants running.   Labor agencies of this kind are
not popular on the "stem"; neither are the men
who hire out as strike-breakers.   But in spite of this
stigma they survive as during the railroad strike
in the summer of 1922.   These railroad agencies
crowded even to the heart of the Madison Street
mart and eventually forced the private agencies to
deal in strike jobs.

Strike-breakers or "scabs" are of four varieties:
(1) men who are innocently attracted to the job
(it is generally charged that this was the case in the
Herrin affair); (2) men who are "too proud to beg
and too honest to steal"; (3) men who have a grudge
against some striking union, or against organized
labor in general; and (4) men who hire out as
bona fide workers but really "bore from within"
and in the language of the radical "work sabotage."

A NATIONAL PROBLEM

All the problems of the homeless man go back in
one way or another to the conditions of his work.
The irregularity of his employment is reflected in the
irregularity of all phases of his existence.   To deal
with him even as an individual, society must deal
also with the economic forces which have formed his
behavior, with the seasonal and cyclical fluctuations
in industry.   This means that the problem of the
homeless man is not local but national.

The establishment during the war of the United
States Employment Service gave promise of an
attempt to cope with the problem nationally.   The
curtailment of this service since 1919 through inade-

quate appropriations has prevented its functioning on a scale which the situation demands.

The emphasis upon the development of a national program means no lack of recognition of the service of local employment agencies. They are indispensable units in any effective plan of nation-wide organization. The bureaus and branches, in Chicago, of the Illinois Free Employment offices are now co-operating with the United States Employment Service.

A CLEARING HOUSE FOR HOMELESS MEN

The accumulated experience of the local employment agencies will be valuable not only in the future expansion of the national employment service, but in pointing the way to the next steps to be taken locally in dealing with the homeless man as a worker. The officials of these agencies have learned that the problem of adjusting the migratory casual worker in industry involves human nature as well as economics. A conviction is growing that in connection with, or in addition to, the public employment agency designed to bring together the man and the job, there is need of a clearing house which offers medical, psychological, and sociological diagnosis as a basis for vocational guidance, after-care service, and industrial rehabilitation.

PART III
THE HOBO PROBLEM

CHAPTER IX
HEALTH

NO EXTENDED study has ever been made that would afford an adequate index for the physical fitness of homeless men. Municipal lodging-houses, jails, hospitals, and other institutions have collected certain data. But such information is indicative of the physical and mental condition of those only who have become problems of charity or correction. They do not represent the whole group of homeless men. However, it is evident from these studies that a large proportion of the entire group is below par physically. They indicate at least that defective individuals are comparatively numerous among hobos and tramps.

THE PHYSICALLY DEFECTIVE

Mrs. Alice W. Solenberger found that two-thirds of her 1,000 cases were either physically or mentally defective. Of these, 627 men and boys were suffering from a total of 722 physical and mental deficiencies.[1]

Condition	Instances
Insanity	52
Feeble-mindedness	19
Epilepsy	18
Paralysis	40
Other nervous disorders	21
Tuberculosis	93
Rheumatism	37
Venereal diseases	21
Other infectious diseases	15
Heart disease	14
Disorders of organs other than heart	19

[1] Alice W. Solenberger, *One Thousand Homeless Men*, p. 36.

Condition	Instances
Crippled, maimed, or deformed; from birth or accident	168
Rupture	11
Cancer	6
Blind, including partly blind	43
Deaf, including partly deaf	14
Defective health through use of drugs and drink	16
Defective health from lack of nourishment and other causes	24
Convalescent	33
Aged	35
All other diseases and defects	7
Doubtful	16
Total instances	722
Total number of different men in defective health or condition	627

She tells us that of the 222 more or less permanently handicapped, 106 men had been entirely self-supporting before their injuries while 127 were entirely dependent after injury.

A careful study of 100 homeless men made in the Municipal Lodging House of New York City by F. C. Laubach showed the following defects:[1]

Tubercular	7	Maimed	14
Venereal	26	Malnutrition	13
Bronchial	4	Poor sight	9
Feeble	14	Poor hearing	1
Senile	16	Impediment of speech	2
Deformed	4	Physically sound	28

Laubach's 100 cases were selected from more than 400 men. They represented the 100 who remained longest to be examined (perhaps the 100 the least able to get away). He found 28 per cent able-bodied

[1] F. C. Laubach, *Why There Are Vagrants*, p. 21

while Mrs. Solenberger reported 37.3 per cent without observable defects. That this per cent of
defectives is high for more unselected groups will be
shown by the following extract from the report of
the Municipal Lodging House of New York City for
1915.

. . . . Fifteen hundred men were studied by a staff of fifteen
investigators. At the same time a medical examination of two
thousand men was conducted by fifteen medical examiners.
This investigation represented the first large attempt in America
to find out about the men who take refuge in a municipal lodging
house. . . . .

Of the 2,000 men who were given a medical examination,
1,774, approximately 9 out of every 10, were, according to the
adjudgments of the examining physicians, physically able to
work. Twelve hundred and forty-seven, or 62 per cent of the
total, were considered physically able to do regular hard manual
labor; 254, or 18 per cent, to do medium hard work; and 173,
or 9 per cent, to do light work only. Two hundred and twenty-
six, 1 out of every 10, were adjudged physically unable to
work.[1]

This investigation showed that in a lean year,
when many men were out of work, a large proportion
of the lodging-house population is composed of handicapped men. The physical condition of 400 tramps
interviewed by the writer is not so much in contra-
diction as in supplement to the foregoing studies.[2]
Only men in transit were tabulated. Nearly all of
them were the typical migratory workers or hobos.
Observation was limited to apparent defects that

---

[1] *Report of the Advisory Social Service Committee of the Municipal Lodging
House*, pp. 9–11. New York City: September, 1915.

[2] This unpublished study of 400 tramps was made while riding freight
trains from Salt Lake City, Utah, to Chicago in the summer of 1921. All the
cases tabulated were cases in transit. A large part of them were men who
regularly beat their way about the country. Document 115.

would hinder in a noticeable manner the working capacity of the men.

Senile................	6	Tuberculosis..........	2
Maimed.............	8	Feeble-minded........	7
Eye lost or partly blind	5	Chronic poor health...	4
Eye trouble..........	5	Impediment of speech	2
Venereal disease......	1	Temporarily injured...	4
Partly paralyzed......	2	Oversized or undersized	4

These 50 defects were distributed among 48 persons

Subtracting those who could be classed mentally defective, we have but forty-one persons who were apparently physically handicapped. It will be noted that the percentage of the aged is considerably lower than the previous tables show. The same is true of the maimed and injured. They were all men who were able to "get over the road." One of the maimed men had lost an arm while the two others had each lost a foot.

Eye trouble was listed separately because these were ailments that were passing. Three of the men had weak eyes and this condition had been aggravated by train riding and loss of sleep. One man had been gassed in the army and his eyes suffered from the wind and bright light. Only one man admitted that he was suffering from a venereal disease.

Both men suffering from tuberculosis were miners. Both had been in hospitals for treatment. One of them was in a precarious condition. The men listed as oversized and undersized might be properly considered physically handicapped. Two of them were uncomfortably fat while the other two were conspicuously under weight and height.

THE HOBO'S HEALTH ON THE JOB

Often the seasonal work sought by the migratory worker is located in out-of-the-way places or with little or no medical or sanitary supervision. Sometimes there are not even tents for the men to sleep in. Life and work in the open, so conducive to health on bright, warm days, involves exposure in cold and stormy weather. In the northwest, where rain is so abundant that workers suffer considerably from exposure, strikes have even been called to enforce demands for warm, dry bunkhouses.

In addition to the exposure to the elements there are other hazards the migratory and casual workers run. On most of his jobs, whether in the woods, the swamps, in the sawmills, or the mines and quarries, in the harvest, on bridges or on the highways, the hobo faces danger. Since he is in the habit of working only a few days at the time, a well-paying, hazardous job appeals to him. The not infrequent accidents are serious since few of these foot-loose men carry insurance.

Seasonal labor generally consists of hard work like shoveling or lifting and carrying heavy loads. Only men who can do hard work are wanted. Not much so-called "light work" aside from a few jobs in kitchens, in stables, or about camps is open to the transient. Many homeless men are not physically able to do eight or ten hours' hard labor without suffering. They are often weak from eating poor food or from dissipation. Even if they go on a job with their minds made up to remain one or two months they are often obliged to leave after a few days. Often the hobo works on jobs where there is no medical attention. Sometimes, where the job includes large numbers of men, a physician is hired to go from camp to camp. He is usually known as a "pill peddler" and all he pretends to do is give first aid to the injured and treat passing ailments. Serious cases he sends to the hospital.

Big industrial organizations usually carry some sort of medical insurance and in some cases accident insurance. This system of workingmen's compensation for industrial accidents is maintained sometimes by fees taken from the pay of the men, sometimes entirely by the employer. The accident compensation, the hospital, and medical privileges apply only to ailments and injuries caused by his work.

The food the hobo receives on the job is not always palatable, nor does it always come up to the requirements of a balanced diet or the caloric needs of a workingman. In the business of feeding the men, considerable exploitation enters which the men are powerless to prevent. The boarding contracts are often let to boarding companies that agree to feed the men and furnish bunks for prices ranging (since the war) from five to eight dollars a week. For the privilege of boarding the workers, they agree to keep the gangs filled. Often in the West the men furnish their own beds, but private "bundle beds" are passing. Some companies furnish good beds, but the general rule is to supply a tick that may be filled with straw and a couple of quilts which are charged to the worker until he returns them. These quilts and blankets are often used again and again by different men without being cleaned during a whole season.

Several boarding companies maintain free employment agencies in Chicago, well known to the hobo

and generally disliked. The chief complaint against
them is that in hard times, when men are plentiful,
there is a tendency to drop on the quality and the
quantity of the food. In such an event the monotony of the menu and the unsavory manner in which
food is prepared is a scandal in Hoboland. However,
all complaints against boarding companies are not
due to bad food. Poor cooking is another ground for
much dissatisfaction. Efficient camp cooks are rare
and too high priced for the average boarding company.

THE HEALTH OF THE MAN ON THE "STEM"

The hazards the homeless man takes while at
work in the city are far less than on the seasonal
out-of-town work. The health problem of the
transient "on the stem" is nevertheless serious. It
is not so much a problem of work conditions as of
hotels and lodging accommodations and restaurants.

The cheap lodging-houses and hotels in Chicago
are under the surveillance of the Chicago Department of Health. The department has done much
to keep down contagion and to raise the standards of
these places. Infectious diseases have been more
rare here than in hotels in the Loop. These hotels
survived the influenza epidemics as well as any in the
city. There has been a gradual rise in the standards
of health and sanitation of the hotels and lodging-
houses, but just how much this is due to the watchful
care of the Department of Health cannot be said.
Other factors, such as business competition, may also
have entered in to improve conditions.

In many respects the cheap workingmen's hotels
still fall far below the standards set by law. Indeed,
if all of them lived up to the letter of the law in every

respect, many would find it unprofitable to operate. These hotels are in buildings that were erected for other purposes, buildings that cannot be adequately made over to accommodate comfortably hundreds of men.

The problem of ventilation is present in the older hotels for men. In some corners, in hallways and isolated rooms, there is never any circulation of air. The smells accumulate from day to day so that the guest on entering a room is greeted by a variety of odors to which each of his predecessors has contributed.

The following statement of an investigator indicates what is one of the most objectionable features of the cheap hotel.

The lack of adequate toilet facilities is deplorable. In one hotel I found two toilets for one hundred and eighty men and in another seven for three hundred and eighty. Some of the toilets have absolutely no outside ventilation, opening on sleeping rooms. Some of them are located in halls with no partition separating them from sleeping rooms and are a source of foul and nauseating odors.[1]

With respect to wash basins and bath facilities the condition is no better. Many do not even have hot water. In some places from twenty to forty men use the same wash bowl.

The Department of Health has taken an active part in the campaign against vermin, and co-operates whenever a complaint is made. Their task seems hopeless since the patrons are so transient and so frequently carry vermin from one place to another. The very buildings are often breeding places for bedbugs, lice, and roaches.

[1] George S. Sobel, *Report to Committee*, summer, 1922.

SICKNESS AND DISEASE

If the homeless man becomes sick or injured while at work he likely will be cared for by the hospital maintained by the industry. But he is in dire distress when he has no job and is in need of medical attention. Occasionally men without funds go to private physicians and not infrequently they get free treatment, but the traditional and easier method of meeting such situations is to go to an institution. Chicago, with its numerous hospitals and medical colleges, is a Mecca for the sick and the afflicted of the "floating fraternity." Homeless men come sometimes several hundred miles for treatment to this great healing center of trampdom. They have no scruples against entering an institution as a charity patient. To them it is not charity, but something due to the sick.

VENEREAL DISEASE

Venereal disease and ailments growing out of venereal disease play a considerable rôle among the tramp population. The Chicago Health Department on the basis of the medical examination of inmates of the House of Correction estimates that 10 per cent of the homeless men are venereally infected.[1] This is double the rate of infection found in drafted men.[2]

The transient does not take venereal disease seriously. He takes no precautions to protect himself after exposure. Necessity forces him out on some job where he must work, sometimes even in an

[1] Letter from Chicago Health Department to Committee on Homeless Men.

[2] U.S. Surgeon General's Office, *Defects Found in Drafted Men.*

active stage of infection. **Often** he tries to treat himself with remedies recommended by druggists or friends. Once the transient submits to treatment in a hospital or by a physician he will seldom continue it after the active stage of his case has been passed.

Along the "stem," sex perversion is not infrequent and occasionally from such contacts infections occur. Embarrassing as it is for the homeless man to apply to a hospital or clinic for treatment for social disease, it is doubly so when thus infected. That such cases are not numerous is true, but they do exist, and they provide an answer to the pervert who holds that homosexuality is safe from disease.[1]

ALCOHOLISM AND HEALTH

Practically all homeless men drink when liquor is available. The only sober moments for many hobos and tramps are when they are without funds.[2] The majority, however, are periodic drinkers who have sober periods of a week, a month or two, or

[1] Unpublished Document 87 is a statement from Dr. Ben L. Reitman, based upon cases in his practice of veneral infection caused by homosexual relations.

[2] It is of interest to note the findings of the study of 2,000 men in connection with the Municipal Lodging House of New York City, 1914:

"Of 1,482 men who made statements regarding their habits, 1,292—approximately 9 out of every 10—said they drank alcoholic liquors. Six hundred and fifty-seven or 44 per cent said that they drank excessively; 635, or 43 per cent, said that they drank moderately; and 190, or 13 per cent, claimed to be total abstainers.

"Of the 2,000 who were given a medical examination, 775, or 39 per cent, were diagnosed as suffering from alcoholism. According to Dr. James Alexander Miller, these 'figures probably do not represent by any means the number of individuals who were alcoholic . . . . but rather indicate only the number who manifested acute evidence at the time of investigation.'"—From the *Report of the Advisory Social Service Committee of the Municipal Lodging House*, pp. 9–22. New York: September, 1915.

Here we have in a few words a cross-section of the drinking population among the homeless men in New York where conditions are not materially different and where the population is essentially the same as in Hobohemia.

even a year.   These are the men who often work all
summer with the avowed purpose of going to some
lodging-house and living quietly during the winter,
but usually they find themselves in the midst of a
drunken debauch before they have been in town more
than a day or two.   Rarely does one meet a man
among migratory workers who does not indulge in
an occasional "spree"; the teetotalers are few indeed.

The homeless man on a spree usually drinks as
long as his money lasts, and then he usually employs
all the devices at his command to get money to
prolong the debauch.   For the time being he will
disregard all other wants.   After he sobers up and
finds himself sick, weak, and nervous, his plight is a
sad one.   He has no appetite for the only food he is
able to buy and the food he craves he cannot afford.
He is too weak and shaky to work, and too disheart-
ened to beg.   In summer he can go to the parks or
the docks and sleep it off.   Getting drunk in winter
means more or less exposure for these men, and their
sobering up not infrequently takes place in the hospital—or in jail.   In view of these after-effects, drinking is more serious for the homeless man than for
any other.

Chronic or periodic drunkenness with its accom-
panying exposure leaves a stamp on the constitution
of the homeless man that is not easily erased.   It
aggravates any latent weaknesses that he may have,
and if he does not go to the hospital after a debauch
with lung trouble, nervous diseases, heart trouble, or
rheumatism, he is at least lowering his resistance to
these and other diseases.   The man who survives best
spends long periods on the job and only occasionally
visits the city.

When the amount of exposure, the extent of dissipation, and the malnutrition that falls to the lot of the homeless man are taken into consideration, it is remarkable that he is as free from sickness as he is. The fact that he is outdoors much of the time may have something to do with this.

THE PROBLEM OF HEALTH

Disease, physical disability, and insanitary living conditions seem to be, as things are, the natural and inevitable consequences of the migratory risk-taking and irregular life of the homeless man. These effects of his work and life upon his physical constitution will be considered by many the most appalling of all the problems affecting the hobo and the tramp. Municipal provision and philanthropic effort have been and will continue to be directed to the treatment of his diseases and defects and to the improvement of his living conditions. The efficiency of the homeless man as a worker and his chance of regaining his lost economic and social status depend upon his physical rehabilitation. A clearing house for the homeless man when established should, therefore, include as one of its activities facilities for diagnosis of the needs, medical, vocational, social, of each individual.

The living conditions of the homeless man, although revolting to the public, are intolerable to him, chiefly as a symbol of his degradation. Lodging-house sanitation and personal hygiene are of minor import, in his thinking, as compared with working conditions, or, for that matter, with the problems of his social and political status, to be discussed in the next two chapters.

CHAPTER X
SEX LIFE OF THE HOMELESS MAN

TRAMPING is a man's game. Few women are ever found on the road. The inconveniences and hazards of tramping prevent it. Women do wander from city to city but convention forbids them to ride the roads and move about as men do. One tramp who had traveled 8,000 miles in six months said: "I even saw two women on the road, and last summer I saw a woman beating her way in a box car."

Tramping is a man's game. Few pre-adolescent boys are tramps. They do not break away permanently until later in their teens. How does the absence of women and children affect the life of the migratory worker? What difference would it make if tramps traveled like gypsies, taking their women and children with them? How does the absence of women and children affect the fantasy and the reveries and eventually the behavior of the homeless man?

The majority of homeless men are unmarried. Those who are married are separated, at least temporarily, from their families.[1] Most homeless men in the city are older than the average man on the road and would be expected, therefore, to have had marital experience. They are content to live in town while the younger men are eager to move in the restless search for adventure and new experience.

[1] Of the 1,000 men studied by Mrs. Solenberger, 74 per cent gave their marital status as single. Of the 400 interviewed by the writer 86 per cent stated that they were unmarried. Only 8 per cent of the former and 5 per cent of the latter survey claimed they were married. The others claimed to be widowed, divorced, or separated from their wives. Unpublished Document 142.

THE TRAMP AND HIS ASSOCIATIONS
WITH WOMEN

The homeless man has not always been homeless. Like most of us, he was reared in a home and is so far a product of home life. He enters upon the life of the road in his late teens or early twenties. He brings with him, as a rule, the habits and memories gained in the more stable existence in the family and community. Frequently it has been his conflict with, and rebellion against, that more stable existence that set him on the road.

Most of these men have mothers living. If their mothers are dead, they speak of them reverently. The mission workers often direct their appeals to these early memories, "the religion of our mothers." The only correspondence that some homeless men carry on is with their mothers. Some of them only write one or two letters a year but these are letters home. In most of the missions there is a sign with the inscription, "When Did You Write to Mother Last ?"

Other women may, and sometimes do, exert a wholesome influence upon him. He is often profoundly touched by the women of the missions who stand on the street corner and plead with him for his soul's sake. Young and attractive women invite more attention because of their sex than their message. Though he may have little or no interest in the religious appeal, feeling for these women is generally idealized and wholesome. The missions have learned the value of young and attractive women and employ them extensively as evangelists.

Women in places where the hobo has worked or boarded, generally older women, frequently take a mother's interest in him. "Mother" Greenstein, who keeps a restaurant on South State Street, is the idol of a great many "bos." She never turns a hungry man away. She is known far and near by tramps and hobos. Many men know her by reputation who have never seen her.

Another woman who has become well known to many homeless men is "Aunt" Nina S. She kept a rooming-house for years and always gave any man who came to her in winter some place to sleep. She could always find room. Her only compensation was the good will of the homeless man.

51. Another woman who has won a place in the hearts of men of West Madison Street is an old lady whom the "bos" call "Mother." She does not give them anything; on the contrary she begs from them but she takes a motherly interest in all the "boys." She is against anyone who makes life hard for them and hates the bootleggers, the gypsies, the gamblers, and all who exploit them. She will denounce and curse anyone who dares to call them "bums" in her presence. Her hobby is cats. She spends several hours a day going up and down the street feeding cats. All the "boys" are tolerant of all cats on the street because they belong to "Mother." He is a poor "bo," indeed, who will not spare "Mother" a dime now and then for milk for her "kitties."

When the tramp works he usually goes out on some job where there are no women. He may spend six months in a lumber camp and not see a woman during all that time. He may work for a whole summer, along with hundreds like himself, and never meet a woman. Sometimes there are women on such jobs, but they are generally the wives of the bosses and have no interest in the common workers. Children in such families frequently strike up a more intimate acquaintance with them. The only com-

pany for such a man is men, and men who are living
the same unnatural life as himself.

There are jobs open to the homeless man that are
more wholesome. Sometimes he finds himself in
communities where he is neither isolated nor an outcast. The tramp is not often interested in small-
town or country associations, because they generally
tend to terminate seriously and he does not want to
be taken seriously. If he has the money to spend,
and he usually has while he is working, he can meet
women, but he meets them in town when he has
leisure. He may have a hundred reasons for going
to town, but the major reason, whether he admits it
or not, is to meet women. The types of women he
meets depends upon his personality, his taste, and
his purse. In this he is like the soldier or the sailor.

The younger hobos, especially those who are on
the road and off again by turns, are able at times to
save money and put on a "front." These younger
men are frequently able, therefore, to get into the
social life of the communities in which they find
themselves. When they are in town with money
to spend they "go the limit" while it lasts, and then
they go out to work and save up another "stake."
Usually they have a number of women on their
correspondence lists. As they go from one city to
another they make new acquaintances and forget
the old friends. Usually they are as transient in
their attachments to women as to their jobs.

Many of these younger men ultimately settle
down, but they do not always have the ability to
make permanent attachments though they may try
again and again. They invariably seek greener
pastures. Wherever they are, they will be found

"burning the candles at both ends." As long as they
are young and attractive they have little difficulty
in finding girls who are willing to assist them in
scattering their cash.

Among these are the show girls who sing or dance
in the cheap burlesque theaters on South State and
West Madison streets. Thousands of hobos, who
never can hope to come in personal contact with
chorus girls, throng the cheap playhouses of Hobohemia. The titillations of a State Street vaudeville
are vulgar and inexpensive. The men, many of
them, at least, would not and could not appreciate
a higher grade of entertainment.

The hobo has few ideal associations with women.
Since most of them are unmarried, or living apart
from their wives, their sex relations are naturally
illicit. The tramp is not a marrying man, though he
does enter into transient free unions with women
when the occasion offers. There are many women
in the larger cities who have no scruples against
living with a man during the winter, or for even a
year or two, without insisting upon the marriage rite.
They are not prostitutes, not even "kept women."

52. M. lived with Mrs. S. N. for four or five years, off and
on, whenever he was in town. What little money he earned he
brought home, though he took money from Mrs. N. more frequently. She worked and usually when she came home very
tired he would have the house work done and a meal ready.
When she was sick he waited on her. He listened to her troubles
and was patient and good natured. In winter he always got up
and made the fires. She was always jealous of him and when he
would leave town for a month or two she fancied that it was to
get away from her and to live with some other woman. Finally
they separated, but they are still good friends. He is living with
another woman and she with another man. Of late he is only
in Chicago in winter.

The tramp who succeeds in living in idleness with a woman in such a companionship considers himself fortunate. The woman who can find a man like M. is often content, provided he is faithful to her, although she prefers a man who can be depended upon to earn a little money. The women who enter these free unions have the least to gain and the most to lose. The general experience of women who keep their "men" is that when they are in the direst need the men will desert them; on the other hand, when the men are in need they will return.

A certain class of detached men makes a practice of getting into the good graces of some prostitute for the winter. The panderer is not a characteristic tramp type, but certain homeless men are not averse to becoming pimps for a season. These attachments between homeless men and prostitutes are often quite real. Some of them even become permanent, others last a year or two, but most of them are only of a few months' duration. While they do persist they are often more or less sentimental.

THE HOBO AND PROSTITUTION

Most hobos and tramps because of drink, unpresentable appearance, or unattractive personality, do not succeed in establishing permanent, or even quasi-permanent, relationships with women. For them the only accessible women are prostitutes and the prostitutes who solicit the patronage of the homeless man are usually forlorn and bedraggled creatures who have not been able to hold out in the fierce competition in higher circles.

These women, otherwise so isolated and so hard pressed by their exigent wants, do not live on the "main stem," but adjacent to it. They are conveniently located so that even the "floater," who comes to town with a few months' savings, has no trouble in finding them. The upper-class prostitutes keep men on the street getting the business for them. Pandering is an art, and many of these pimps have become adepts in catching the men who come to town with "rolls." Only a small part of the commerce of the homeless man is with the "live ones." He usually has so little money that he is forced to bargain for the attention of the lowest women that walk the streets.

Men with "rolls" are scarce in Hobohemia. One man met on West Madison Street said: "I came in last night with $380 and now I'm flatter'n a pancake. I didn't even get a pair of sox. Hallelujah! I'm a bum." He was still too drunk to realize the situation, but next day he was uncertain whether he had been robbed by a woman or by a "jack roller." He did not even know whether he had been robbed or had lost his money. He had worked all winter and spring on a ranch near Casper, Wyoming, and had come to town with a trainload of cattle.[1] It is seldom that the second-rate prostitute gets hold of so much money.

From these "second raters" the tramp is doubly liable to infection. Most of them have been diseased at some time while some of them are infected all the time. More than one-third of them, according to Dr. Ben L. Reitman, of the Chicago Health Department, are constantly spreading infection. The homeless man is well aware of the risk he runs when he patronizes the prostitute, but he does not realize the gravity of the danger.

[1] Unpublished Document 114.

PERVERSION AMONG THE TRAMPS

All studies indicate that homosexual practices among homeless men are widespread. They are especially prevalent among men on the road among whom there is a tendency to idealize and justify the practice. Homosexuality is not more common among tramps than among other one-sex groups. In the prison and jail population, the authorities are forced to wage a constant warfare against it. The same condition prevails also in the navy or merchant marine, and, to a lesser extent, in the army.[1]

Among tramps there are, it seems, two types of perverts. There are those who are subjects, in the words of Havelock Ellis, "of a congenital predisposition, or complexus of abnormalities." Ellis contends that certain individuals, different temperamentally and physically from the rest of us, are not attracted by the opposite sex but are easily attracted by their own sex. Most of them are men who have developed from childhood feminine traits and tastes, and they may be regarded as predisposed to homosexuality. The second group is composed of individuals who have temporarily substituted homosexual for heterosexual behavior. Most of these perverts by conversion are men who, under the pressure of sex isolation, have substituted boy for woman as the object of their desires. This is chiefly because boys are accessible while women are not.

THE BOY TRAMP AND PERVERSION

The boy does not need to remain long in hobo society to learn of homosexual practices. The average boy on the road is invariably approached

[1] Iwan Bloch, *Sexual Life of Our Times*, p. 540.

by men who get into his good graces. Some
"homos" claim that every boy is a potential homosexual. This is without doubt an exaggeration as
well as a defense, for not all boys are subject to
persuasion. Sometimes boys will travel alone or with
other boys to avoid the approaches of older men.
Often boys will refrain from traveling with adults,
even well-behaved adults, because they realize that
they will be under suspicion. It is not uncommon
to hear a boy who is seen traveling with an older man
spoken of as the "wife" or "woman." It is only
natural that many boys fear to be alone with adult
tramps.

53. The case of M. is typical. He is a sixteen year old boy
who travels alone. He is a handsome lad; small for his age and
neat in appearance. He is just the type of boy that would
attract the average "wolf" who idealizes pink cheeks and an
innocent appearance. He travels alone because of his fear of
"wolves." He had not been away from home three weeks and
he says that he has been accosted several times. Although he
had been in Chicago but a day he had received advances from
two men who tried to persuade him to go to a room.

Many devices are employed by them to place the
lad in their debt or under their protection. If
methods of persuasion do not work, force is sometimes used. One man gave a brakeman a dollar to put
a boy off the train at a lonely siding. Another man
learned which direction a certain boy was traveling
and followed him from town to town, "accidentally"
meeting him at each place. The lad was without
funds, and so was the man, but the latter was able to
beg and usually had a "lump" when he met the boy
and he always divided. Another man led a boy a
mile or so out in the country to a place where he

claimed he had worked during the previous year and where he knew they could both get something to eat.

Another common ruse is to take a boy to a room or a box car to sleep. The man suggests that he knows a clean car in a safe place with plenty of straw or paper on the floor. In a big city the boy is often enticed to a room for the same purpose. There are many cases on record in the Chicago courts.[1]

54. A. F., a boy sixteen years old, was being held in a room on West Ohio Street to which he had been enticed for immoral purposes by John M. J. M. was arrested on complaint of one F. He was found in company with another boy in a room in the E. Hotel on South State Street. John was held for trial on $3,000 bonds which he could not furnish. He died in jail waiting for trial.

55. C. J. This man worked on a boat plying between Michigan ports and Chicago. He persuaded a Michigan boy whose home was near Lansing but who had run away and was loafing about the docks on the lake front, to come with him to Chicago. He promised to help the boy get a job, etc. He took him to a room on South State Street where he held him for three days and had improper relations with him. Prior to his apprehension he had turned the boy over to another man for the same purpose.

Josiah Flynt, who was familiar with tramp life, seems to be of the opinion that most boys are forced into the practice. However, it does not seem probable that force is so extensively employed as is sometimes believed. These accounts serve as a defense reaction on their part, yet we cannot say that such forced initiations do not occur. But even those who at the outset were the victims of "strong arm" methods often become reconciled to the practice and continue it. Often they become promiscuous in their relations and many of them even commercialize themselves.

[1] Unpublished Document 32.

Writers on the sex behavior of men and boys often refer to the relationship as it exists among tramps as a sort of slavery. By slavery is meant that boys are held in bondage to men and forced to steal and beg for them. This condition may exist in isolated instances but it is not general. It is even suggested by some authorities that there exists some sort of organization among tramps through which boys have been "caught" and kept in servitude. The best evidence that such an organization does not exist is the fact that perverted sex practices are frowned upon by the tramps themselves.

The court records show, however, that not infrequently boys are held in rooms, or taken to lonely buildings, or out on the lake front, or in the parks, but the case that gets into court is seldom one in which both parties were free agents. If there is slavery in these latter cases it is slavery to their passions, or to a state of mind growing out of their habits and their isolation.

The duration of an intimacy of this kind in the city is seldom more than a few days. On the road, however, the "partnership" may last for weeks. Whereas, out of town the pair can travel as companions aiding each other, in the city they can get along better alone. It is difficult for partners to remain together long in the city, especially if one has money and the other none, or if one drinks and the other does not. Living in a metropolis is a problem the tramp can solve better alone.

ATTITUDES OF THE PERVERT

Tramp perverts argue that homosexual intercourse is "clean" and that homosexuals are less liable to become infected with venereal disease. The Vice Commission of Chicago, in its report for 1911, states that homosexual individuals "are not known in their true character to any extent by the physicians because of the fact that their habits do not, as a rule, produce bodily disease."[1]

It is also urged by perverts that in the homosexual relation there is the absence of the eternal complications in which one becomes involved with women. They want to avoid intimacies that complicate the free life to which they are by temperament and habit committed. Homosexual attachments are generally short lived, but they are real while they last. Sometimes a man will assume a priority over a boy and will even fight to maintain it. The investigator during his study of this phase of the tramp problem made two unsuccessful attempts to step between men and their boys, or "lambs." In one case his interference was resented by both the man and the boy, but in the other it was rather enjoyed by the boy, though he would not be separated from his "wolf."

The investigator met S., a veteran "wolf" on Madison Street. When he was asked why his face was so badly bruised he said that he and another man had fought over a boy. "He was trying to get my kid into a room with him." He claimed that he hit the man and ran but that he was arrested. He was held over night in the Desplaines Street Station on a charge of disorderly conduct, but was discharged the next morning. What hurt him most was not the night in jail or his bruised face but the fact that the other man had left town with the boy.

[1] *The Social Evil in Chicago*, pp. 296–97.

In his sex life, as in his whole existence, the homeless man moves in a vicious circle. Industrially inadequate, his migratory habits render him the more economically inefficient. A social outcast, he still wants the companionship which his mode of life denies him. Debarred from family life, he hungers for intimate associations and affection. The women that he knows, with few exceptions, are repulsive to him. Attractive women live in social worlds infinitely remote from his. With him the fundamental wishes of the person for response and status have been denied expression. The prevalence of sexual perversion among the homeless men is, therefore, but the extreme expression of their unnatural sex life. Homosexual practices arise almost inevitably in similar situations of sex isolation. A constructive solution for the problems of the sex life of the homeless man strikes deeper into our social life than this study can carry us.

CHAPTER XI
THE HOBO AS A CITIZEN

WHERE are we to place the hobo as a citizen ? What is his actual status as a member of society or as a functioning unit in the state ? Where does he stand in relation to organized society and its laws and its mores ?

The public dismisses these questions by assigning the hobo and the tramp to the class of "undesirables." This reaction of the public is, of course, emotional and superficial, based partly on the shabby and unkempt appearance of the men of the road and partly on their reputation as beggars, vagrants, drunkards, and petty thieves. Any study of the homeless man as a citizen must go farther and take into account such factors as nativity, naturalization, and patriotism; legal residence and the right and opportunity to vote; obedience to law; and his political aspirations.

NATIVITY, NATURALIZATION, AND PATRIOTISM

Students of hobos and tramps have been struck by the fact that the great majority of homeless men are native-born Americans. Mrs. Solenberger found that of 1,000, 623 were native born. Of the 400 tramps interviewed by the writer during the summer of 1921, only 61 were foreign born and 23 of these had taken out naturalization papers. From these and other studies it appears that from 60 to 90 per cent of hobos and tramps are native born.

The tramp is an American product. The foreign-born in this group are chiefly of the older immigration. Among these, Englishmen, proverbial as "globe-trotters," are conspicuous. The number of homeless men from the newer immigration is small, and the individuals who are found in the tramp and hobo group seem often out of place.

One test of patriotism is military service. The writer found that of the 400 he interviewed, 92 had seen military service. This figure is high, since there were only 183 men of the whole group between the ages of twenty and thirty-four. These men were listed in 1921 and would include many who were not in the draft age when the allotments were drawn in 1918. There were of the 400, 58 who were probably under the draft age in 1918. When we consider the proportion of physically and mentally unfit, it seems that this figure is high.[1]

THE HOBO AND HIS VOTE

What is the status of the hobo as a voter? He seldom remains in one place long enough to acquire legal residence. His work, because of its seasonal character, often takes him away from his legal residence just at the time when he should be there to register or vote. Whether he has a desire to cast his ballot or not, he is seldom able to do so.

A canvass of thirty-five Hobohemian hotels in Chicago has shown that about a third of the guests are voters. In March, 1923, there were 3,029 registered voters from these hotels, which have a total capacity of 9,480. Many of these, though they are in the city only in winter or for a few weeks at

---

[1] It must be remembered that the 400 include tramps in transit who are, perhaps, the better and most fit of all the types. At least there would be in such a group a greater number of able-bodied men than in any 400 selected at random in the "stem" of one of our cities. Again, 400 is not a sufficient number to permit more than a tentative conclusion.

a time, manage to maintain a residence here and, if they are in the city during an election, they vote.

Charges are even made that tramps and hobos sell their votes, that they often engage in "repeating." There is not as much ground for such charges as one would expect. The average tramp does not have the courage to take the chances that the "repeater" must expect to run. He realizes also that he is always under more or less suspicion even when he is going straight, and this serves as a brake.

Homeless men as a group make much of the fact that they are excluded from the ballot, and they remind all who have the patience to listen that the exclusion is unjust because they perform an important and legitimate function in the labor world. They seem to protest against their exclusion more than to demand the ballot. One man said that he did not know if he would vote if he had a chance, "but it's the principle of the thing."

The International Brotherhood Welfare Association has repeatedly stood for some form of universal suffrage that would permit migratory workers to vote, regardless of the length of their residence in a community.

During the latter part of May, 1922, a convention of the Farmer-Labor Party was held in Chicago. Certain members of the hobo group failed in the attempt to get a resolution through the convention in favor of giving the vote to migratory workers. Certain delegates feared that the hobo was too irresponsible to use the ballot. The farmer element in the Farmer-Labor Party resented the idea of giving support to the tramp group by whom they had been harassed so much in the harvest fields. Nor is the I.W.W. particularly interested in "votes for the hobos," because in their opinion the ballot is at best an indirect method of accomplishing what can be easier secured by direct action.

Forty-eight of the 400 homeless men studied by the writer claimed to have voted in the presidential election of 1920.

56. One of the men interviewed in this study said: "I happened to drop into Salt Lake the last day of the registration so I got my name on the dotted line. I swore I had been in the state a year. They couldn't prove I wasn't, so it passed. I'd been in ten or fifteen states that year. Well, when election came I was working in Bingham. My boss was short of help and didn't want me to lay off to vote, so I quit and went to Salt Lake. Got there just before the polls closed."

One man said that he beat his way 1,000 miles to cast his ballot. Most of the 48, however, had voted because at election time they were living in or near their legal residence. What was the attitude of the 352 who did not vote ? The following are the reasons given (with reference to 1920 election):[1]

No desire to vote and no legal residence	28
Having legal residence but no desire to vote	54
No legal residence but desire to vote	129
Under twenty-one	88
Aliens	38*
In military service	9
Disfranchised	2
Not known	4
Total	352

*Sixty-one foreign-born in 400; 23 naturalized.

There were 28 men both ineligible to vote and indifferent to the ballot. The group of 54 who had no desire to vote included men who were at home, or near their legal residence, and could have voted had they been interested. The two listed as disfran-

[1] From an unpublished study by the author of 400 tramps, Document 115.

chised were both men who had been dishonorably
discharged from the navy. Both were under twenty-
one and had enlisted under the pressure of wartime
enthusiasm. One of these was not interested in voting and the other said that the vote was a joke
anyway.

THE HOMELESS MAN AND THE LAW

The migratory worker is not saddled with responsibility for law and order. As he makes his way
about the country, he is unincumbered. He has
nothing to lose and nothing to protect but his person, and that he protects best by constantly moving.
The homeless man has no interest in common with
the settled man of the community who has attachments and property, and at whose expense he often
lives. The migratory worker, for a time, may be
physically a part of a community, but he actually
does not become absorbed into its social life. The
wanderer who fails to win a place in the life of a
community often takes his own course. This
course is sometimes in harmony with the interests
of the community, but more often counter to them,
and he fails under the surveillance of the law.

To the tramp and the hobo the police are the
guardian angels of organized society, created to
protect the community against criminals and
migrants. To him there are two varieties of
police—civil and private. The uniformed upholder
of the law, the civil police, is given the uncomplimentary epithet, "harness bull." The plain-clothes men
are called "dicks," "fly cops," and "stool pigeons."
The private police who protect the property of the
railroad are held in even lower contempt.

THE PRIVATE POLICE

The chief job of the "dicks" is to keep the "bos" off the trains. The private police are unpopular, not only among homeless men, but also among the employees of the railroads. Brakemen and switchmen will often aid tramps in their effort to avoid the police. Railroad police must often contend with a lack of co-operation by the civil police. The town police, or "town clown" as he is called, may order the tramps to leave on the "next train," while the railroad police may be making every effort to prevent their riding the trains. The town police are not anxious to fill the jail; they prefer that the transients move on; they reason that the railroad should take away what the railroad brought.

The railroad policeman shows results, not by the number of convictions as the civil police, but by his ability to keep at a minimum the number of offenses against railroad property. His endeavor is to put fear into the hearts of all trespassers on the right-of-way. He becomes a hunter of men, not to seize and detain them, but to pursue and terrorize them. He is to the railroad property what the scarecrow is to the cornfield.

Railroad police sometimes drive men off fast-moving trains by throwing stones or shooting at them. Not infrequently they catch and maltreat a tramp; however, they are seldom able to get hold of a veteran tramp. The inexperienced man or the boy is more likely to be caught. These means of putting fear into men do not stop tramping. As they become fearful of the railroad "bull," they become more cautious, and the "bull's" problem is increasingly difficult.

WHAT THE TRAMP THINKS OF THE
PRIVATE POLICE

To migrants the railroad is "the tramp's traditional highway." The tramp, however, expects opposition from the railroad police and even from the train crews; nevertheless he measures his success as a "boomer" by his ability to outwit this opposition. Encounters with the railroad police are a favorite theme of conversation in the "jungles" and along the "stem."

One man tells of being held in Hutchinson, Kansas, on suspicion:

57. A bunch of us came in on a freight and started up town. It was about midnight and the moon was shining. We were sneaking along the shade of a row of box cars. A couple of men halted us and ordered us to come out into the light. I had a notion to run but one of the other fellows said they had "gats" and we'd better take no chances. It was a good thing we didn't run because we found out that a couple of men had escaped from the jail. All the police and a lot of the citizens had been drafted to find them. Most of them carried guns and nothing would have suited them better than to have had some one to shoot at.

They rounded up about ten "bos" out of the yards and took us to a room in the depot where they held us for about an hour till one of the guards came from the jail. He did not see the escaped men in the crowd so we were turned loose. The railroad "bull" ordered us to walk out of town. We walked out a ways and then sneaked back and caught a freight.

I think we got off easy. I had a buddy once who was held a week until the police could get a picture. He was caught by the railroad "bull" and turned over to the "town clown." They are always sorry if they can't get someting on a "bo" they hold.

Youths in their first adventures on the road accept with zest the conflict with the private police. A student who made a practice of "working the harvest" each summer gives the following statement:

58. My first experience with a bull was at Marshalltown, Iowa. I had been selling books up near Mason City, Iowa, and after three weeks of that loathsome occupation, I threw my prospectus into the ditch and started for home. Late one night I caught an express train on the Northwestern from Ames, Iowa, bound for Chicago, and rode from there to Marshalltown; unfortunately the train pulled into the station very slowly and the long string of lights on the station platform shed a great deal of light on the train. I started to get off when a rough voice cursing loudly told me to get off on that side. He took me by the shoulder and asked me what in hell I was doing riding on that train. "Don't you know," he said, "what we do with fellows who ride the front ends of these trains?" He gave me a kick and told me to get out of the yards. It was my first encounter with the "bulls" and I have since learned that "bull" tactics are very much the same.

Another time I crawled off the train into the waiting arms of a Rock Island "bull" in Council Bluffs, Iowa. He showed me his star and searched me over carefully, feeling every lump in my clothing. During the search he said, "Will you give me all I find on you?" The question rather startled me but I quickly replied, "Yes." Finding nothing, he seemed disappointed and said, "I can't understand why you haven't more money on you! What are you, anyway?" I told him I was a college student looking for work. "The hell you are!" he sneered, "you're a Weary Willie, now get out of here, quick."

At Grand Island some fifty of us tried to ride a merchandise freight out of the yards, when an energetic "bull" pulled himself out of a car and waved a revolver wildly warning all not to get on. It was a long freight and the men strung themselves up and down the track the full length of it. In spite of his efforts, several got aboard. My companion and I were quite close to him and made no effort to get on.

My next encounter occurred at Bureau, Illinois, a division point on the Rock Island. There were four of us on the tender (behind the engine), my room mate and I and two lads who had jumped on some miles down the line. They had been jumping on and off and having a good time generally. Both of them had on white shirts and could be easily recognized by the train men. At Bureau a rough looking "bull" poked his head over the tender, waved a gun, cursed madly and told us to get down from there. We were lying flat on one corner and I did not believe he had seen us. The two boys did as they were told while I held my room mate down and told him not to move. I heard him swearing at the boys as the train pulled out.

With a companion I left a Rock Island freight one afternoon to get a drink of water. We came back to see our train far up the track toward Des Moines. I noticed by my table that an express train would soon be in. My companion was a long, lean individual, a bluffing, blustering type probably weighing about 175 pounds. A "bull" was waiting for us at Valley Junction, just outside of Des Moines. He pulled us off and marched us out in front of all the passengers and into the station. We both noticed that we had climbed a mail train and that our future was not very bright. The station agent was not in and I sized Mr. "Bull" up as he searched us. He was a young fellow, not over twenty-five and did not look nearly as hard as he talked. My companion was as pale as a sheet and would say nothing. I talked to him as best I could, and after scaring us to the best of his ability he finally turned us loose, actually buying us a ticket on the auto bus to Des Moines. He acted almost human toward us.

A man, prominent in Hobohemia as a soap-boxer, recites this experience out of a great number that he has had with railroad and other private police.

59. I was traveling in Indiana with a man by the name of Sullivan, known around the country as "Sully." We got off at Flora, a railroad town in Indiana. It was cold and the town was "hostile" because so many "bos" had been there that the people were hardened to them. We knew better than to hang around the railroad yards so we decided to go out of town a ways and build a fire to keep warm while we waited for a train. We started out but Sully decided to return and learn from the switchman when a train would be leaving. I said that I would go out along the track and build a wind break with some old ties and make a fire.

I dragged some ties together and had the wind break up by the time Sully returned. I had the fire going too and was taking off my shoes. I had stepped in some water while dragging ties and my feet were wet and cold.

Everything went fine for about half an hour. I was drying my shoes and socks and Sully and I were talking about where we were going and what to do. It was at the time of the Steel Strike, and Sully was planning on going up there to get a job as a "scab herder." He said that by that means he would get in with the company and that he could work some "sabotage" in the interest of the workers. At that time I was traveling and selling literature, and holding street meetings in the interests of the I.B.W.A.

All of a sudden something hit me in the back between the shoulder blades. I looked around quickly and there were two "bulls." We were on railroad property and I knew we were in for it. Sully ducked and went over the fence. I had my shoes off and couldn't run. One of them gave me another tap on the back with a black jack. "What are you here for?" "I am drying my shoes," was the only answer I could think of. As I hurried to get my shoes on one of them slapped me on the side of the head. I jumped and ran while they cursed me and told me never to let them catch me again. I met Sully an hour later and together we cursed all railroad "bulls" as cowards and sneaks.

Sometime after that I was told by a friend that Sully was an employee of the Pinkerton agency. I did not believe it but before a year was out I heard it from two or three sources. I made an effort to find out and I learned it was true; that he was in their employ at the time we got chased. Then it came to me why he went back to talk to the switchmen and how he got away without being hit. He was traveling with me because he was trying to get a line on me as an agitator.

These stories are typical of those that any experienced tramp can tell.

The private police "talks by hand" because it is the most practical method at his command. The argument of the club coincides most admirably with the mood he is in when on duty searching trains and keeping trespassers off railroad property. He is a hunter and the tramp is his prey. If it is a game to the police, it is no less so to the tramp. One lad who had been caught a time or two said: "I get a lot of 'kick' out of riding trains out of a place when I know the 'dicks' are trying to keep me off."

When a town has a railroad policeman who is "hard," the fact is soon noised about. A few years ago, Galesburg, Illinois, was known throughout the country for the "bad" colored policeman who guarded the yards. The hobo who could tell a story of an encounter with the big "nigger bull" had an exploit to be proud of. For some time Green River, Wyoming, boasted a "hard bull" known to the "floating fraternity" as "Green River Slim." As the reputation of a "bad" policeman travels ahead, so the information about his tactics and methods. Where he may be found, how avoided, how he watches the trains, are usually common knowledge to the average "bo" before he reaches a town.

ATTITUDE OF THE PRIVATE POLICE

The *Hobo News* for April, 1922, reprinted an article "The Hobo; a Real Problem to the Railroad," by T. T. Kelihor, chief special agent of the Illinois Central Railroad. The article was given space in the *News* in order that the hobos might see how the "bulls" regarded them. It was followed by a caustic criticism from the editor who charged that the writer "like the rest of his fraternity cannot distinguish between Hobos and Bums and Tramps and Yeggs."

The railroads of this country are the chief sufferers from this cancerous social growth. There is no property right or other

rights of the railroad that the modern hobo feels called upon
to consider or respect. Millions of dollars' worth of railway property and merchandise in transit are destroyed and
stolen annually by this class. The actual value of merchandise stolen is only a small part of the loss of merchandise
in trains.

The average hobo realizes that he is not provided with means
of carrying away a large amount of bulky goods. Consequently
when hobos enter a merchandise car, they break open a great
many cases and dump or throw out the contents on the floor in
searching for small, compact, valuable goods that they can carry
off concealed about their persons. It often happens that they
will not take more than $50.00 value in valuable articles, but
they will destroy and damage $500.00 worth of goods by destroy-
ing the original containers and soiling the contents by trampling
on them on the dirty floor of the car and otherwise damaging
them.

The amount of property the tramp actually steals
and destroys is not known. He probably is blamed
for more damage than he does. Those who speak for
the hobo class claim that most of the goods stolen
from cars is taken by train crews who shield themselves by pointing to the tramp, who is already an
outlaw as far as the railroad is concerned, because he
steals rides. Aside from the loss of property, Mr.
Kelihor calls attention to the great loss of life attrib-
uted to tramping.

The loss of life and limb on account of hobos riding
trains and trespassing on the right-of-way, and the
consequent financial and economic loss to the country
and the railroads, is appalling. The reports for all
railroads during 1919 show:

Trespassers killed........... 2,553
Trespassers injured.......... 2,658

Total.................. 5,211

And during 1920:

Trespassers killed........... 2,166
Trespassers injured.......... 2,362
Total.................. 4,528

During 1921, on the Illinois Central and the Yazoo and Mississippi railroads, 98 trespassers were killed and 221 injured.

How many of these persons killed were actually hobos, perhaps even the railroads could not say. To the railroad officials anyone is a trespasser on railroad property who is not a patron or an employee. On the other hand, all the instances of tramps killed or injured on the railroad are not recorded.

In a communication of August 2, 1922, to the Homeless Man Committee, W. P. Riggs, chief special agent of the American Express Company, says in part:

On our more important exclusive trains we have inspectors employed to ride them for the purpose of keeping tramps and other unauthorized persons off such trains. As in the past we have suffered serious loss through such parties breaking into our sealed cars and robbing them. There have also been instances where parties under the guise of tramps beating their way around the country turned out to be real bandits, who would at the opportune time hold up the mail clerks and messengers.

The tramp situation is the worst in this section during the spring, summer, and fall; yet we also have more or less trouble with them in winter months.

Generally speaking, we do not receive much assistance from civil authorities in combatting tramps.

J. H. Hustin, Jr., superintendent of property protection for the New York Central Railroad, writes the committee as follows:

It is the endeavor of our police officers to keep the tramp off our right-of-way. Many of our freight trains on the Western

territory are protected by police officers enroute between termi-
nals, and it is part of their duty to keep such train riders off our
trains. Usually the tramp is placed under arrest and taken
before the local authorities for disposition.

During the spring and fall we experience most of our difficulties with train riders, especially in connection with the opening
and closing of navigation.

In general, we receive the co-operation of the city authorities.
When business is quiet and a large number of men are out of
work, we obtain little direct assistance from the local police and
courts; while, when business is good and there is little unemployment, such co-operation is very satisfactory.

THE CIVIL AUTHORITIES AND THE TRAMP

The average man on the street, or the average
housewife, sees in the tramp either a parasite or a
predacious individual. The average man may admit
that there are many migratory men who would
work, but he feels that most of them will not, and
that they have neither permanent habits nor good
intentions; they need to be watched. If the public
opinion decrees that the town needs to be protected
against tramps, it is the duty of the police to do it.
There seems to be a relation between the pressure
that the police bring to bear on the tramp and the
pressure that the tramps impose upon the community
which is reflected in the pressure the residents place
on the police. In towns where vagrancy has become
a problem, the police are very energetic in keeping
down the number of apparently idle men.

In small towns, especially railroad towns, through
which many tramps move, the police are "hostile."
A policeman in a Wyoming town on the Union Pacific
Railroad asserts: "We've got to be hard on these
fellows or they will eat us out of house and home in
a week." In the larger towns the police are sporadic

in their harshness. Men of the road will ask one
another about the attitude of the police in certain
cities. "Omaha was good the first part of the
winter," reported a man in a circle about a camp
fire, "I think I'll go to Chi this winter if I don't go
to the Coast. I heard they were pretty easy on
them there last winter." Again, "I was in Chicago
the most of the winter. They are all right there if
you stay on the 'stem.'" "How has K. C. been
lately ? I haven't been there for five years."

The average hobo will often avoid certain towns
because he has heard that the "bo" will not be well
received. He will sometimes go to a town even when
he has heard of its drastic method of treating the
transients. A "hard" police force and a drastic
policy of repression do not keep tramps away. It
selects out those who are willing to run the risk.
Timid and inexperienced men are kept away, but the
daring and veteran tramps who cause the police the
most trouble are not so readily frightened off.

The police do not regard the tramp as a serious
offender. If he steals, it is generally for something
to eat or to wear. Every man on the road steals
potatoes or green corn from the nearby fields, or
fruit from the neighboring orchard, or chickens that
stray within reach of the jungle.

Tramps will boast about what they will do when
times get hard and cold weather crowds them. "I
won't starve. I worked all summer, and I won't go
hungry this winter." This man was "broke" in
spite of a summer's hard labor in the harvest fields.
His earnings quickly went for drink. He did get
hungry, and his clothes were torn to tatters before
spring, but he did not break in any windows as he had

threatened. There are "crooks" among the tramps, but not so many as might be supposed. The average tramp does not possess the courage to be a first-class crook.

Warden Wesley Westbrook, of the Cook County jail, supports this estimate of the tramp as an offender:

> I am convinced that the tramp does not have the courage to be a criminal. He will steal something to eat or wear, and he may steal a door mat or some article he may sell for a quarter to get a coffee an'; or, if he is drinking, to get the price of a pint of whiskey. But tramps do not become criminal in the serious sense. They make noise and threats sometimes but I have found them an easy group to get along with. It takes considerable courage to break into a house or to hold a person up and the tramp will not do this. He seems to think that he can get a living easier and with less risk.

But whether a major offender or not, the fact is that the homeless man is almost always liable to arrest as a vagrant. He is marked as a potential offender. He always faces the possibility of being arrested on suspicion. Where the ex-convict is harassed by the authorities because they have his record, the tramp is often held because they do not have his record. Often migrants are taken from freight trains and transported many miles to the scenes of some offense only to be turned loose. Often they are held for days in local jails until they can prove an alibi or their identity can be established. For them there is no redress.[1]

[1] The following case, though extreme, is not unusual: Martin Tabert, a farmer boy from South Dakota, left home in 1921 in search of work and adventure. In December of the same year he was arrested for vagrancy in Florida and bound out to a lumber camp as a convict laborer. In January, 1922, 30 days later, he died from the effects of whippings administered by officials of the company. His death was officially reported as the result of malaria. More than a year passed before the facts were known and the senate of South Dakota demanded an investigation. The radical press has put up a

The status of the homeless man in the courts is not high. Again and again men are arraigned before the judge for vagrancy, fighting, drunkenness, begging, petty stealing, and other minor offenses. Any policeman can walk along West Madison Street any day and see some man or perhaps a dozen who could be arrested on some charge. If all policemen did this the jails would be full and the police courts in which these cases are tried would be continually overflowing. Only the most conspicuous cases are arrested. Those are numerous enough to keep an average judge busy in an average police court.

The judge who sits in the Desplaines Street police court, where more tramps are arraigned than in any other court in Chicago, faces sometimes as many as 100 men whose cases must be disposed of within a few hours. One morning the investigator visited Judge LaBuy's court in the Desplaines Street station and saw more than fifty cases of vagrancy, disorderly conduct, drunkenness, etc., disposed of in less than half an hour. There was little material at hand by which the judge could arrive at a just decision, consequently he disposed of the cases with only that evidence that was apparent. Apparently neither the needs of the individual were being met nor the demands of justice satisfied.[1]

The experiences of the tramp or hobo in the police court do not increase his respect for the law and the administration of justice. He finds the administra-

---

continuous but rather ineffectual fight against this form of convict labor which the migrant has endured for years. The Tabert case furnished colorful news items and consequently attracted widespread attention (see *Literary Digest*, April 21, 1923, pp. 39–44).

[1] Unpublished Document 80.

tion of justice a mechanical process. At the points
where the law touches his life it has lost every trace
of the human touch unless it be the brutal "third
degree" or the traditional "sixty days." The courts
sometimes put fear into his heart but they do not
reform him.

What status as a citizen does the hobo wish ? His
attitude toward the police and his reaction toward
the civil authorities that represent organized society
seem to be tempered with antipathy. Most of the
songs he sings are songs of protest. The organizations to which he allies himself are antagonistic to
things as they are.

In many ways, the migratory worker is "a man
without a country." By the very nature of his
occupation he is deprived of the ballot, and liable
when not at work to arrest for vagrancy and trespassing. The public ignores him generally, but now
and again pities or is hostile to him. With no status
in organized society, he longs for a classless society
where all inequalities shall be abolished. In the
I.W.W. and other radical organizations, he finds in
association with restless men of his own kind the
recognition everywhere else denied him.

PART IV
HOW THE HOBO MEETS HIS PROBLEM

CHAPTER XII
PERSONALITIES OF HOBOHEMIA

LIKE other communities, Hobohemia has its eminent persons. In the flux and flow of the life on the "main stem" certain individuals are conspicuous. They are for the most part the soap-box orators, the organizers and promoters of utopias. These men are the most loved or the most hated of all the Hobohemian celebrities. They are either overwhelmingly approved or are unsparingly condemned as grafters and parasites. But whether exploiters or benefactors they are centers of interest. They are powers. Among the many men of this group are: James Eads How, Dr. Ben L. Reitman, John X. Kelly, Michael C. Walsh, Daniel Horsley, and A. W. Dragstedt.

Outside of these leaders of the migratory workers are mission workers, like Charles W. Langsman, of the Bible Rescue Mission; and John Van de Water, of the Helping Hand Mission; and Brigadier J. E. Atkins, of the Salvation Army, which is neither a mission nor a church.

It has been the policy of the Baptist Church on North LaSalle Street and the Immanuel Baptist Church on South Michigan Avenue more than other churches to feed homeless men. Dr. Johnston Myers is pastor of the latter church, and probably the most talked-of minister in Hobohemia when times are hard. Dr. Myers is contrasted by homeless men with the Greensteins on South State Street. "Mother" Greenstein's "bread line" is known the country over.

These or their counterparts may be found in any city where hobos gather.

DR. JAMES EADS HOW, "THE MILLIONAIRE HOBO"

How, a man of wealth and education, renounced all to share the lot of the hobos. He is not an imposing personality, but he is a kindly, ingratiating, almost saintly man. He is a dreamer and a visionary with a program for reforming the world. Every cent that he does not spend for doughnuts and twenty-five-cent flops goes to the "cause." He hopes that other millionaires will see his good works and imitate him.

How is a bachelor in his late forties. According to rumor, which he neither affirms nor denies, he has two college degrees, one of them in medicine. He plans soon to enter a college for a year to study law, so as to be the better prepared to promote the interests of the International Brotherhood Welfare Association and the "Hobo College." The I.W.W. believes the world will be reformed by organization and direct action first, and education second. How puts education first. He hopes to establish a central hobo university to which the numerous hobo colleges in the large cities will be feeders.

To How the hobos are a "chosen people" who have been denied their own. They will come into their own in time. All his repeated failures to build up a strong organization of migratory workers have not shaken his faith in his vision. How still believes that hobos and millionaires will sooner or later work together in harmony to construct the House of Happiness for humanity.

DR. BEN L. REITMAN, "THE KING OF THE HOBOS"

With the exception of James Eads How, "the millionaire hobo," Reitman is known to more migratory workers than any other man in the country.

DR. BEN L. REITMAN

MEMBERS OF THE JEFFERSON PARK INTELLIGENTSIA

THE HOBO READS PROGRESSIVE LITERATURE

Several years ago, while he was roaming casually over the United States, Reitman was dubbed by the papers the "King of the Hobos." This title was well earned by more than twenty years on the road, including two or three tramps around the world.

His own description of himself given to the papers several years ago still holds:

> I am an American by birth, a Jew by parentage, a Baptist by adoption, a physician and teacher by profession, cosmopolitan by choice, a Socialist by inclination, a celebrity by accident, a tramp by twenty years' experience, and a reformer by inspiration.

The only modification that he would make today is that he has settled into the routine of his profession. He still lectures at the "Hobo College." He still intercedes for hobos and guarantees their bills in case they do not make good. He is still a refuge for the sick and afflicted and not a day passes that he does not treat some down-and-outer free. He is still a reformer but he has lost that "lean, hungry look" of his hobo days, and since he owns a Ford, the hobos charge him with being an aristocrat.

JOHN X. KELLY, SOAP-BOXER AND ORGANIZER

John Kelly has been associated with James Eads How for more than fifteen years. Before he met How he was a curbstone orator. Beating his way from city to city, he has talked in the "slave markets" of every metropolitan city in the United States. He has been jailed many times for his "soap-boxing," and has often been forced to leave town between the suns because of free-speech fights. He has often beaten his way 1,000 miles to be present at a hobo convention and to participate in the demonstrations of the hobo against the upper strata of society.

Kelly is still an organizer, though he is not an enthusiastic or hopeful one. He still has faith, but he is no longer the staunch advocate of democratic hobo organizations he formerly was. Years of bitter experience have taught him that the average hobo will not stand up under any responsibility. At one time he was an I.W.W. soap-boxer, but he no longer believes that the "Wobblies" are doing anything for the hobo, and he frankly tells them so.

From a champion of democracy, he has swung over to an advocate of benevolent autocracy. He is still active in the "Hobo College," but is often at variance with How and opposes him bitterly on some issues.

How, an idealist, has never learned that the ordinary hobo organization is almost sure to fail if left to manage itself. "But," says Kelly, the organizer, "they'll never succeed. They will never be cured of quarreling over trifles. They have got to be saved by some other method than their own power."

MICHAEL C. WALSH, ORGANIZER AND PROMOTER

Walsh has long been a factor in the hobo life of Chicago. At present he is the head of a struggling organization of workers known as the United Brotherhood of American Laborers, which seeks to organize workers around an insurance program. Walsh designates himself "Journalist and Lecturer, Founder of the Famous Hobo College," "The Society of Vagabonds," and "The Mary Garden Forum." He further styles himself, not without reason, a graduate of the "University of Adversity."

Left an orphan at an early age, he began wandering, working casually at his trade as an iron-worker.

He traveled extensively over the United States and went abroad as a tramp worker and a beach-comber. In 1906–7, becoming interested in the problem of the down-and-outs, he conducted the Liberty Hotel in Seattle for the unemployed. Later in San Francisco he was again active in the interest of the unemployed. Still later he joined James Eads How in St. Louis and aided in organizing the "penniless men of his own city." In 1915 he came to Chicago and organized the "Hobo College." Other hobos say that the "college" had been in existence years before Walsh arrived on the scene, but that he did play a part in making it popular.

Walsh, as president of the "college," was able to attract the assistance of many leading citizens. He won the services of Mary Garden, who took special pride in singing there occasionally. He has been active among the unemployed, and at one time attracted considerable public notice which got him into disrepute with the local police.

Walsh has also sought the limelight as a lyceum and chautauqua lecturer. His subjects dealt with the various aspect of the hobo problem. Walsh, like many of the hobo celebrities, only sees in the tramp problem one cause, and that is, unemployment. "Give the boys plenty of jobs and there will be no tramps." This is a popular interpretation among the tramps themselves.

DANIEL HORSLEY, "PROFESSOR" AND BOOKDEALER

Daniel Horsley is a bookseller. His establishment, at 1237 West Madison Street, is called the hobo bookstore. The place is known as the "Pro-

letariat" to the men on the "stem." Here many
men who have no other address receive their mail.
Says one man, "Where is —— lately, Dan ?" "I don't
know, but I suppose he is on his way to Chicago.
I have had some mail for him for two weeks." The
men meet their friends at the "Proletariat," or they
leave things there for safekeeping. They all know
Mr. Horsley, and he has the good will of all the
"bos."

Horsley has been somewhat of a hobo himself, as
the following excerpt will show:

> My occupation during the past 14 years has carried me
> through many grades of labor. First, the coal mining industry
> was for many years my sole occupation. The miner, having more
> dangers to confront than most workers, does not last long. The
> industry claimed two of my brothers. After having received
> a dose of black damps (foul air), my health was not of the best so
> I decided the open air would be the most beneficial.
>
> I started with a picture machine to earn my living as I
> recuperated. I traveled through Nebraska, Dakota, Wyoming,
> Montana, and Alberta, Canada. In every small town we would
> generally come across some of the boys (hobos). Returning from
> the Northwest I came back East without the machine. I
> stayed a while in Iowa and then went back to the West. Pre-
> vious to and during the war I was in the shipbuilding industry.
> Leaving there I worked for a short while in the woods but decided
> to come East again. Visiting the eastern seaboard I saw great
> industries closing down so I finally landed in Chicago.

Dan's work is selling books and periodicals but
he gets his recreation by mounting the soap box
occasionally. He is a devout student of Marxian
economics, and he likes nothing better than to talk
economics to an audience of workers. At the "Hobo
College" he is known as "professor," and he gives
lectures there now and then on economics, or his
other favorite topic, current history.

The *Hobo News* has printed a number of his articles on economic subjects. His writing, like his teaching and soap-boxing, is along Marxian lines. He has little patience for anyone who sees things differently. His hobby is education, and the book business gives him a chance to get to the homeless man and all other workers the kind of literature that he thinks will start them thinking.

A. W. DRAGSTEDT, "THE HOBO INTELLECTUAL"

Mr. Dragstedt is one of the numerous ex-secretaries of the "Hobo College" for the year 1922–23. As secretary of the "college," it was his business to attend to the finances of the institution and to manage the programs. It is the secretary's job to find speakers for various occasions, and to advertise the meetings. In short, the secretary must be a diplomat and an executive. Dragstedt has all the earmarks of a good hobo secretary.

Born in Sweden some forty years ago, he emigrated to this country and settled in Montana before he was out of his teens. He did not remain settled long, but went here and there in search of work until he developed into a regular hobo. He has worked at nearly all the migratory occupations and has seen nearly all the states of the Union. He is now one of the seasoned veterans of the floating fraternity. He is getting over his passion for travel, but he has not yet learned to settle down. He still likes to feel that he is free to go whenever the notion strikes him, although for a year or so he has not gone very far from the city.

Dragstedt is a man of wide and varied experience, but he seldom can be persuaded to talk about him-

self. He did his bit in the late war and went as far
as France. Most hobos who have been across like
to tell about it, but not he. But Dragstedt talks.
He has ideas and he talks about them. He has a
great many ideas, some of them consistent and
others not, but they keep him occupied and he is
generally keeping someone else interested. He is a
type of the hobo intellectual.

As a high brow, Dragstedt is a poet of no mean
ability. His poems either protest against the "system" or idealize tramp life. He is also an artist.
The walls of the "Hobo College" are adorned with
samples of his workmanship such as cartoons and
decorated placards. He has an ambition to become
a cartoonist, but he is a hobo, and hobos are men who
will not apply themselves. He has two or three
scenarios that might be developed into fair picture
plays, but he will not go back to them to polish
them up. This calls for more application than he
cares to give. In this, again, he is a hobo, but he
does not grieve about that.

CHARLES W. LANGSMAN, EXPONENT OF LOVE

Recently, Superintendent Langsman celebrated
his twentieth spiritual birthday. For twenty years
he has been connected with the Bible Rescue Mission.
Before he became converted, to use his words, he was
an "ordinary bad man of the street." He has lived
the life of the tramp. He knows hobos from the
human side. He knows their weaknesses, their
temptations, and their trials. For twenty years he
has worked with them to aid them. Hundreds of
men have been lifted out of the quicksands of a

transient and aimless life by him, while he has inspired thousands to make an effort.

In his official capacity he is the superintendent of the Bible Rescue Mission. He is also vice-president of the midwest district of the International Mission Union. To the men on the street he is known as "Charley." No mission man in Chicago is better known.

The Bible Rescue Mission is the only one that feeds men the year around. Mr. Langsman feels that hungry men need food just as much in summer as in winter. To him feeding is an evidence of the spirit of Christianity. Because of this policy of feeding, he has been severely criticized by the homeless men themselves and by missions. Many of the "bos" say that "Charley" has a "doughnut philosophy." They maintain that religion is not worth much if it can only get into a man's heart through his stomach. These criticisms come back to Superintendent Langsman, but they have not changed his policy.

One of Langsman's hobbies is a homeless man's picnic each year. When "Charley" stages a picnic it is a gala day for West Madison Street. All the "boys" come out for a ride to the country in trucks furnished by various firms and to eat sandwiches provided by the churches.

JOHN VAN DE WATER, THE FRIEND OF THE DESERVING

The Helping Hand Mission at 850 West Madison Street is essentially a family mission with Sunday-school, parents' classes, and other auxiliary activities. It does not, however, neglect the homeless man. Superintendent John Van de Water, for the last eight years superintendent of the Helping Hand Mission, is one of the few practical men in the mission work. Throughout the winter his organization feeds, upon an average, 100 men a day. However, no one is fed who will not work. He operates a wood yard and any able-bodied man who asks for aid is given a chance to work. His is the only mission that has such a test.

Mr. Van de Water does not care for converts that must be "bought" with doughnuts and coffee, and he has little patience with the missions imposed upon by men who become converted only for a place to sleep or something to eat. He is in favor of concerted action among missions, because where they work separately they lay themselves open to exploitation.

The homeless man is often an ungrateful individual, but Mr. Van de Water feels that more than a fourth of the men aided really appreciate the help they get. Many men prefer the mission floor in cold weather to the floor in the "flophouse," which is seldom scrubbed.

BRIGADIER J. E. ATKINS AND THE SALVATION ARMY HOTELS

Most exploited and least loved by the hobos is the Salvation Army. But the Salvation Army does more for the hobo than any other agency. In every city of the country it is the "good Samaritan" to the down-and-outs. Not only is it interested in working upon the hearts of men, but it seeks to help people to walk alone. One of the pioneers in this program of practical salvation is Brigadier J. E. Atkins.

Brigadier Atkins, a native of Wales, enlisted with the Salvation Army forty-three years ago. He was sent to this country in 1886 as a worker at the time when the first split occurred in the ranks. At that time he was a regular officer in the ranks, and later became a division officer. Before the war he was placed in charge of the Salvation Army industrial work in Denver, Kansas City, and Des Moines.

He entered the army as a chaplain, and was assigned to the first division. He was attached to "Young Teddy" Roosevelt's organization, and as a consequence saw considerable action. In this capacity he spent twenty-one months overseas, serving with his organization in all its major offensives. Twice he was gassed, and, as a result, his voice has been permanently impaired.

Since his discharge from the army, Brigadier Atkins has been in charge of the four Salvation Army hotels for men in Chicago which cater to the superior class of homeless men. These hotels are operated on the usual Salvation Army business-like basis. The policy is to make them pay their way, if possible, but not to charge prices greater than the commercial hotels. It is the Atkins aim to give all the service that is consistent with the price: to keep the price as low as possible, and to keep the places clean and orderly. He is insistent on getting clean, sober guests in the Army hotels, and no apparently clean, sober man without funds need go away. The contrary is said to be true by many "bos," but they are generally men who have been "found out."

DR. JOHNSTON MYERS AND THE IMMANUEL PLAN

We have knocked out the heavy stone barrier which stood between us and the people and placed in its stead a glass, business, inviting front, bearing such announcements as, "We worship, we heal, we clothe, we feed, we find employment for those in need"; "Your friends are inside, come in." Between five hundred and one thousand people accept this invitation daily. We are prepared to meet and help them.

This is what Dr. Myers has done with a typical, forbidding, gray-stone church, the Immanuel Baptist Church, at 2320 Michigan Avenue. For twenty-seven years he has been pastor of this church, and all that time he has been adhering to the Immanuel plan outlined above. For ten years previous to his coming to the Immanuel Church, he was pastor of the Ninth Street Baptist Church of Cincinnati, where he followed this scheme of serving humanity as well as God.

Dr. Myers is a practical religionist. He is bringing religion out of the clouds, and has made it an everyday, functioning affair. In his mind it does not hurt a church to have a kitchen in the basement nor to operate a restaurant in the building. His church serves an excellent meal for thirty cents. Many of the workers in the automobile salesrooms and the students from the medical college near by are in the habit of taking lunch at the church.

Most of the churches in the business area have closed their doors, but the Immanuel Baptist is more conspicuous today than ever before. The business men on the street are proud of it. They contributed recently to help rebuild it after the steeple had been blown down by a gale. The church does not serve its members as it used to, because most of the families have moved away and now most of its congregation is composed of homeless men.

Dr. Myers does not try to preach to the men, nor does he try to use the material aid he gives as a means of coaxing men to become converted. He does not believe in such conversions. He and his staff have learned that the average homeless man cannot hold money. The men who apply know this too. "Johnston Myers will feed anyone but it is pretty hard to get any 'jack' from him."

THE GREENSTEINS AND "MOTHER'S RESTAURANT"

Few hobos enter Chicago who have not heard of "Mother" Greenstein. For years Mother and Father Greenstein ran a saloon on South State Street. It was a barrel-house and the "bos" flocked to it when they had money. It was one of the few saloons in that area that was on "the square." Among the hobos it is asserted that "Mother" is the richest woman in Chicago. But her wealth has not changed her habits. She reared a family of seven children, and most of them have gone through college and into business for themselves. The Greensteins are proud of their family, but no less proud of their work. With the coming of prohibition, they closed the saloon and opened a restaurant on the corner of Ninth and State streets.

The place is known as "Mother's Restaurant," and it is one of the few places in Hobohemia that has the right to write "Home Cooking" on the window. Day after day "Mother" is on the job, cooking steaks and chops and French-fried potatoes, while "Father" waits table and serves at the bar. Mother lives in her work. She is proud of her kitchen, and she likes to serve hungry men. The hobos say no chef in the Blackstone or Drake can prepare more savory dishes. The Greensteins did not earn their reputation by serving hungry men who could pay their way, but by serving the penniless and hungry at times when it is hard for hungry men to get food.

A sign is painted on the wall outside the restaurant: "Mother's Restaurant. Don't Go Hungry. See Mother." Last winter another sign placed in the window read: "Attention! Starting Monday, Dec. 20 [1921], 'Mother' Will Serve Hot Coffee and Rolls Free . . . . from 5 A.M. to 7 A.M." Some mornings the bread line at 901 South State Street contained as many as 500 men who were out to get a bowl of coffee and something to eat, but none were ever turned away. There is always plenty of bread and plenty of coffee, and good coffee, too.

The hobos do appreciate "Mother." The old-timers of South State Street swear by her.

HOBO LEADERSHIP

This rapid sketch of a few persons in the *Who's Who* of Hobohemia gives a picture of the local leadership among the homeless men. All these persons, and many others who embody either the aspirations of the hobos or the organized religious and philanthropic impulses of the larger community toward the migrant, must be taken into account in any fundamental policy and program for his welfare. All these leaders are dealing with the homeless man as a human being, that is, with his personal needs, his memories, and his hopes. Working with these leaders, the social agencies may secure both insight into his attitudes and wishes and his co-operation for his own well-being.

CHAPTER XIII
THE INTELLECTUAL LIFE OF THE HOBO

THE homeless man is an extensive reader. This is especially true of the transients, the tramp, and the hobo. The tramp employs his leisure to read everything that comes his way. If he is walking along the railroad track, he picks up the papers that are thrown from the trains; he reads the cast-off magazines. If he is in the city, he hunts out some quiet corner where he may read. The tramp is a man with considerable leisure, but few books.

The libraries are open to them, but comparatively few use them. Public libraries are generally imposing structures and, dressed as he usually is, the tramp hesitates to enter them. Dan Horsley, who is a newsdealer and runs a bookstore on West Madison, in an article in the *Hobo News* for October, 1922, writes:

Just as a hobo would feel out of place in a Fifth Avenue church, so he would feel in the average library. He does not make general use of the libraries because of the menacing fear of the law. He is always watching lest he be caught as a vagrant, and this prevents him seeking recreative study; so he gets his own literature to read and seeks some quiet place.

There are men in the hobo class who are not deterred by these scruples. Some of the most persistent users of the library have been initiated during the winter time when they were forced inside for shelter. The newspaper reading-room of the Chicago Public Library has become for them a favorite retreat during the cold winter days. It is also a good resting-place in the hot summer months.

Lodging-houses sometimes have reading-rooms in which guests may find the local newspapers and

current periodicals.   Such reading material is usually extensively read and much thumb-marked.
Most lodging-houses and rooming-houses do not
provide reading matter for their guests.   Seldom
does a tramp throw away a paper.   He passes it on
to someone else, and after it has served its usefulness
as reading matter, he may use it at night for a bed
either in a "flophouse" or a park, along the docks,
or in box cars.

The hobo reads the daily papers but does not
indorse them.   He looks with disapproval upon the
so-called "capitalist" press.   If he belongs to the
radicals he is sure that the press is against him.   But
in spite of this he reads it.   He reads it for the
news.

Radical papers, to be sure, are steadfast in their
efforts to promote his interests and champion his
cause, but it is a cause that is so well known to the
homeless man that it has lost its novelty.   There are
many radical papers.   Among them are the *Weekly
People*, the *Truth*, the *Industrial Solidarity*, the
Worker, the *Hobo News*, the *Liberator*, the *Voice of
Labor*.   These are not printed primarily for the
homeless man, but have a wide circulation among
the so-called "slum proletariat."

The homeless man reads a certain amount of
religious literature, but little of it is perused in the
spirit hoped for by the mission worker or street
evangelist.   He reads it because it is handed to him
and it kills time.

Short-story magazines are popular. Next to
short-story magazines would come railroad or engineering journals and other magazines dealing with
popular mechanics.

Sex stories are, of course, popular. The tramp has a preference for books of adventure and action. Jack London is the most widely read of novelists among the "bos." Books on mechanics, *How to Run an Automobile*, *Uses of the Steel Square*, *Block Signal Systems*, *Gas Engines*, have a wide sale.

Works on phrenology, palmistry, Christian Science, hypnotism, and the secrets of the stars, etc., are of perennial interest. Joke books and books explaining tricks with cards or riddles, detective stories, and books in the field of the social sciences are surprisingly popular. Bookstores patronized by tramps keep in stock special pocket-size editions of works on sociology, economics, politics, and history. The radical periodicals recommend books to the serious-minded hobo reader. Following is a list from the *Hobo News:*

Easy Outlines on Economics, by Noah Ablett
A Worker Looks at History, by Mark Starr
Philosophical Essays; Positive Outlines of Philosophy, by J. Dietzgen

Among the books recommended for the proletariat in the I.W.W. literature list for April, 1922, are the following:

The Ancient Lowly, C. Osborne Ward
Ancient Society, Lewis H. Morgan
Capital, Karl Marx
Capital Today, Herman Cahn
The Economic Causes of War, Achille Loria
Essays on the Materialistic Conception of History, Antonio Labriola
Evolution of Man, Wilhelm Boelache
Evolution of Property, Paul Lafargue
Social and Philosophical Studies, Paul Lafargue
Stories of the Great Railroads, Charles Edward Russell
The Universal Kinship, J. Howard Moore

History of Great American Fortunes, Gustavus Myers
History of the Supreme Court, Gustavus Myers
Origin of the Family; Private Property and the State, Frederick Engels
The History of the I.W.W., Frederic Brissenden

These books are kept in stock at the I.W.W. headquarters and extensively sold and read by the intellectuals. Soap-box orators get fuel for the fires they seek to kindle from books of this sort. It is common knowledge on the "stem" that one can tell the books a speaker reads by the opinions he expresses and the programs he favors.

THE HOBO WRITER

The hobo who reads sooner or later tries his hand at writing. A surprisingly large number of them eventually realize their ambition to get into print. It is not unusual to meet a man of the road with a number of clippings in his pocket of articles he has contributed to the daily press. Most of the great dailies have columns that are accessible to the free-lance writer, and the pages of the radical press are always open to productions of the hobo pen. Most of these contributions are in the form of letters to editors. One man who writes many such letters proudly exhibited an article recently published in the *Chicago Daily Tribune*. It was signed "F. W. B." He explained that these letters stood for "Fellow Worker Block." That was his nom de plume.

The hobo writer does not concern himself with letters alone. A number of them are ambitious to become novelists, essayists, and even dramatists. Some of these men have manuscripts that they have carried about with them for years in search of a publisher. One such author, an old man, said: "I have material enough together to write a book. All I want is to get someone to help me organize it. I want someone to go over it with me. You see, I never had much schooling and my grammar is not very good." Another man carried about a great roll of manuscript which purported to be a "society novel." It was entitled *The Literary in Literature*. It was written in lead pencil and represented the accumulated effort of several years. When the mood struck him, he added a chapter or a paragraph. Before the last page had been written, however, the first was so badly dimmed from being carried around that it could not be deciphered.

Some hobo writers have visions of a financial success that will put them on "easy street." One man offered to share the proceeds from the publications of a series of essays on economics if the investigator would typewrite it. "Why, this will bring thousands of dollars," he said. "If I can only get a publisher interested, but," he added, "they don't seem to care for live subjects."

Another hobo writes songs and has the same difficulty with publishers. He still feels, after hundreds of failures, that he will eventually get into the limelight.

The hobo writer who plies the pen for the love of it is not unusual. One man has been working on a play for several months. He cannot get anyone interested, but that has not quenched his enthusiasm. Another man spends most of his leisure on the north side of Hobohemia, writing fantastic paragraphs. They are interesting and amusing. He does not try to publish them. He writes them because he

enjoys it.   Most numerous of the hobo writers are
the propagandists and dreamers.   They are the
chief contributors to the rebel press.   Many of them
care to be identified with no other.   They are not
artists nor do they write for gain.   They have little
patience for the writer who lives for the so-called
"filthy lucre."

But whatever their motive, most of these hobo
writers, for the want of a better medium, become
contributors to the radical press.   Without them
radical sheets like the I.W.W. publications and the
Hobo News would not appeal to the homeless man.
The radical press in turn serves as a pattern by
which hobo writers fashion and color their literary
productions.

THE "INDUSTRIAL SOLIDARITY"

The *Industrial Solidarity* is a typical I.W.W.
paper.   It comes nearer than any other I.W.W. paper to reflecting the mind and the spirit of the
average hobo.   It is a six- or eight-page weekly and
sells for five cents.   It is published in Chicago from
where it is distributed to individual subscribers or
in bundles to the peddlers or newsdealers.

The issue of July 1, 1922, contains the following
articles:

In bold headlines across the front page under the caption,
"Company Brought on Herrin Mine War" is a detailed narrative
of the whole affair written by George Williams who is supposed
to have been an eye-witness.   This article contains four full
columns, two of them on the front page.   Another front-page
article is devoted to the freeing of political prisoners.   It has
special reference to the fifty-two I.W.W. in Leavenworth who
refused to ask the President for pardon.   The article is headed,
"Hundreds of Cities in Million Signature Petition Drive."

The slogan was "Let Them Go Free." Attorney-General Daugherty, who at best is not popular with the floating population, is shown in a cartoon on the front page marching in a parade carrying a banner on which is inscribed, "Please, Let Morse out of Prison." Over the cartoon is written the ironical legend, which harks back to some remark that had been used against the "Wobblies," "This is no Children's Crusade."

Considerable space is devoted to the spring drive for membership. At the time of the publication of this number the drive was on in full blast in the harvest fields where the so-called "slugging committees" were out enrolling members. One long article was published telling of "conditions" in Kansas and Oklahoma where the Ku Klux Klan was offering active opposition to the I.W.W. The articles had been sent in by some "bo" who told in detail how the "Wobblies" outwitted the "town clowns," or local police, and the K.K.K.

According to the I.W.W. literature list for April, 1922, the following periodicals are issued regularly:

Name	Issued	Where Published	No. Each Issue	Language
Industrial Solidarity....	Weekly	Chicago	12,000	English
Industrial Worker......	Weekly	Seattle	10,000	English
Industrial Unionist.....	Bi-weekly	New York	(?)	English
Golos Truzenika........	Bi-weekly	Chicago	3,000	Russian
A Felszabadulas........	Weekly	Chicago	5,000	Hungarian
Il Proletario...........	Weekly	Chicago	6,000	Italian
Solidaridad............	Weekly	Chicago	5,500	Spanish
Rahotnicheska Mysl....	Weekly	Chicago	2,800	Bulgarian
Muncitorul............	Bi-weekly	Chicago	4,200	Roumanian
Jedna Velka Unie......	Monthly	Chicago	2,700	Czecho-Slovak
Tie Vapauteen.........	Monthly	Chicago	7,000	Finnish
Industrialisti..........	Daily	Duluth	16,000	Finnish
Snaga Radnika........	Bi-weekly	Duluth	3,500	Croatian

"Wobbly" papers are extensively used as lesson sheets. *Solidarity* has one long article of this character which is an analysis and criticism of craft unionism. Finally, there are several communications from members on the road and four or five editorials on questions of the day.

The *Solidarity* is only one of a number of I.W.W. publications, but the most important as far as the hobos are concerned. The organization maintains a publishing company of its own, the Equity Press, which is situated at the I.W.W. headquarters in Chicago.

THE "HOBO NEWS"

The *Hobo News*, published in St. Louis, contains sixteen pages and carries no advertising. It is published monthly and sells for ten cents. It is distributed, like *Solidarity*, by bundle orders or subscription. The July, 1922, issue of the *Hobo News* has the following contents:

An article by Laura Irwin entitled, "Half Dead (Unnecessary Movement a Crime)." It laments the fact that more care is given to machines and animals than to men by the big interests. Another article is a reprint entitled, "Hobos in Missouri" It is a description of life on the road. Daniel Horsley, a Chicagoan, has an article on "Hobo Life and Death: Something to Think About." It is a discussion of the struggle for existence. There is also a short story entitled "Callahans's Castle" depicting jungle pastimes.

Under the heading "Near Poetry" are several short poems by different hobo contributors. Some of the titles are: "History," "Adrift," "To a Hobo," "Labor's March," "Our Boss," "The Hobo: of Course," and "The Glory of Toil." Several letters to the editor deal with subjects of general interest to the hobos. The editor writes on the prospects for work the coming winter. There are two cartoons. One shows the figure of a worker hewn out of stone at the top of a mountain. He is being assailed by politicians and capitalists. Over the cartoon is this legend, "These Shall Not Prevail against Him." Another cartoon shows a tramp waiting at the water tank. A train is approaching in the distance. It is entitled, "The Regular Stop."

No class of men are in a better position to know life than the migratory population. These men have a large fund of experience, but they do not seem to have developed any sense of the relative values. With all this experience and with all these contacts with life, they are not able to interpret it. The intellectuals are obsessed by the class struggle, and instead of writing literature, they prefer to repeat the formulas and play with the mental toys which the doctrinaire reformers and revolutionists have fashioned for them.

We cannot say therefore that the radical press in monopolizing the hobo pens has robbed art. Among all these contributors to the radical publications, there are few who might produce literature. Many of them do not have patience to write literature nor the courage to formulate a new idea. They prefer to ride a hobby and repeat familiar formulas.

Writers who do find themselves do not remain in the hobo class. Others have the ability to rise, but because of drink or drugs are unable to do so. These men may find a place on the staff of one of the radical papers. They may even aspire to an editorship. Such a goal is not uncommon among the intellectuals. The *Hobo News* is one paper that the hobo writer likes to be identified with because it is more than a doctrinaire propagandist sheet. It maintains some literary features, and every issue has one or more articles or poems that portray hobo life.

CHAPTER XIV
HOBO SONGS AND BALLADS

MUCH so-called hobo verse which has found its way into print was not written by tramps, but by men who knew enough of the life of the road to enable them to interpret its spirit. The best hobo poems have been written behind prison bars. Many of the songs of the I.W.W. have been written in jail.

The poetry most popular among the men on the road are ballads describing some picturesque and tragic incident of the hobo's adventurous life. The following by an unknown author illustrates the type. Here is an incident told in the language of the road in a manner that every "bo" can understand and appreciate.

THE GILA MONSTER ROUTE

The lingering sunset across the plain
Kissed the rear end of an east-bound train,
And shone on the passing track close by
Where a dingbat sat on a rotten tie.

He was ditched by the "shack," and cruel fate,
The "con" highballed, and the manifest freight,
Pulled out on the stem behind the mail,
And beat it east on a sanded rail.

As she pulled away in the fading night
He could see the gleam of her red tail lights.
Then the moon arose, and the stars came out;
He was ditched on the Gila Monster Route.

There was nothing in sight but sand and space;
No chance for a bo to feed his face;
Not even a shack to beg for a lump.
Nor a hen house there to frisk for a gump.

As he gazed far out on the solitude
He dropped his head and began to brood.
He thought of the time he lost his pal
In the hostile berg of Stockton, Cal.

They had mooched the stem and threw their feet,
And speared four bits on which to eat;
But deprived themselves of their daily bread,
And sluffed the coin for dago-red.

Then, down by the tracks, in the jungle's glade,
On the cool, green grass in the tule's shade,
They shed their coats, and ditched their shoes,
And tanked up full of that colored booze.

Then, they took a flop with their hides plumb full,
And did not hear the harness bull,
Till he shook them out of their boozy nap,
With a husky voice and a loaded sap.

They were charged with vag, for they had no kale,
And the judge said sixty days in jail;
But the john had a bundle, the worker's plea,
So he gave him a floater and set him free.

They had turned him out, but ditched his mate,
So he grabbed the guts of an east-bound freight;
He had held his form to the rusty rods
Till the brakeman hollered, "Hit the sod."

So the bo rolled off and in the ditch,
With two switch lights and a rusty switch,
A poor, old, seedy, half-starved bo
On a hostile pike without a show.

Then all at once from out of the dark
Came the short, sharp notes of a coyote's bark;
The bo looked up and quickly rose,
And shook the dust from his threadbare clothes.

Far off in the west through the moonlight night
He saw the gleam of a big head light;
An east-bound stock run hummed the rail,
It was due at the switch to clear the mail.

As she pulled up close the head-end "shack"
Threw the switch to the passing track,
The stock rolled in and off the main,
The line was clear for the west-bound train.

As she hove in sight far up the track,
She was working steam with the brake shoes slack;
Whistling once at the whistling post,
She flittered by like a frightened ghost.

You could hear the roar of the big six wheel,
As the drivers pounded the polished steel,
And the screech of the flanges on the rail,
As she beat it west o'er the desert trail.

The john got busy and took a risk,
He climbed aboard and began to frisk,
He reached up high and began to feel
For an end-door pin, then he cracked a seal.

'Twas a double-deck stock loaded with sheep;
The john got in and went to sleep;
The "con" highballed, and she whistled out,
They were off—down the Gila Monster Route.

The following ballad by Harry Kemp, the "tramp poet," describes a situation that is familiar to those who know Hobohemia. Many men in the tramp class, to escape cold and hunger, have yielded to a similar temptation.

THE TRAMP CONFESSION

We huddled in the mission
    Fer it was cold outside
And listened to the preacher
    Tell of the Crucified;

        Without a sleety drizzle
            Cut deep each ragged form,
        An' so we stood the talkin'
            Fer shelter from the storm.

They sang of Gods and Angels
An' Heaven's eternal joy
An' things I stopped believin'
When I was still a boy;

They spoke of good an' evil
An' offered savin' grace
An' some showed love for mankind
Ashinin' in their face.

An' some their graft was workin'
The same as me and you;
But some was urgin' on us
What they believed was true.

We sang an' dozed an' listened,
But only feared, us men
The time when, service over,
We'd have to mooch again.

An' walk the icy pavements,
An' breast the snow storm gray,
Till the saloons was opened,
An' there was hints of day.

So, when they called out, "Sinners,
Won't you come ?" I came . . . .
But in my face was pallor
An' in my heart was shame . . . .
An' so fergive me, Jesus,
Fer mockin' of thy name.

Fer I was cold an' hungry;
They gave me food and bed
After I kneeled there with them,
An' many prayers was said.

An' so fergive me, Jesus,
I didn't mean no harm . . . .
Fer outside it was zero
An' inside it was warm.

Yes, I was cold an' hungry
An' Oh, Thou Crucified,
Thou Friend of all the Lowly,
Fergive the lie I lied.[1]

WANDERLUST

Many men have seen charms in the life on the
road; Walt Whitman and Vachel Lindsay are or were
tramp poets. For men who cannot endure the
security and the tyranny of convention, this care-
free existence has an irresistible appeal. The following swinging poem by H. H. Knibbs vibrates with
the call of the road.

NOTHING TO DO BUT GO

I'm the wandering son with the nervous feet,
That never were meant for a steady beat;
I've had many a job for a little while,
I've been on the bum and I've lived in style;
And there was the road, stretchin' mile after mile,
And nothing to do but go.

So, beat it, Bo, while your feet are mates;
Take a look at the whole United States;
There's the little fire and the pipe at night;
And up again when the morning's bright;
With nothin' but road and sky in sight,
And nothin' to do but go.

So, beat it, Bo, while the goin's good,
While the birds in the trees are sawin' wood;
If today ain't the finest for you and me,
Then there's tomorrow that's going to be,
And the day after that, that's comin', see,
And nothin' to do but go.

[1] H. Kemp, *The Cry of Youth*, p. 60. By special permission of the publisher, Mitchell Kennerley.

> Then beat it, Bo, while you're young and strong;
> See all you can, for it won't last long;
> You can tarry for only a little spell,
> On the long, gray road to Fare-Ye-Well,
> That leads to Heaven or maybe Hell,
> And nothin' to do but go.[1]

"Away from Town," by Harry Kemp, is a vivid picture of the springtime yearning that the hobo feels to be off to the country after spending the winter in the city's slums. Not all tramps who feel, with the passing of winter, the urge to move, are enticed from the "gaunt, gray city" in search of "country cheer," but a goodly number love the grass and shade and a season in the "jungles." It is the same call that makes truants of school boys and fishermen of staid business men.

High perched upon a box-car, I speed, I speed today;
I leave the gaunt, gray city some good, green miles away,
A terrible dream in granite, a riot of streets and brick
A frantic nightmare of people until the soul turns sick—
Such is the high, gray city with the live green waters 'round
Oozing up from the Ocean, slipping in from the Sound.
I'd put up in the Bowery for nights in a ten-cent bed
Where the dinky "L" trains thunder and rattle overhead;
I'd traipsed the barren pavements with pain of frost in my feet;
I'd sidled to hotel kitchens and asked for something to eat.
But when the snow went dripping, and the young spring came as one
Who weeps because of the winter, laughs because of the sun
I thought of a limpid brooklet that bickers through weeds all day,
And I made a streak for the ferry, and rode across in a dray,

[1] H. H. Knibbs, *Songs of the Outlands*, p. 50. By permission, and special arrangement with, Houghton, Mifflin Company, the authorized publishers.

And dodged into the Erie where they bunt the box-cars round.
I peeled my eye for detectives, and boarded an outward bound.
For you know when a man's been cabined in walls for part of
     a year,
He longs for a place to stretch in, he hankers for country cheer.[1]

POEMS OF PROTEST

In spite of its transient charms, the life of the
tramp is a hard one. It is fine to be free, but it is
good to have a home. The hobo likes freedom, but
is not satisfied to be an Ishmaelite. His speeches
and his poetry are filled with protests against the
social order which refuses to make a place for him;
against the system that makes him an outcast.

The following poem entitled "The Dishwasher"
was written by Jim Seymour, the "Hobo poet."
The second half, omitted here, is a prophecy of the
overthrow of the "system."

Alone in the kitchen, in grease laden steam,
I pause for a moment—a moment to dream:
For even a dishwasher thinks of a day,
Wherein there'll be leisure for rest and for play.
And now that I pause, o'er the transom there floats,
A strain of the Traumerei's soul stirring notes.
Engulfed in a blending of sorrow and glee,
I wonder that music can reach even me.

But now I am thinking; my brain has been stirred.
The voice of a master, the lowly has heard.
The heart breaking sobs of the sad violin,
Arouse the thoughts of the sweet might have been.
Had men been born equal, the use of their brain,
Would shield them from poverty: free them from pain,
Nor would I have sunk into the black social mire,
Because of poor judgment in choosing a sire.

[1] H. Kemp, *The Cry of Youth*, p. 78. By permission of the publisher,
Mitchell Kennerley.

But now I am only a slave of the mill,
That plies and remodels me just as it will;
That makes me a dullard in brain burning heat;
That looks at rich viands not daring to eat;
That works with his red, blistered hands ever stuck,
Down deep in the foul indescribable muck;
Where dishes are plunged seventeen at a time;
And washed in a tubful of sickening slime.

But on with your clatter; no more must I shirk.
The world is to me but a nightmare of work.
For me not the music, the laughter and song;
For no toiler is welcome amid the gay throng.
For me not the smiles of the ladies who dine;
Nor the sweet, clinging kisses, begotten of wine.
For me but the venting of low, sweated groans,
That twelve hours a night have instilled in my bones.

Arturo Giovannitti won his reputation as a poet by a poem in blank verse which pictures the monotony of prison life. "The Walker" was written in jail, as was "The Bum," the poem by which Giovannitti is best known among the hobos. As an I.W.W. and a radical, his writings breathe the spirit of protest. "The Bum," the first three verses of which follow, is an eloquent tirade against religion:

The dust of a thousand roads, the grease
    And grime of slums, were on his face;
The fangs of hunger and disease
    Upon his throat had left their trace;
The smell of death was in his breath,
    But in his eye no resting place.

Along the gutters, shapeless, fagged,
    With drooping head and bleeding feet,
Throughout the Christmas night he dragged,
    His care, his woe, and his defeat;
Till, gasping hard, with face downward
    He fell upon the trafficked street.

The midnight revelry aloud
    Cried out its glut of wine and lust
The happy, clean, indifferent crowd
    Passed him in anger and disgust:
For—fit or rum—he was a bum,
    And if he died 'twas nothing lost.[1]

In the following poem, by an unknown writer, "The Bum on the Rods and the Bum on the Plush" states the case of labor against capital in the language and accents of the hobo:

The bum on the rods is hunted down
    As the enemy of mankind,
The other is driven around to his club
    Is feted, wined, and dined.
And they who curse the bum on the rods
    As the essence of all that is bad,
Will greet the other with a winning smile,
    And extend the hand so glad.

The bum on the rods is a social flea
    Who gets an occasional bite,
The bum on the plush is a social leech,
    Blood-sucking day and night.
The bum on the rod is a load so light
    That his weight we scarcely feel,
But it takes the labor of dozens of men
    To furnish the other a meal.

As long as you sanction the bum on the plush
    The other will always be there,
But rid yourself of the bum on the plush
    And the other will disappear.
Then make an intelligent, organized kick,
    Get rid of the weights that crush.
Don't worry about the bum on the rods,
    Get rid of the bum on the plush.

<hr>

[1] Arturo Giovannitti, *Arrows in the Gale*, p. 40.

The following verses are taken from a selection written by Henry A. White, who is a veteran of the road and for many years connected with the publication of the *Hobo News*. It is entitled "The Hobo Knows." In it one can detect an unfamiliar note of resignation, the resignation of an old man who has hoped and struggled, and learned.

> He knows the whirr of the rolling wheels,
>   And their click on the time-worn joints;
> His ear is attuned to the snap and snarl
>   Of the train, at the rickety points.
>
> He knows the camp by the side of the road,
>   And the "java" and "mulligan" too;
> The siding long, and the water tank
>   Are as home to me and you.
>
> He knows the fright of hunger and thirst,
>   And of cold and of rain as well;
> Of raggedy clothes and out-worn shoes,
>   An awful tale he can tell.
>
> He knows what it means to slave all day,
>   And at night eat the vilest of fare;
> What a tale he can tell of loathsome bunks,
>   Cramped quarters, and noisome air.
>
> He knows what the end of it all will be
>   When he crosses the line at the goal;
> A rough, pine box, and a pauper's grave
>   And he has paid his toll.

THE HOBO'S OBSERVATIONS AND REFLECTIONS ON LIFE

The poets who have written best about the tramp are those who have recorded their reflections on their own life and his. Robert W. Service sees in "The

Men That Don't Fit In" a great group of wanderers who move here and there in response to an imperious wanderlust.

> There's a race of men that don't fit in,
>   A race that can't stay still;
> So they break the hearts of kith and kin,
>   And roam the world at will.
> They range the field and they rove the flood,
>   And they climb the mountain crest,
> Theirs is the curse of the gypsy blood,
>   And they don't know how to rest.
>
> If they just went straight they might go far;
>   They are strong and brave and true;
> But they're always tired of the things that are
>   And they want the strange and new.
> They say, "Could I find my proper groove
>   What a deep mark I would make!"
> So they chop and change, and each fresh move
>   Is only a fresh mistake.
>
> And each forgets as he strips and runs
>   With a brilliant, fitful pace,
> It's the steady, quiet, plodding ones
>   Who win the lifelong race.
> And each forgets that his youth has fled,
>   Forgets that his prime is past,
> Till he stands one day with a hope that's dead,
>   In the glare of the truth at last.[1]

There are men in the tramp class who are always chasing rainbows, always expecting to "strike it rich" sometime and somewhere. Bill Quirke, for many years contributor to the *Hobo News*, gives expression to this sentiment in the poem, "One Day; Some Way, I'll Make a Stake." This poem was

[1] From *The Spell of the Yukon*, p. 15, by Robert W. Service, author of *Ballads of a Cheechako, Rhymes of a Red Cross Man*, and *Ballads of a Bohemian*, published by Barse & Hopkins, Newark, N.J.

written a few months before Bill was killed by an automobile in California. From the heart of it we quote:

> For years I've drilled the rough pathway,
>   And weathered many a wintry blast,
> I'll make another stake some day
>   For luck must turn my way at last.
> I'm far too old for working, too
> They say my work is almost through;
> My ore assesses never a flake
> But still I hope to make a stake.

In the *Hobo News* of August, 1921, Charles Thornburn records his reflections while he contemplates the empty, beaten faces of the men of the "stem":

> With ever restless tread, they come and go,
>   Or lean intent against the grimy wall,
> These men whom fate has battered to and fro,
>   In the grim game of life, from which they all
> Have found so much of that which is unkind,
>   Still hoping on, that fortune yet may mend,
> With sullen stare, and features hard and lined,
>   They wander off to nowhere, and the end.
>
> Their thoughts we may not fathom, in their eyes
>   One seems to sense a vision, as though fate
> Had let one little glimpse of fairer skies
>   Brighten their souls before she closed the gate.
> Yet have they hopes and dreams which bring them peace,
>   Adding to life's flat liquor just the blend
> Called courage, that their efforts may not cease
>   To seek the gold, hid at the rainbow's end.

"The Wanderer" is from the pen of Charles Ashleigh. It is said to have been written in jail. It is a justification, not complete, of the hobo principle of living for the day and by the day, of enjoying the sweets of life, if they can be secured, and of avoiding its problems.

> Is there no voice to speak for these, our kin;
>   The strange, wild sorrows for the wanderer's soul;
> The shining comradeship we sometimes win
>   When on our wilful way to visioned goals?
>
> We are the ones to whom the forests speak,
>   For whom the little by-streets run awry;
> Ships are our mistresses, and vaulted peaks
>   Draw us unconquered to the tyrant sky.
>
> And what if we in sordid corners sink,
>   Or perish in the crash of lawless fight;
> Our souls have had the wine of life to drink,
>   We've had our blazing day. Let come the night.

The hobo characterizes the district where the employment agencies are located as the "slave market." Louis Melis, prominent in Hobohemia as a soap-boxer, has written a poem entitled "The Slave Market" from which the following verses have been taken:

The Slave Market

> This is the city of lost dreams and defeated hopes;
> Always you are the mecca of the Jobless,
> The seekers after life and the sweet illusions of happiness.
> Within your walls there are the consuming
> Fires of pain, sorrow and eternal regrets.
> Roses never bloom here; silken petals
> Cannot be defiled.
>
> Streets in ragged attire, sang-froid in their violence;
> Years come and go; still your hideousness goes on
> And mute outcasts garnish
> Your every rendezvous.
> Blind pigs, reeking with a nauseous smell everywhere;
> The so-called "flops," the lousy beds

Where slaves of mill and mine and rail and shop
Curl up and drop away unconscious,
In fair pretense of sleep.
Employment sharks entrapping men,
Human vultures in benign disguise,
Auctioning labor at a pittance per day.
And it's always "What will you give ?"
"What will you take ?"
The pocketing of fat commissions;
Old men, young men, tramps, bums, hobos,
Laborers seeking jobs or charity
Each visioning happiness from afar.

They swarm the city streets, these slaves,
For all must live and strive,
And always the elusive job sign
Greets their contemplative glance.
A job—food, clothing, shelter;
Wage slaves selling their power;
Oh, you Slave Market, I know you!

From timbered lands, North, East, South and West
From distant golden grain belts,
From endless miles of rail,
These workers float to the city.
Timber beasts, harvesters, gandy dancers—
Adventurers all.   From every clime and zone,
Each comes with hope of work or
Else to blow his pile.

BATTLE SONGS OF THE HOBOS

There are many types of tramp songs but most conspicuous are the songs of protest.   The I.W.W. have done much to stimulate song writing, mostly songs of the struggle between the masses and the classes.

Most hobo songs are parodies on certain popular airs or on hymns.   One can easily determine when certain songs were written if he knows when certain popular airs, to which they are fitted, were the rage.

The tunes most used by the tramp song writers are those that are so well known that the song may be sung by any group of transients. When the songs are parodies on hymns there is usually a note of irony running through them. The following is called the hobo's "Harvest War Song." It was written by Pat Brennan and is sung to the tune of "Tipperary."

We are coming home, John Farmer; We are coming back to stay.
For nigh on fifty years or more, we've gathered up your hay.
We have slept out in your hayfields; we have heard your morning shout;
We've heard you wondering where in hell's them pesky go-abouts?

Chorus

It's a long way, now understand me; it's a long way to town;
It's a long way across the prairies, and to hell with Farmer Brown.
Here goes for better wages, and the hours must come down,
For we're out for a winter's stake this summer, and we want no scabs around.

You've paid the going wages, that's what kept us on the bum
You say you've done your duty, you chin-whiskered son-of-a-gun.
We have sent your kids to college, but still you rave and shout
And call us tramps and hobos, and pesky go-abouts.

But now the long wintry breezes are a-shaking our poor frames,
And the long drawn days of hunger try to drive us bos insane,
It is driving us to action; we are organized today;
Us pesky tramps and hobos are coming back to stay.

Joe Hill, whose real name was Joseph Hilstrom, holds the place of honor among the I.W.W.'s as a song writer. Before his death he was one of the most enthusiastic of the I.W.W. organizers. His execution in Utah in 1915 has not lessened his popularity among the "Wobblies." Most of his songs are parodies. "The Tramp" is a parody on the old tune: "Tramp, Tramp, Tramp; the Boys Are Marching."

> If you will shut your trap,
> I will tell you 'bout a chap,
> That was broke and up aginst it too for fair;
> He was not the kind to shirk,
> He was looking hard for work,
> But he heard the same old story everywhere.

> *Chorus*
>
> Tramp, tramp, tramp, keep on a-tramping,
> Nothing doing here for you;
> If I catch you 'round again;
> You will wear the ball and chain,
> Keep on tramping, that's the best thing you can do.

> He walked up and down the street,
> 'Till the shoes fell off his feet;
> In a house he spied a lady cooking stew,
> And he said, "How do you do,
> May I chop some wood for you?"
> What the lady told him made him feel so blue.

> 'Cross the street a sign he read,
> "Work for Jesus," so it said,
> And he said, "Here is my chance, I'll surely try,"
> And he kneeled upon the floor,
> Till his knees got rather sore,
> But at eating time he heard the preacher say:

> Down the street he met a cop,
> And the copper made him stop,
> And he asked him, "When did you blow into town?"
> "Come with me to the judge."
> But the judge he said, "Oh fudge!
> Bums that have no money needn't come around."

"The Preacher and the Slave," also written by Joe Hill and sung to the tune of "Sweet Bye and

Bye," is especially popular among the malcontents because of its attack upon religion:

> Long haired preachers come out every night,
> Try to tell you what's wrong and what's right;
> But when asked how 'bout something to eat
> They will answer in voices so sweet:

> *Chorus*

> You will eat bye and bye
> In that glorious land above the sky;
> Work and pray, live on hay,
> You'll get pie in the sky when you die.

> And the starvation army, they play,
> And they sing and they clap and they pray,
> Till they get all your coin on the drum,
> Then they'll tell you when you're on the bum:

> Workingmen of all countries, unite,
> Side by side we for freedom will fight;
> When the world and its wealth we have gained
> To the grafters we'll sing this refrain:

> *Last Chorus*

> You will eat bye and bye
> When you've learned how to cook and to fry;
> Chop some wood, 'twill do you good,
> And you will eat in the sweet bye and bye.

The "Portland County Jail" is one of the few songs of the road that does not wear out.

> I'm a stranger in your city,
>   My name is Paddy Flynn;
> I got drunk the other evening,
>   And the coppers run me in.

I had no money to pay my fine,
  No friends to go my bail,
So I got soaked for ninety days
  In the Portland County Jail.

Chorus

Oh, such a lot of devils,
  The like I never saw;
Robbers, thieves, and highwaymen,
  And breakers of the law.
They sang a song the whole night long,
  And the curses fell like hail,
I'll bless the day they take me away
  From the Portland County Jail.

The only friend that I had left,
  Was Happy Sailor Jack;
He told me all the lies he knew,
  And all the safes he's cracked.
He cracked them in Seattle;
  He'd robbed the Western Mail;
It would freeze the blood of an honest man,
  In the Portland County Jail.

HOBO VERSE IN A LIGHTER VEIN

The characteristic hobo is an optimist who sees
the humorous side of many an unpleasant or dangerous situation. The average seasoned "bo" with full
stomach and money in his pocket can enjoy to the
full the never-ending series of happenings on West
Madison Street. If there is nothing else, he can be
amused at the other man's predicament. Many of
these humorous experiences have found their way into
poetry.

The hobo is ironic even in the face of death. The
following poem, by an unknown writer, caricatures
the contrast between the sentiment and the reality
of the hobo's existence.

The Hobo's Last Lament

Beside a Western water-tank
  One cold November day,
Inside an empty box-car,
  A dying hobo lay;
His old pal stood beside him,
  With low and drooping head,
Listening to the last words,
  As the dying hobo said:

"I am going to a better land,
  Where everything is bright,
Where beef-stews grow on bushes
  And you sleep out every night;
And you do not have to work at all,
  And never change your socks,
And streams of goodly whiskey
  Come trickling down the rocks.

"Tell the bunch around Market street,
  That my face, no more, they'll view;
Tell them I've caught a fast freight,
  And that I'm going straight on through.
Tell them not to weep for me,
  No tears in their eyes must lurk;
For I'm going to a better land,
  Where they hate the word called work.

"Hark! I hear her whistling,
  I must catch her on the fly;
I would like one scoop of beer
  Once more before I die."
The hobo stopped, his head fell back,
  He'd sung his last refrain;
His old pal stole his coat and hat
  And caught an East-bound train.[1]

A. W. Dragstedt, a prominent personality in Chicago's Hobohemia, is a man who goes and comes

[1] *Hobo News*, June, 1917.

when he pleases. According to hobo custom, he goes to the country each summer, but he usually spends his leisure in town. He is an optimist. The following two verses were written at a time when he was down but not downhearted.

> It takes a very little for me to be happy;
>   The world has a smile for each day that goes by;
> My diet of coffee and doughnuts so snappy,
>   Makes me very clever and mentally spry.
>
> My shoes are but uppers, pants full of patches;
>   My stomach feels pleased when I fill it with soup;
> When sleepy and tired my slumber I snatches,
>   In haystacks and hallways; sometimes in the coop.

"No Matter Where You Go" is a humorous presentation of the futility of wandering. Where to go next when the hobo wants to move is always a problem. Usually the "bo" gives an unfavorable report of the district he has just left.

> Things are dull in San Francisco,
>   "On the bum" in New Orleans;
> "Rawther punk" in cultured Boston,
>   Famed for codfish, pork, and beans.
> "On the hog" in Kansas City;
>   Out in Denver things are jarred;
> And they're "beefing" in Chicago
>   That the times are rather hard.
>
> Not much doing in St. Louis;
>   It's the same in Baltimore;
> Coin don't rattle in Seattle
>   As it did in days of yore.
> Jobs are scarce around Atlanta
>   All through Texas it is still.
> And there's very little stirring
>   In the town of Louisville.

There's a howl from Cincinnati,
New York City, Brooklyn too;
In Milwaukee's foamy limits
There is little work to do.
In the face of all such rumors,
It seems not amiss to say
That no matter where you're going
You had better stay away.

POETRY AND HOBO SOLIDARITY

In song and ballad the hobo expresses life as he feels and sees it. Through poetry he creates a background of tradition and culture which unifies and gives significance to all his experiences. His ballads of the road and his battle songs of protest induce a unanimity of sentiment and attitudes, the strongest form of group solidarity in the hobo world.

Through the universal language of poetry the homeless man bridges the chasm of isolation that separates him from his fellows. In song and ballad he communicates his memories and his hopes to men everywhere who, fascinated by his experiences, perceive in them only a different expression of the human wishes of every person.

CHAPTER XV
THE SOAP BOX AND THE OPEN FORUM

"KILLING time" is a problem with the homeless man. The movie and the burlesque are the only forms of commercialized amusements within the range of his purse. Even these are only patronized infrequently and by a few. For the vast majority there is no pastime save the passing show of the crowded thoroughfare. Most of them spend their leisure time shuffling along the street reading the menu cards in the cheap restaurants, or in other forms of "window shopping." Sometimes they stray out of the "stem" into the Loop. Perhaps they will go to the parks and lie on the grass, or to the lake front where they may sit down and look out on the water.

The homeless man, as he meanders along the street, is looking for something to break the monotony. He will stand on the curb for hours, watching people pass. He notices every conspicuous person and follows with interest, perhaps sometimes with envy, the wavering movements of every passing drunk. If a policeman stops anyone on the street, he also stops and listens in. If he notices a man running into an alley his curiosity is aroused. Wherever he sees a group gathered, he lingers. He will stop to listen if two men are arguing. He will spend hours sitting on the curb talking with a congenial companion.

During the summer, time hangs heavier on the hobo's hands than in winter. In cold weather, he is usually hard pressed to find food and shelter. If the inclement weather overtakes him without funds and jobless, and this is generally the case, he is absorbed with the problem of "getting by." He is driven to his wits' end to find a warm place to sleep at night and a comfortable place to loaf during the day. It oftens takes a whole day's scouting to find a place to sleep at night and food enough to appease his gnawing and growling stomach.

There are homeless men who have time on their hands even in winter. They are those who have the rare ability to save enough in summer to live in winter. The parks are no longer inviting. The soap-box orators have either gone out of business or are forced indoors. The hobo follows them and, where he can afford it, helps to support them inside much as he did in the open. He spends more time in the movies and burlesques and will sit for half a day at times watching one show.

Listening to speeches is a popular pastime in Hobohemia. Nothing, unless it is reading, occupies so much of the homeless man's leisure time.

STREET SPEAKING IN HOBOHEMIA

Hobohemia knows but two types of speakers— the soap-box orator and the evangelist. The evangelist has been longer on the job. Religious speakers are usually associated with established organizations, or they represent mission groups of which there are many varieties on the "stem." There are evangelists who adhere to no faith or creed. They are "free lances," as most hobo speakers are, only their message is a religious one. Few of these latter take contributions, and seldom do they essay to make converts in the sense of having a following. They are enthusiasts driven into the streets with the irresistible

THE SOAP-BOX ORATOR—THE ECONOMIC ARGUMENT

AN OUTDOOR MISSION MEETING—THE RELIGIOUS PLEA

JAMES EADS HOW

urgency of their message. In Hobohemia, where time hangs heavy on the hobo's hands, there is an audience for every message.

In a later chapter[1] the rôle of the evangelist in the life of Hobohemia is considered; here we are interested in the soap-box orators whose message is secular rather than other-worldly. The man on the soap box is a reformer or a revolutionist, seeking to change conditions. The missionary, on the other hand, is seeking less to change conditions than to change mankind. This is the basis of the conflict between their rival doctrines. The soap-boxers may contend with each other concerning what is best for the down-and-out in the here and now, but they are unanimous in their opposition to the "sky pilots" and the "mission squawkers." They maintain that it is more important to enjoy life here than to live on the prospect of joy hereafter. They have lost patience with the preacher because he only promises "pie in the sky when you die," and they want the pie now.

The men and women who bring religion to the tramp in Hobohemia have taken root in the life of the "stem." Their street singing, their preaching and praying, although little heeded by the hobo, would be greatly missed if absent. But the missionary, transplanted from another area of life, remains more or less of an alien. The soap-box reformer is no less of an institution and he is, moreover, native to the soil. He is closer to the actual life and mundane interests of the homeless man. He stands on the curbstone and publishes his opinions on the great questions of the day in a positive and convincing

[1] Chapter xvii, "Missions and Welfare Organizations."

manner, and his ideas are generally couched in language that the man on the street can understand. The hobo's intellectual interests revolve about the problem of labor. The soap-box orator is the hobo's principal source of information on this topic.

Soap-boxers are "free lances" most of the time. Either they are out of harmony with all organizations or no organization has been willing to adopt them. Those who make street speaking a profession are a great deal like the ancient sophists. They are able to plead one cause today and a different cause tomorrow. Their allegiance is to be had by any group that can make the proper bid. With some of them the inducement must be a financial one, while others are interested only in ideas. If the idea attracts them they will take up the new angle of the subject with the same enthusiasm that they did the old. In this respect they are influenced by public opinion. They love to harangue the crowds but they like to have the crowd on their side.

EDUCATING THE PROLETARIAT

Soap-boxers usually take themselves seriously, though their audiences do not always do so. They take themselves seriously in spite of their frequent and often abrupt changes in positions on the issues they discuss. They are usually made to explain these changes, and these explanations, if not always logical, are usually sincere. They invariably give their best thoughts on the subject they discuss. Whatever they have gleaned from the available sources they are striving to express in language that is live and understandable to the man on the street. These efforts to clear the issues, to spread propaganda or whatever it may be called, is termed by the soap-boxers, "education."

Not all the "stem" intellectuals who assume the burden of educating the proletariat use the soap box. Many of them wield the pen. The latter are, in the main, free-lance writers, and most of their productions are tinctured with "red." But they are generally able to catch the ear of the down-and-out, whether he is a hobo or not. The writings of these cloistered radicals, who are striving to bring the chaotic proletariat to a unity of the faith, provide the soap-box pulpiteer with facts and ideas which he interprets and passes on to his curbstone audience in the shape of poems, songs, articles, and essays. The writers provide, for them, an abundance of material out of which the orators build their castles. Most of these literary radicals are optimistic about the success of their efforts to "get the worker's mind right," and thus prepare him for the new order. The masses must be educated, but the soap-boxer, whose burden it is, must himself be educated, and that is the job of the writer who works behind the scenes.

Just how much education the Hobohemian proletariat gets from this speaking and reading is not easily estimated. They learn something about the class struggle, industrial organization, and politics. Sometimes an observation on science or literature or art will fall from a speaker's lips, but most of these observations are new only to the stranger in the class. The old-timer, however, hears only old ideas restated; or, at best, new facts and figures interpreted to support old ideas. It is like a game with a limited number of pieces and a limited number

of moves. Sometimes, to be sure, a speaker
endeavors to serve "science" to the "floating fraternity." Lectures on biology, psychology, sociology,
or economics may be heard any evening or holiday
during the summer. Most of these lectures go over
the heads of the audience, and it is questionable
whether the speakers have sufficient background to
speak intelligently of the sciences they are attempting
to expound.

This effort to educate the proletariat is, nevertheless, not altogether without results. It gives
men something to occupy their minds. It gives them
some understanding of their common interests;
creates a certain amount of solidarity and, perhaps,
best of all, "kills time." Some speakers realize this
and declare that the soap box is primarily a kind of
entertainment. One man makes it a point to try
to amuse his crowd as well as to "instruct" them.
"You've got to keep 'em interested. You have to
amuse them and make 'em laugh before you can get
any ideas into their heads. Whenever things get
dry, I leave an opening for a drunk or someone to
ask me a question or crack a joke, and interest picks
up again."

An Afternoon Series of Soap-Box Orations

60. During a Sunday in July, 1922, no less than twenty men
spoke on the box at the corner of Jefferson and Madison streets;
and as many topics were treated. In the afternoon the following
speakers shared the time:

1. The meeting was opened by a man who borrowed a box
from a nearby fruit stand. He tried to get another man to
speak first so that he would not have to hurt his voice gathering
the crowd, but no one cared to start. He talked for twenty
minutes about graft in the patent-medicine trade. He had a very
catchy speech well tempered with humor and he gathered a big

crowd. Evidently he had made a study of the patent-medicine business and his speech was an "exposure" of the game. He finished by selling some pamphlets dealing with the subject.

2. The second speaker was an I.W.W. who talked for fifteen minutes on education. He was a good talker and held the crowd. He wound up by selling some I.W.W. literature and periodicals in which the thoughts of economists had been reduced from the difficult academic language to the understanding of the man on the street. He also passed out some literature, i.e., old issues of the *Solidarity*, and I.W.W. papers.

3. Another I.W.W. talked twenty minutes on organization. He argued that the rich man organizes and for that reason is successful. He does not want the poor man at the bottom to organize because he fears that he will not be able to keep him at the bottom. He didn't blame the rich man for organizing; he blamed the poor man for not organizing. He gave some literature away and sold some.

4. A speech on superstition followed. It lasted twenty minutes and was aimed at a mission group that was holding a meeting across the street. The argument was that the Bible and the church were the most powerful instruments in the hands of rich men for keeping the poor man down. No collection was taken.

5. A twenty-minute speech on the economic organization of industry was given by a man who took great pains to remind the crowd that he had spent seven years to learn all about it. He made a plea for the co-operation of labor to combat the organization of capital. No collection was taken.

6. The next man argued that the unemployment problem is caused by two things; the overcrowding of population and the concentration of wealth into the hands of a few. Eighty-five per cent of the people had but 15 per cent of the wealth and 15 per cent of the people had 85 per cent of the wealth or more than they could possibly consume. This man usually takes up a collection on the ground that he is handicapped physically, but he did not on this occasion. He spoke for twenty minutes.

7. No more speakers wanted the box so a drunk got on the stand and asked for the attention of the crowd. He furnished amusement for fifteen minutes. He was witty but easily led from subject to subject.

No speaker talked long enough to bore the crowd. Each speaker, when he had finished, yielded the box to his successor.

The crowd was a characteristic Hobohemian gathering, willing
to stand so long as they could be interested. Like most such
gatherings, it kept diminishing and increasing in size. Some
would stand in front and listen for an hour while others would
only stop a few minutes on the outer edge of the gathering. The
reaction to the speakers was for the most part sympathetic.
Occasionally a man on the sidelines would be seen to frown
disapproval but it is the habit of those who are not interested
to worm their way out of the group and go their way.

While the sixth speaker of the above list was talking the
crowd was attracted to the side by a discussion between one of
the previous speakers and another man. The argument attracted
so many listeners that the speaker was irritated and he called to
one of the men engaged in the discussion, "Say B—, do you
think that's a square deal?" "Sorry C—, I didn't know we were
disturbing you." The crowd on the side dispersed and gathered
around the speaker on the box.

SOAP-BOX ETHICS AND TACTICS

Just as there are certain unwritten laws that are
found in the jungle camps, so there are unwritten
laws that the soap-boxer observes. Regardless of
how much they differ in their schemes, they are
seldom personal in their opposition to one another.
Soap-boxers behave toward one another when not on
the box much as lawyers do when they are out of the
courtroom, and even while on the box they consider
one another's interests. For example, a speaker
in resigning the rostrum to his successor will frequently close with some such statement as this:
"I'd like to talk longer on this subject but there are
other speakers here and they have something to say
that you might like to hear."

The practice of taking up personal collections is
looked down upon by most curbstone speakers.
They feel that the soap box should not be exploited.
Collections are not always approved by the audiences.

Some men label their speeches "lectures" and "pass the hat" on the ground that they have spent years in getting the information. When they "perform the hat trick on the 'simpoleons' [simpletons]" they regard it as a compensation for the rôle they play as educators. They chew fine the complex intellectual food so that it may be taken up by the untrained and unlearned. But unpopular as is the practice of collecting money, it is not a barrier. The audience is exceedingly tolerant toward the hat-passer and more so if he has a good "line" of talk, or if he is handicapped.

Most men who talk to Hobohemian crowds make their living by selling some kind of literature. Sometimes they sell pamphlets they have written themselves, or they sell pamphlets or periodicals on a commission. Getting money in this way is not unpopular among the soap-boxers. It is a practice that is rather favored, for it is the best way of getting the down-and-out to thinking, and if the soap-box orators are united on any one thing it is this: that the proletariat must be educated.

One of the favorite methods of distributing literature is to sell it from the box. Enthusiastic persons in the crowd often buy a paper and pay for several others to be distributed from the box. Sometimes a man will take the stand and dispose of a hundred papers or pamphlets in a few moments by persuading those who have money to buy for those who have none.

A man who entertains the "slum proletariat" need not be without status because he lives by street speaking. Most of them either directly or indirectly earn their living in this way, though many of them would not admit it. If a man can plead the cause of the under dog to the satisfaction of the man on the street, if he has a philosophy that pleases the crowd, and if he can present it in an attractive manner, very few resent his passing the hat.

So with all their contentiousness the soap-box orators manage to keep on speaking terms, and rather informally turn favors to one another. Seldom do they "knock" one another, and seldom do they crowd one another away from a corner or place one another in embarrassing positions. In this they have gone farther toward reaching a unity of purpose than the various mission groups who compete on opposite corners for the same crowds.

It must not be thought that soap-boxing is a game that is without its tricks. There are tricks for getting the crowds, tricks of holding the crowds, and tricks for exploiting the crowds. Speakers do not like to be the first one up on the box, nor do they like to be the last one up when the crowd has become tired. If a man wants to pass the hat, it is to his advantage to get the first chance at the crowd. Men will do considerable jockeying to get on the box just when they think it will be to their advantage.

FREE-LANCE VERSATILITY

Street speakers who stand before the same audiences one or more times a week throughout the year tend to wear out. Some of them are resourceful enough to find something new to say, but others find it difficult to say old things in a new way, so they are likely to fall into the habit of repeating themselves. Sometimes they try to keep from growing stale by speaking in as many places as possible, but since their audiences are limited to the Hobo-

hemian population they are always talking to a
number who have heard them say the same things
before. After a speaker has made the rounds of all
the corners he is forced to get a new "line."

Some men, however, persist in delivering old
thread-bare messages in their old, well-worn way.
The speeches of some· men are so well known that
the only interest is one of curiosity. The crowd
listens to see if anything was left out. The hobby
of one free-lance speaker is Henry George and the
Single Tax. To the crowd he is the "P and P"
man, because he usually ends his speeches by selling
copies of *Progress and Poverty* at "cost." Everyone
who has been in town long enough to become
acquainted with the principal soap-boxers is familiar
with this man's "line," but usually he hears him again,
partly, perhaps, because of his apparent sincerity.

Most soap-boxers, when they find themselves
growing stale, are able to change. B's hobby for
a long time has been a speech on birth control,
which he followed by selling some books on sex, but
he wore this subject out and recently changed to a
speech on superstition at the close of which he sells
literature of an anti-religious nature. Another
speaker whose speech on patent medicine and quack
doctors finally lost its novelty is now talking on
birth control. Another has gone from trade unionism to the Ku Klux Klan. An old-timer on Madison
Street said of a certain speaker: "That man used
to be with the I.W.W.; then he went over to How's
organization and now he's free lancing." "What is
his line now?" is a question that is commonly
asked in regard to a soap-box pulpiteer. They are
expected to change.

In search of variety and for financial reasons, free lancers of ability hire out as campaigners for the political parties. "Where is John L. now?" asks one man. "Oh, he's up in Wisconsin campaigning for Senator LaFollette. Last month he was in Missouri stumping for Senator Reed." John carried credentials from both the Democrats and Republicans and he can plead the cause of either.

The rôle of the soap-boxer, like that of the ancient sophist, is that of instructor or entertainer. Men go in search of these curbstone gatherings. On Sundays and holidays the crowd expects them. Homeless men who have a job in the city during the week spend the Sunday on the "stem" partly in order to hear the evangelists and soap-boxers. It is their life. They like to see old friends on the street, but they like especially to see familiar faces on the box.

THE OPEN FORUM

The open forum is a place, usually indoors, where persons may gather in formal meeting to discuss topics of interest. It is usually a winter retreat for the soap-boxers and their followers. In order to maintain a forum it is necessary to hire a hall and govern themselves by some sort of organization. The "Hobo College" is probably the most conspicuous open forum in Chicago. It is but a branch of a chain of "colleges" that are maintained in the larger cities of the country by the wealth of James Eads How, the "millionaire hobo." It has operated in Chicago nearly every winter since 1907. Scarcely a soap-boxer in Chicago has not at some time been associated with this institution. Many of them at some time have either been officers or leading lights of the "college." The I.W.W. generally maintains a hall where a forum is conducted during the winter, though it does not offer the variety of discussion and subjects that the "college" does.

The forum is far from being a harmonious nestling ground for hibernating soap-boxers. It is rather a veritable battle ground of contending factions. These advocates of the "new society" who agree and disagree so smilingly in the open often become caustic and bitter in their attacks when forced to share the same hall. There close association generates factions and cliques. There are always the "ins" and the "outs." New leaders are ever getting the chair, and old policies are constantly replaced. The "Hobo College" for the winter of 1922–23 had no less than six secretaries in as many months and three complete "house cleanings."

The order of procedure at the "Hobo College" is practically the same as in most of the open forums. Meetings are held on the afternoons or evenings at set dates, or there is a regular program of a certain number of meetings a week. On Sunday two meetings are often held. Meetings and programs are advertised in conspicuous places. The meetings are so arranged that there is time at the end of the principal speech for criticism, remarks, or questions from the floor, after which the speaker has an opportunity to defend himself. If distinguished visitors are present, they are usually called upon. Meetings at the "Hobo College" are different from most forums in that they usually terminate with a lunch.

The open forum has some advantages over the street meetings. The group is more select and less transient. A subject for discussion is viewed from

various angles by different speakers who have come
at least partially prepared. On the soap box the
problem of disciplining the crowd is left entirely to
the speaker. Once he loses their interest they either
harass him or desert him. In the forum the audience
is honor bound to remain until the speaker has
finished. In the open forum speakers may be invited
who are supposed to lend a certain distinction to the
occasion. No one can lend distinction to a soap box.
Not the least advantage of the forum over the soap
box is that most of the audience can participate in the
meeting. The disadvantage is that it is not so
accessible and hence becomes exclusive.

The question is often asked, "How do soap-
boxers get initiated into the game of outdoor speaking?" For most of them the answer is, "In the
open forum." In the open forum the beginners, the
aspirants, learn to take part in the discussions.
They learn here to find words to express themselves.
In the forum they take sides and learn to defend
or oppose propositions, and they learn to order and
present their thoughts.

The forum has been described as a refuge for
the hibernating soap-boxer. It is more than a
refuge; it is a study center. It is to the free-lance
speaker what a summer school is to the teacher;
an opportunity to relax and "polish up."

THE SOAP BOX AND HOBO OPINION

Soap-boxers all say that they have enjoyed more
liberty in Chicago than in most cities. Chicago
police have always taken a generous and liberal
attitude toward the curbstone forum. A man who
has been prominent in several free-speech fights says:

The free-lance speaker is a great help to the police in this town.   It's easier to handle these crowds when they have some- one to listen to.   When a man gets restless, it gives him some- thing to think about.   If you don't believe it just go into a town where the soap-boxer is suppressed and see how bitter the "bos" are.

The rôle of the soap-boxer is to make hobos think.   He succeeds to a greater extent in this than we realize.   In his efforts to hold his audience for half an hour he throws off a great many ideas.   Much of this ammunition is fired in the air, but not all of it.   What he actually does is to keep the minds of his hearers on objective things.   Otherwise their thoughts would turn inward, and for the homeless man introspection is not a pleasant pastime.

It is probably true that the soap-box orator makes no permanent impression on his audience. He does, to be sure, give voice to some ill-defined sentiments in which all are agreed.   But no practical unanimity is ever achieved.   This agitation starts no mass movement.   There has never been an effec- tive permanent organization among hobos.   The very nature of the hobo mind resents every kind of discipline that any form of organization would impose.   He is by circumstance, tradition, and temperament an individualist.

What of the soap-box reformer and revolutionist ? Is he a menace or merely a joke ?   The curbstone orator is not an agitator in the ordinary sense of that word.   He is merely a thinking hobo.   In him the homeless man becomes articulate.   It is something to these outcast men to hear in these curbstone forums the reverberations of their own unuttered thoughts. It is something to the homeless man merely to have a voice.

CHAPTER XVI
SOCIAL AND POLITICAL HOBO ORGANIZATION

THE hobo is an individualistic person. Not even the actors and artists can boast a higher proportion of egocentrics. They are the modern Ishmaels who refuse to fit into the routine of conventional social life. Resenting every sort of social discipline, they have "cut loose" from organized society.

For them there is only the open road which offers an existence without discipline, without organization, without control. To the restless and dissatisfied the life of a vagabondage is a challenge, the most elementary way by which men seek to escape from reality.

Out of this unrest, efforts have arisen through which the hobo has striven to materialize his dreams. Among the organizations initiated or promoted by migrants are the Industrial Workers of the World (I.W.W.), the International Brotherhood Welfare Association (I.B.W.A.), the Migratory Workers' Union (M.W.U.), the United Brotherhood of American Laborers, and the Ramblers.

INDUSTRIAL WORKERS OF THE WORLD

The I.W.W. was formed in Chicago in July, 1905. Its headquarters are here and its conventions have almost invariably been held here. Chicago has been favored by the migratory radicals because it is a transportation center, and because of its tolerant attitude toward street speakers.

Theoretically, the I.W.W. is an organization of all industrial workers, but it has been most enthusiastically supported, however, by the hobos. It was conceived in the "stem," and cradled and nurtured by the floating workers. The hobo has always been identified with it and, in the West, has played a militant rôle in fighting its battles.

"The backwardness and unprogressiveness of trade unions as organized in the American Federation of Labor, and the impotency of trade union as organized in the American Federation of Labor, and the impotency of political socialism to safeguard the ballot and provide the organs necessary to carry on production in the future society," are the reasons, on paper at least, for the existence of the I.W.W. It is an effort to organize the workers along industrial lines, that is, to substitute, for trade unions, industrial unions for all the workers in one industry. All the industrial unions, metal-workers, construction-workers, seamen, agricultural-workers, it seeks to combine into one mammoth organization called the "One Big Union."

The structure of the I.W.W. is simple. The unit is the industrial local, which is composed of all the workers of an industry in a locality. The various locals of an industry combine to form an industrial department. The departments join together to form the "One Big Union." The organization is managed by a general secretary who is virtually the executive head. The general secretary-treasurer is assisted by an executive board elected by the six unions having the largest membership. A seventh member is elected by the other smaller unions.

Some of the "wobbly" spokesmen boast of 100,000 members, but that is an overestimate. The membership is fluctuating and rises and falls with the seasons, but perhaps it has reached 100,000 at times. The membership is "on the road" most of the time, and even the locals are migratory, so that definite figures are not always at hand. The dues are fifty cents a month, so that many loyal members are not always in good standing. The members in good standing represent probably but a third or a fourth of the men who designate themselves I.W.W.'s.[1]

When certain seasonal occupations begin, as the harvest fields, the construction camps, and lumbering camps, the organizers set to work enrolling members. Rumors circulate that no one will be permitted to work on certain jobs unless he carries a red card; that the "wobblies" will throw all non-members off freight trains; that all the other workers are taking out membership cards; that the employers of a certain district are going to cut the wages of transient labor, or that in other localities the wages are good because the I.W.W. will not permit anyone without a red card to work.

The I.W.W. as an organization does not officially sanction methods of intimidation, and will take action against any cases brought to its attention. However, force and fear get members. Men who are seeking work in a community on jobs over which the "wobblies" have assumed control will take out cards to avoid conflict. Men will join the organization to facilitate "riding the rods." Memberships for convenience only are short lived, seldom enduring over the summer.

APPEAL OF THE I.W.W.

The I.W.W. does not depend wholly on fear to win its members. The great appeal of the I.W.W.,

[1] According to the financial statement for the I.W.W. for May and June of 1922, there were in good standing 18,234 members. This, it must be remembered, was just before the summer membership drive, which is said to have recruited over 18,000 additional members.

as of all other radical organizations, is to the spirit
of unrest that is a part of every hobo's make-up.
The I.W.W. program offers a ray of hope to the man
who is down and out. Why the "wobbly" creed
makes so stirring an appeal to the hobo may be best
understood by quoting the preamble of its constitution:

The working class and the employing class have nothing in
common. There can be no peace as long as hunger and want are
found among millions of the working people and the few, who
make up the employing class, have all the good things of life.

Between these two classes a struggle must go on until the
workers of the world organize as a class, take possession of the
earth and machinery of production, and abolish the wage
system.

We find that the centering of the management of industries
into fewer and fewer hands makes the trade unions unable to
cope with the ever growing power of the employing class. The
trade unions foster a state of affairs which allows one set of
workers to be pitted against another set of workers in the same
industry, thereby helping to defeat one another in wage wars.
Moreover the trade unions aid the employing class to mislead
the workers into the belief that the working class have interests
in common with their employers.

These conditions can be changed and the interest of the working class upheld only by an organization formed in such a way
that all its members in any one industry, or in all industries if
necessary, cease work whenever a strike or lockout is on in any
department thereof, thus making an injury to one an injury
to all.

Instead of the conservative motto, "A fair day's wage for
a fair day's work," we must inscribe on our banner the revolutionary watchword, "Abolition of the wage system."

It is the historic mission of the working class to do away with
capitalism. The army of production must be organized, not
only for the everyday struggle with capitalists, but also to carry
on production when capitalism shall have been overthrown.
By organizing industrially we are forming the structure of the
new society within the shell of the old.

The hobo, dissatisfied with things as they are, has no time to wait for the slow-moving processes of evolution. The preamble appeals to him because it is anti-evolutionary; it preaches the gospel of struggle and revolt. It is opposed to compromise and reconciliation, and affirms that the fight must go on as long as there is an employing class. No man, down-and-out, can hear this doctrine without a thrill. The declaration that no quarter shall be given to the capitalist is music to his ears.

Every member of the I.W.W. is expected to be an agitator. Wherever he goes it is the mission of the "wobbly" to sow seeds of discontent and to harass the employer. Certain members go from job to job as "investigators." They usually remain long enough to start a disturbance among the regular employees, and to get discharged. Agitators regard a long list of dismissals as evidence of their success.

Official agitators make no effort at organizing. They merely "fan the flames of discontent" and pass on. They are followed by the pioneer organizer, an aggressive individual who starts the work of forming a local. He is of the militant type and often gets no farther than to arouse the men to the need of organization. Sooner or later he also gets discharged, which is to him evidence that he has "put it over."

In the third stage of the offensive comes the real organizer. He follows the militants and reaps what they have sown. He works coolly and quietly in organizing the workers. He persuades and argues, but not in the open. The employer only learns of his presence when he has won over the men and is ready to make a demand.

CHICAGO'S ATTITUDE TO I.W.W.

The I.W.W. is little understood by society in general. The public believes that it is an organization of "tramps who won't work," and that the initials stand for "I Won't Work," or "I Want Whiskey." It is true that many "wobblies" do want whiskey and many do not want work, but the organization is neither pro-whiskey nor anti-work. During the war the opposition to the organization was intense, and Chicago was a center of arrests and prosecutions. At present, however, the I.W.W. in Chicago enjoys a freedom for its activities not found in many other cities.

There are two reasons for this tolerant attitude. In the first place, West Madison Street, where the I.W.W. is most active, is virtually isolated from other parts of the city. It is hemmed in on the north and south by factories, and on the east by the river. Then, too, Chicago is situated far from the battle grounds of the organization. The "wobblies" wage a yearly war, but it is with the farmers in the harvest belt, the lumber barons of the northwest, the contractors, the mine operators; but all these are remote from Chicago. If Chicago serves any part in this warfare it is the rôle of a winter training camp where the tactics of the summer campaign are worked out.

INTERNATIONAL BROTHERHOOD WELFARE ASSOCIATION

Next in importance to the I.W.W. is the hobo organization known as the International Brotherhood Welfare Association, or the I.B.W.A. Like the I.W.W. it started in 1905, but its membership at no time has exceeded 5,000. The I.B.W.A., like the I.W.W., looks forward to a new social order, a society in which there will be no classes. But where the I.W.W. proposes to use force and direct action or industrial organization to accomplish its purposes, the I.B.W.A. would use education. The I.B.W.A. stresses welfare work, brotherhood, and co-operation among the hobos. It aims to organize and educate the unorganized and uneducated homeless and migratory workers.

The I.B.W.A. is largely the creation of James Eads How, a member of a wealthy St. Louis family, How, dissatisfied with the ease and comfort of a rich man's life, left home and drifted into the group of hobos and tramps. Becoming interested in their problems, he set to work to better their condition. He conceived the idea of a great international hobo organization and converted several hobo "soapboxers" to his cause. The program of the I.B.W.A. is set forth in Article III of the constitution:

A. To bring together the unorganized workers.

B. To co-operate with persons and organizations who desire to better social conditions.

C. To utilize unused land and machinery in order to provide work for the unemployed.

D. To furnish medical, legal and other aid to its members.

E. To organize the unorganized and assist them in obtaining work at remunerative wages and transportation when required.

F. To educate the public mind to the right of collective ownership in production and distribution.

G. To bring about the scientific, industrial, intellectual, moral and spiritual development of the masses.

Another section of the constitution states that the organization aims to "unite the migratory

workers, the *Disemployed* and the unorganized
workers of both sexes for mutual betterment and
development, with the final object of abolishing
poverty and introducing a classless society."

"HOBO COLLEGE"

The most important of the auxiliary institutions
of the I.B.W.A. is the "Hobo College." This unique
institution is How's idea. How, as a strong believer
in progress through education, desires to bring to the
hobo worker the rudiments of the natural and social
sciences. The "Hobo College" affords the migrant
an opportunity to discuss topics of practical and
vital interest to him, and to attend lectures by
professors, preachers, and free-lance intellectuals.

The "Hobo College" in Chicago[1] has received
considerable newspaper publicity. Like all the hobo
colleges, the Chicago branch only operates in winter.
During the summer most of the "students" are out
of town at work on different migratory occupations.

HOLDING COMMITTEE

How's income, which he inherited, is at the disposal
of the hobos, but it is "fed out" by degrees, according
to the terms of the will. As the money comes into
How's hands it is distributed and apportioned by
the Holding Committee, which is composed of a
member of the How family, a member of the "Hobo
College," a member of the Junior League (a non-

[1] The Chicago branch of the "Hobo College" is located at present (1922–23)
at 913 West Washington Boulevard. It has taken the name temporarily of
"Brotherhood College," because the owners of the property would not rent the
hall so long as the word "hobo" was connected with the movement. The
change was made rather reluctantly. The second and third floors are in use;
the second floor for reading-room and kitchen, the third floor is a lecture-hall.

functioning organization for boy tramps), and the acting secretary and all previous secretaries of the I.B.W.A. Most of this money goes to the support of the various organizations of the I.B.W.A., including the *Hobo News*.

The Holding Committee also may contribute at times to the purchase of halls and other property, to transport delegates to and from conventions, or rather to pay their fare back after they have "beaten their way" to the meeting, and to promote propaganda. A plan is now on foot to maintain a lobby at Washington to support legislation in behalf of the hobo. One proposal is a federal labor exchange. The Holding Committee may and often does contribute to other causes.

CO-OPERATIVE "FLOPS"

One of How's ambitions is to establish hobo stopping places in all the principal cities of the country. Already he has opened "Hotels de Bum" in more than twenty cities. Some of them are owned by the I.B.W.A., but most of them only rented for the winter months. The "hotel" in Cincinnati is typical. It is a two-story frame building, located in the Hobohemian section of the city. The second floor, designed for "flopping," is equipped with about forty cots. The first floor is divided into a loafing- or reading-room and a kitchen. In the kitchen there are a gas range and enough pots and kettles to "boil up" clothes or cook a "mulligan." At the rear of the building is a small wood yard where ties and other wood are cut for the heater. The management of these hotels is left to the men who select a house committee from their number.

The committee looks after the building and insists that the men keep the place clean. A small tax is imposed now and then to meet current expenses and to pay one man a small fee for looking after the accounts. The ordinary "mission stiff" cannot survive long in an I.B.W.A. hotel. He usually leaves when asked to contribute his share toward the upkeep. But a man without money is welcome, if he does his part. Some of these hotels pay their way. Most of them, however, never meet expenses, but the deficit generally is made good by How.

RÔLE PLAYED BY HOW

Whatever the future of the I.B.W.A., at present it is almost a one-man organization. Regardless of the ideals How entertains about democracy, he really controls the I.B.W.A. He does all this because he holds the purse. The I.B.W.A., with all its auxiliaries, are dependent in the last analysis upon the funds of Dr. How. None of these institutions is self-supporting. The membership fees are not sufficient in many cases to cover the running expenses. The Chicago branch of the "Hobo College," for instance, has been one of the most active in the country, but it has never paid its way. How does not take advantage of the fact that his money maintains the institution. He does not have as much to say about the disposition of funds as certain other members of the Holding Committee, but his right to impose his will upon the organization is ever present with the leaders.

How has been persuaded at times to withhold funds from certain locals thought to be radical. He fears the I.W.W. who sometimes crowd into a local group and outvote the non-I.W.W. In such cases, How's money is used to spread their propaganda. The initiation fee of the I.B.W.A. is so small (ten cents and ten cents a month dues) that a large number of men may be enrolled for a few dollars. When the I.W.W. recently lost one of their halls in Chicago, they tried to work their way into the I.B.W.A., but the plot was found out and the books for the time being were closed. When How cuts off the rent allowance to a local it soon closes its doors.

The fact that the I.B.W.A. is virtually How's organization has had interesting effects on the behavior of the members. Certain officials compete with one another to get into his good graces. Others take a stand in bitter opposition to him. There is always jealousy between those "who sit on the right hand and those who sit on the left hand." Individuals in the various locals with a grievance write directly to How. Complaints go to him more often than to general headquarters.

MIGRATORY WORKERS' UNION

The Migratory Workers' Union, or the M.W.U., composed wholly of hobos, was organized within the I.B.W.A. in 1918. Some of the leaders of the I.B.W.A. felt that the older organization was neglecting the interests of the migratory worker. They charged that it was too much concerned with welfare work and too little with the organization of the workers. They converted How to the idea of a migratory workers' union and he contributed to its establishment.

The originators of the M.W.U. had other ends in mind. They wanted to organize a powerful group

of workers within the I.B.W.A. that would be able
to dominate the conventions and bring pressure to
bear on How.   They hoped that the M.W.U. would
grow to such proportions that How would fear it,
and that he would not dare to use it as a "play-
thing."   Secondly, the M.W.U. was a scheme to
get funds independently of the How allowance.
Thirdly, the originators planned to organize the
workers along industrial lines more effectively than
had the I.W.W., which at the time was unpopular
on account of its opposition to the war.   Fourthly,
the M.W.U., starting with a "clean slate" and a less
radical program than the I.W.W., might attract the
more moderate of its members who had lost faith in
the revolutionary movement.   The thought of winning over the lukewarm members of the I.W.W. was
probably the argument that appealed to How.

The "Aims and Objects" of the organization con-
tain a decidedly less radical program than the
preamble to the I.W.W. constitution.

1. A national agitation against the unconstitutional laws as
they affect the migratory worker.
2. Federal inspection of all construction camps by the United
States Public Health Service.
3. To work in favor of the abolition of the chain-gang system
and all prison contract labor.
4. Free transportation to and from the jobs for all migratory
workers.
5. The abolition of privately owned employment agencies.
6. A shorter work day.

The M.W.U. has not been active in Chicago,
though one of its officers has always been a Chicago
man.   It has been most active in Ohio and Indiana
but is even dying there.

UNITED BROTHERHOOD OF AMERICAN LABORERS

Michael C. Walsh is the general secretary-treasurer and the chief promoter of the United Brotherhood of American Laborers. Walsh, an old organizer for the I.W.W., is not in harmony with the "wobblies" at present. Although at one time the president of the "Hobo College," he has also withdrawn from that institution.

The aim of the Brotherhood is to unite all migratory and even non-migratory workers with the slogan, "What is the concern of one is the concern of all." Its program promises reading-rooms, picture shows, lectures, but the chief attraction is an accident and life insurance policy which every member takes out.

Members of the M.W.U. and the I.B.W.A. accuse Walsh of drawing up an impractical program for economic and legislative reform, and charge that the "aims" of the Brotherhood were borrowed from their organizations and only slightly modified.

BENEVOLENT AND PROTECTIVE ORDER OF RAMBLERS

The Benevolent and Protective Order of Ramblers is supposed to be a semi-secret organization of the floating fraternity, but its membership is composed of a small number of Chicago's "home guards." It was organized by John X. Kelly and has no benefits nor program except that the members agree to help one another when in trouble. It holds meetings (for members only) now and then, but it does not aim to deal with any economic or social problems. The "Ramblers" endeavors to add a human touch to the migrant's life. It is, in short, a hobo good-fellowship club that meets where and when it is con-

venient to drink the "milk o' human kindness" and
to sing "Hail! Hail! You Ought to Be a Rambler."

HOBO CO-OPERATIVE MOVEMENTS

Dissatisfied with things as they are, the hobo
experiments now and again with co-operative projects. Most of these are attempts to do on a small
scale what the dreamers hope to accomplish in the
future on a larger, a national, or an international
scale. That co-operative organizations failed is no
discredit to the leaders nor any conclusive proof
against the value of co-operative movements as a
motive in economic life. The failure is to be explained at least in part by the egocentricity and
individualism or the irresponsibility of the migratory workers.

Of the following five interesting cases of co-
operative projects among migratory workers, only
one took place in Chicago. The story of all of these
attempts has, however, been written by the prime
mover of them, John X. Kelly. Sooner or later all
hobo co-operative experiments end the same way.
They fail because of suspicion and lack of harmony.

61. My first attempt to organize a co-operative scheme was
in 1909 in Redlands, California. I knew a group of men; some
of them radical and all of them idealists. It occurred to me
that they were the very types to make a communistic plan work.
I knew of a tract of land, one hundred and sixty acres, open for
settlement. Fourteen dollars to file a claim and a little additional expense and labor would have put the place in working
condition.

I presented my plan to these men and ten of them approved
the idea. They had all been soap-boxers and agitators and I
felt that here at last is a group of men who can make a co-
operative organization a success. Our scheme was very simple,

everyone was to bear his share of the burden and to receive his share of the profits. No matter what a man did as long as it was part of the work of running the farm would be considered as important as any other part. The government of the place would be absolutely democratic. A manager would be elected from the number and he would remain manager for a certain term or as long as he gave satisfaction. The land was to be divided up as follows: each man was to have a five acre plot as his individual property and the other hundred and ten acres of ground was to be worked co-operatively.

We had scarcely got organized when dissensions arose. Some were satisfied with the manager but others feared him and mistrusted him. Some declared that it was impossible to determine how much of one kind of work was equal to another kind of work. Some were not satisfied because they felt that they were going to be imposed on and they would not join an organization in which there was no assurance that they would get a square deal. The result of this disputation was the breakup of the movement. Each man went his way.

My second endeavor to promote a hobo co-operative movement was in 1917 in St. Louis. It was in the winter time and there were many idle men in town. I conceived what I thought was the most modern and up to date plan ever brought into being to promote the interests of the down-and-outs. Knowing that the unemployed were being exploited by semi-religious and charitable organizations who gave little in return for much work, I set about to solve the problem in another way. Dr. James Eads How of St. Louis, founder of the International Brotherhood Welfare Association, contributed $200 to be used as follows: $100 to be spent for a horse and wagon, $50 for a gasoline engine and a saw, while the rest was to be used to buy food until funds could be had for the sale of wood. It was a reserve fund only to be used in case of emergency. A saloon-keeper gave us the use of a yard in East St. Louis free of charge. There was an old store in connection with the yard that could also be used. The place was in the heart of East St. Louis and accessible to any part of the city. The American Car Repairing Company gave us all the wood we cared to haul away. Eleven policemen sent in orders for wood. They were willing to pay three dollars a load for this wood sawed and split into kindling.

The conditions under which the men entered the program were similar to the first venture. They were all to have an equal share in the profits. The manager, the man who operated the saw; all who worked in and around the wood yard, after expenses were deducted, were to share alike. Everything was to be democratic, no one was to be an exploiter, and nobody was to be exploited. Everyone agreed and after I had remained with the project a day or so until it got under way, I left them to work out their own problems.

Within a week a committee of three came to me in St. Louis with a story of confusion and a cry of being buncoed by the manager. They said that some of the members would not work. I sent them back to straighten out matters but conditions seemed to get worse in so far as finances were concerned, and within six weeks the co-operative wood yard disbanded.

A short time later I went over to East St. Louis and took the horse and wagon and other property of the wood yard to St. Louis where I had interested a number of the St. Louis Group of the I.B.W.A. to take a chance with the communistic scheme. Instead of selling the wood by the load this time they were going to sell small bundles of kindling coated with pitch. The men did not care this time to use the buzz saw and engine so I bought six hand saws and six hatchets. I also bought a half barrel of pitch into which the kindling could be dipped. I succeeded in raising $32.00 as a jungle fund so that the boys could "get by" while working to get a start.

A start was all that was made as the entire group got intoxicated with "joy" with some of the jungle fund. Next morning the secretary, who was handling the fund returned half of it with the statement that the co-operative wood yard was a fizzle. The man who had been elected manager died while on this drunk.

Here was a group of men that I was satisfied would make a success of a communistic scheme if one could be put over, but they failed miserably. Some men in both these wood yard experiences blamed me because the schemes did not succeed.

The fourth venture was in Chicago in 1920. I tried to put over a co-operative lodging house scheme in the "Slave Market District" where thousands of migratory workers congregate because of the cheap living conditions. Instead of the Scissors Bill class this group was made up of radicals who at some time in their unhappy lives had taken part in some co-operative experiment. Again I went to Dr. How with my new idea and at my suggestion he agreed to pay three months rent in advance to help the movement along by retaining one of the rooms as an office for the I.B.W.A. Five rooms were rented for twenty-five dollars and the I.B.W.A. took one of them at half the price or twelve and a half dollars a month. Later we rented four additional rooms at fifteen dollars making the total rent for nine rooms forty dollars of which nearly a third was paid by the I.B.W.A.

As national secretary of the I.B.W.A. I was supposed to have my office there, but I could do most of my work at home so I turned the room rented for office over to the club for a sitting room. The I.B.W.A. contributed fifty-eight dollars to buy furniture. Some other furniture was also bought by money contributed by the men. The place was to be operated on a fifty-fifty basis. All the profits and the expenses were to be equally shared. Everyone agreed and the organization was effected.

Now the funny part comes. Quarrels soon arose over trifles, and the members began calling each other grafters, and parasites. I was even called a parasite though the only part I played was to start the project and to encourage it to operate smoothly. Before six months had elapsed the co-operative flat was a thing of the past. The men sneaked away all of the furniture, that of the I.B.W.A. as well as some that belonged to the members of the group. They hauled it all away to furnish two small flats. They also left an eighteen-dollar gas bill which the amateur promoter had to pay.

The fifth and last experiment is not a case of co-operation but it illustrates what might be expected from the hobo.

During the winter of 1916 a St. Louis lady, Dr. Innis, conducted a free dispensary for the "bos" who could not get hospital treatment. Dr. How paid the bill for conducting the place. Dr. Innis took a great interest in the migratory worker and co-operated with us in working out a scheme by which the hobo could save some money during the summer to hold him over the winter months. She agreed to receive and hold in trust all the money that any man would send to her and in the fall when he came to town turn it over to him. We got out a lot of letters and cards by which this correspondence banking could be carried on and about a hundred and fifty men agreed that it was a good scheme and that they would take advantage of it.

The result was amusing. Out of all the men who approved the plan only one sent in any money. That one man sent in one dollar. Shortly after Dr. Innis got a letter from this man. He said he was "broke" and would like to have his dollar back.

My conclusion is that it is impossible to accomplish anything along co-operative lines and in a democratic manner. I know the hobo worker fairly well and I tried patiently to put over schemes that they have, for the most part, favored, and I worked with fair representatives of the group, but they will not co-operate. They are suspicious and selfish when it comes to the final test of their pet ideas. Co-operative schemes may work but I don't think they will be a success along democratic lines.

FAILURE OF HOBO ORGANIZATIONS

Hobo organizations have never been a success in this country. It is proverbial that conventions of the I.W.W. and the I.B.W.A. have always been veritable battle grounds of contending interests. The I.B.W.A. has had four conventions during the winter of 1921–22 and the summer of 1922 and they all failed to accomplish anything because of jealousies and bitter feelings. The convention in Cincinnati on May Day, 1922, continued in session for three days and did not get any farther than to argue about the power of the convention to act in the name of the I.B.W.A. One whole session was spent in a quarrel about the election of a chairman.

Between the M.W.U. and the I.B.W.A. there is considerable antipathy, yet the M.W.U. cannot stand alone and will not co-operate with the parent organization. The I.W.W. is against both, but even in the I.W.W. there is a perpetual clash between the migratory workers and the "home guards." Active and zealous organizers usually find room for complaint against the office force.

The hobo, like other egocentric types, is suspicious. The I.W.W. at its inception spent days arguing whether the name of its chief officer should be that of president. Some felt that to model the organization after others would be a step in imitation that might lead to other forms of imitation. Some reasoned that most presidents of organizations they had known were "parasites" and their head officer might become one also if given the name. The hobo's suspicious attitude toward all organizations and persons in power is not altogether without ground. As a group the migratory workers usually get the "short end" of every bargain they drive with organized society. Every contractor they work for "does" them for something. If he does not charge them for tools they lost or destroyed he may charge them for rent on a pair of boots or a blanket they may have used. They may buy a job from some private agency and later lose the job because the agency and the contractor have an understanding to sell as many jobs as possible. The hobo gets the opinion that most officers in most organizations are playing the game for what they can get out of it and he concludes that it is the natural thing to do.

The mobility and instability of the hobo or tramp, which is both cause and consequence of his migratory existence, unfits him for organized group life. Moreover, he is propertyless, and therefore the incentive of fixed ownership and fixed residence to remain faithful to any institution is gone. While the man of property secures himself best by associating with his neighbor and remaining in one locality, the hobo

safeguards himself by moving away from every difficulty. Then, too, the hobo is without wife and
child. His womanless existence increases his mobility and his instability.

In pointing out the repeated and seemingly inevitable failures of hobo organizations, the fact must
not be lost sight of that they are absolutely necessary
to his social existence. Only in these social and
political organizations can the migratory worker
regain his lost status. Only in association with his
fellows can he again hope and dream of an ideal world
of co-operation. These organizations will either
survive repeated failures or take new forms, because
they satisfy this fundamental need of the social outcast for status. Then, too, in these groups, his
rebellious attitudes against society are sublimated
into a radical idealism. Were these organizations
destroyed, the anti-social grudge of the individual
would undoubtedly be reflected in criminality.

CHAPTER XVII
MISSIONS AND WELFARE ORGANIZATIONS

IN THE winter of 1921–22 there were twenty-five missions in the Hobohemian areas of the city. This number tends to expand and to contract with the increase or the decrease in number of men out of work. The number of missions in the West Madison Street section is larger than the number in the South State Street and North Clark Street regions combined. The influence of the Salvation Army, which has outgrown the status of a mission, upon similar organizations is profound. The names of many of the missions suggest their origin in imitation of this pioneer body in religious work for the "down-and-outs": Christian Army, Samaritan Army, Saved Army, Volunteer Rescue Army. The names of other missions are as interesting: Bible Rescue Mission, Cathedral Shelter, Helping Hand Mission, Pacific Garden Mission, Sunshine Gospel Mission.

The uniforms of the "armies" that make up the working force of certain of the missions are often so nearly alike that it is difficult to tell them apart. A short time ago the Salvation Army brought suit against the Saved Army to prevent it from using the poke bonnets, the blue uniform, the song "The War Cry" on the ground that they were so similar to those of the Salvation Army that the public was confused. It is claimed by representatives of the Salvation Army that individuals contribute to these other missions and "armies" under the impression that the contribution is for the Salvation Army.

TYPES OF MISSIONS[1]

Aside from the religious work of the Salvation Army and the Volunteers of America, three types of missions are to be found in Hobohemia: (1) the permanently established local mission, (2) the migratory national mission, and (3) the "wild cat" local mission.

1) The permanently established local mission either owns its building or holds it on a long lease. These missions are sponsored by some church or by a board of directors composed of business men of more or less local prominence. Not infrequently these contributors are successful converts.

These local missions dispense charity in the form of food, clothing, and beds for homeless men.[2] They differ, however, in their methods of relief as well as in their policies of relief. One mission may care for every man who asks for aid without question as to his worthiness, another feels that better service can be done by helping only those who are willing to work, or those who are incapacitated for manual labor. Only the verbose intoxicant is ever ejected from the mission—all others may come and go as they wish.

In the permanently established mission is found the better type of mission worker who is compensated by a definite salary rather than paid on a

[1] In the section on "Types of Missions" and "Permanent, Periodic, and Temporary Converts," the writer is indebted to material furnished by Mr. L. Guy Brown from an unpublished study of "Missions in Chicago."

[2] One mission of this type on West Madison Street records that during the year ending September, 1921, 56,718 homeless men visited the mission. During this time 4,016 men knelt at the altar (were converted). Nearly 29,000 meals were served to hungry and unemployed men, while 4,145 tickets were issued which entitled the bearer to sleep at a flophouse or cheap rooming-house.

commission basis. The permanent workers consist
of a superintendent and a secretary assisted by converts who have made good, usually old men who use
the mission as a refuge. Still further help comes
from students of the various religious institutions
in the city and from the friends of the mission.

2) The national migratory missions may have
headquarters in Chicago or some other metropolitan
center with branches or sub-missions in nearby
towns and cities. These organizations are generally
financed by solicitations. Men and women are
employed to canvass places of business; to "drum"
on the streets and to make house-to-house calls.
This practice of drumming on the streets is known
as "ballyhooing." These solicitors receive, in most
cases, as much as 50 per cent of the amount they
collect, which greatly lessens the sum to be used for
the homeless men after the rent for the building,
the salaries of the men in charge, and other expenses
have been deducted from the remaining 50 per cent.

The shifting of these missions is proverbial. If
they are not moving from city to city they are moving
from one street to another, or from one location to
another on the same street. The workers are as
transient as the institutions themselves: migrating
back and forth between cities, and affiliating themselves first with one mission and then with another.
Often they are rural folk who, through urban mission
work, find expression for the wishes of adventure and
recognition. The fascination of the city has an
attraction for the migratory mission worker as for
the migratory laborer. They prefer this life, even
under adverse conditions, to any other field of service.
Others are veterans, who have been in mission work

for years with four or five different organizations in as many cities.

3) The "wild cat" local mission, more or less ephemeral in nature, springs up during some crisis as an unemployment situation. Using the crisis as an excuse for soliciting funds to aid the unemployed, they operate for awhile, and when conditions have been ameliorated, they go out of existence. The workers, enthralled by a few months in the service, then affiliate with another mission.

MAKING CONVERTS

The following narrative by an observer in the Bible Rescue Mission one Sunday evening early in April, 1922, describes the technique of conversion.

62. More than a hundred men were in the audience. The night was cold and they were glad to be inside. Then, too, there were rolls and coffee to be served after the meeting. Near the close of the service the evangelist stept down from the stand and asked if anyone in the audience wished to be prayed for. Surely out of an audience of so many men, all sinners, someone was concerned about his soul. All a man would have to do was to raise his hand. That was easy; just believe with all your heart, raise your hand for prayer. It was worth taking a chance on anyway. Three hands went up.

"That's fine! Three men have asked to be remembered before the Lord. Is there anyone else? Just one more, let's make it four. Won't someone else raise his hand. Yes, there's another hand. God bless you, brother. Now, will the four men who raised their hands please stand?"

This was more than they had bargained for, but they stood. All eyes were on the four, all homeless men with the characteristic beaten look. They were self-conscious and uncomfortable. One of the men, somewhat older than the others, seemed to be stirred by emotion.

"Now," continued the evangelist, "will the four brothers who just stood up kindly come forward and kneel with us in

prayer ?" There was a moment of hesitation. Finally, the old
man led the way. One of the others followed in a halting fashion.
A worker came down from the stand and escorted to the front the
younger of the remaining two. The fourth man sat down.
Another worker sat down beside him and pleaded with him for
some time. The man seemed to resent it at first, but at length
he yielded and was led into the circle. He had a sheepish look
as he slumped to his knees between two of the other converts.

Several of the workers began to labor with members of the
audience while the little circle kneeled on the floor and prayed.
No other converts were made so the meeting came to an end with
handshakes and congratulations for the new converts. Then
the lunch was passed and the tension relaxed.

Once outside I asked a man who had been inside what he
thought of the meeting. He laughed, "Oh, it's just like all of
them. I wanted to laugh out loud when I saw that old duck
get saved. He gets saved every winter. This winter he got
saved twice. He always manages to get saved in missions where
there is something to eat."

Women play a leading rôle in mission work. The
homeless man, who remembers his home and mother,
listens with respect to the prayers and appeals of
the women workers, and is stirred by the singing of
young girls. A religious plea by a woman of strong
personality will sometimes overwhelm a despondent
and homesick man.

63. Probably the most interesting event of our investigation
was a Salvation Army revival meeting, held in a little auditorium
behind the smoking room. Each Sunday night at about 8:00,
these services are held. Eight or nine girls, one the leader, and
one the pianist, make up the cast and chorus. When they are
ready the invitation is extended to those in the smoking room and
anywhere from six to thirty are likely to go into the "church."

The leader is a very versatile lady. She can utter a fervent
prayer, sing louder than all the rest of the girls together, play a
tambourine at the same time, and make a stirring appeal to
the audience that they "come forward to Jesus and be saved."
The girls join in the chorus, clapping as they sing. They have

all been saved, and testify as to the truth of the leader's words. "Isn't that true, girls?" and they all nod their heads in perfect accord.

The old songs are sung, songs with simple tune and words as "He's the Lily of the Valley." Anyone hearing these songs once can join in, and all are asked to do so, but few respond. Yet it is inspiring to see some forlorn looking bum concentrate on the little book and sing forth earnestly, as some of them do. Very few, however, wish to be saved. They are willing to attend the services, and maybe to sing, but they will not volunteer to join the army of God, and when personal solicitation is undertaken, few remain in the room.

During warm weather the missions hold street meetings. Headed by the mission band, the company marches outside to get the crowd. A few songs are sung, several testimonials are given, and the curbstone audience is invited to the hall.

Few mission workers are able to gather and hold a crowd on the street. It is more difficult to preach on account of the noise of passing street cars and automobiles. The crowd outside is less stable and not so considerate as the indoor audience. Often the meetings are disturbed by drunken men or by competing mission groups on the same street. A mission band may not be able to gather any crowd, even though hundreds of men are passing or loafing on the streets. Sometimes their audiences will be stolen by soap-boxers who start near by with the "economic arguments."

PERMANENT, PERIODIC, AND TEMPORARY CONVERTS

Every mission has its permanent, periodic, and temporary converts; its "alumni." Some of these linger about the mission doing odd jobs, others go

to work or into business, only returning occasionally
to bear testimony. Many of these have prospered
both spiritually and materially, and assist the mission
in its work. Certain missions celebrate the "spiritual
birthdays" of these converts. A bouquet of flowers is
placed on the pulpit and a special program is arranged
in honor of the occasion. The anniversary of the
conversion of a permanent convert is a time of
rejoicing. The "twice-born man" bears his testimony to the saving power of the gospel that snatches
"a brand from the burning," and asks the prayers of
the saints that he may continue "faithful until the
end." Each of the "saved" who are present wears
a flower in the lapel of his coat and takes advantage of
the occasion to add his testimony.

The following typical cases of converts were
secured through hearing the testimony of men in the
missions and by later interviews with each of the
converts. The information given was also verified
by mission workers who knew the men.

64. H. M., in his own words, was once "one of the worst
jail birds and boozers" in this part of the country. For years,
he declares, he was never sober. His arrival home usually
meant the beating of his wife. At the end of every month he
was in debt to the saloon keeper. He gravitated from one house
to another unable to pay his rent, until his family was living in
an old dilapidated shack. His religious transformation changed
the whole situation. He is now in business for himself. He is
considered one of the most competent and reliable in his field.
He and his wife work at the mission and are among its largest
financial contributors.

65. About twenty years ago T. S., a typical "down-and-out,"
wandered into a Chicago mission. He had deserted his family
in an eastern state and started on the bum. Exposure and
"booze" had almost completely enervated him. He was dirty,
unshaved, and in rags. His visit to the mission led to his

conversion and subsequently to reconciliation with his wife and three children. He is now superintendent of a business concern in the city.

66. P. W., a man of foreign birth and a graduate from one of the leading universities of his native country, became addicted to drink, deserted his wife, and leaving her in dire need came to this country. He became so low a bum that he was taking his food from garbage cans in the alleys of Chicago, spending every cent he could get for "booze." He was so debilitated from alcohol, exposure, and lack of nourishment when he came to the mission that he was hardly able to walk. He was converted and restored to health. His wife later joined him. He became nationally known as a worker in missions.

67. Some years ago a young lad left his home in Germany and came to the United States. His associates here were persons who spent their leisure time in dissipation. One morning he awoke after a drunken night and decided to go down on West Madison Street with the bums where he thought he belonged. He despaired of life. He wandered into one of the missions to get warm and was converted. Although he had a meager education he is now studying in one of the religious institutions of the city with the expressed purpose of doing religious work.

68. P. D. came into the mission drunk one night and was converted. Several times previous to this he had been thrown out for disturbing the meeting. According to his own statement he entered the mission one time and was "saved and stayed saved." He is now general labor foreman for a large construction company.

Of course there are temporary converts who become victims of their old environment. For awhile they go straight, but eventually they yield to "the world, the flesh, and the devil." Some periodic converts kneel before the altar every year and each time go out with renewed determination to avoid sin, but they often succumb the first time they are subjected to temptation. The mission workers expect this periodicity of conversion with some of these men just as they expect the winter.

"Backsliders" are usually well meaning men but weak. Any convert who remains on the "stem" is likely to become a "backslider." The emotional nature of many of these men may induce a mood of sincere repentance, but it is difficult to keep the resolution to reform.

69. L. S. is a youth of the city. He is twenty-three. His parents are strict German Lutherans and he spent several years in a Lutheran parochial school. He left home over a month ago (April, 1922) because of some trouble he had with his folks. Shortly after he entered the ―― ―― Mission on Madison Street where he "got religion" but in a week he "back slid." He was melted into consenting and was rushed to the front and "saved" before he knew what had happened. After the men on the outside laughed at him he "weakened." Now he feels that there is "nothing to religion anyway," though he admits that the mission worker at one time kept him out of jail.

MISSION BREAD LINES

During the winter of 1921–22, twelve of the missions in Chicago, maintained "bread lines," that is, dispensed food, as coffee and doughnuts, or a bowl of soup and vegetables. The term "bread line," used figuratively for "free lunch," originally described the long lines of men during years of want and unemployment waiting outside relief stations for bread and soup.

Missions without "bread lines" claim that the food is given as a bait to get conversions. They hold that "meal ticket" converts lose their religion as soon as they become economically self-sustaining. The unregenerate homeless man looks down upon the regular attendants at the mission, and accuses them of getting converted for "pie card" reasons. He calls them "mission stiffs," a term as uncomplimentary as for an Indian to be called a "squaw man."

A FREE LUNCH AT A MISSION

A WINTER'S NIGHT IN A MISSION

WELFARE ORGANIZATIONS

The mission is not the only institution to which the homeless man turns. Social-service agencies, public and private, many of which are organized primarily for family rehabilitation, have given assistance to the homeless man.

The United Charities, although engaged chiefly in work with families, has a homeless-men division. During the year ending September 30, 1922, 1,026 non-family men received assistance. Of these, 629 were given material or personal service, and 397 were referred to other organizations. The Jewish Social Service Bureau also maintains a homeless men's department which, in the year 1921, gave personal and material aid to 1,333 men. During 1922, the number of men helped fell to less than half this number, largely as a result of the improved industrial situation. The Bureau works in close association with two Jewish sheltering-homes, which together house about 70 men. Homeless men who apply for assistance are cared for here until their cases are carefully investigated. The Central Bureau of (Catholic) Charities, in conjunction with the Mission of the Holy Cross, provides shelter and food for destitute men, and aids them to become self-supporting.

The Chicago Urban League, organized to promote co-ordination and co-operation among existing agencies for the welfare of Negroes, maintains an employment bureau for men out of work. During the winters of 1920–21 and 1921–22, when thousands of men[1] were without house accommodations, the League took the lead in co-operating with churches

---

[1] The officials of the League estimate that there were 7,000 homeless men among the Negroes in the winter of 1921–22.

and other organizations to secure temporary housing quarters.

The hotels for homeless men maintained by the Salvation Army and by the Christian Industrial League have already been described.[1] In addition, both organizations maintain industrial homes where men are given temporary work and are helped to become self-supporting.

The American Legion has been active in behalf of unemployed ex-service men, many of whom are also homeless men. Its work has consisted chiefly in getting jobs for the unemployed, and in this it has had the hearty co-operation of the newspapers. The Legion Hall was turned over to homeless veterans for sleeping quarters during the winter of 1921–22.

The Chicago Municipal Lodging House was first opened on December 21, 1901. It provided free temporary shelter and food for destitute, homeless men. At first it was operated under the Department of Police, but was transferred on January 1, 1908, to the Department of Health, and later, on April 17, 1917, transferred to the Department of Public Welfare. In its early history, the Municipal Lodging House was fortunate in having as its superintendent men like Raymond Robins, James Mullenbach, and Charles B. Ball, who set high standards for its administration.[2] The Municipal Lodging House met the severe test of the unemployment years of 1908 and 1914 by showing how its organization could expand to meet extraordinary situations. For example, while only 23,642 lodgings were given in 1907,

[1] See pp. 27–28.

[2] See Raymond Robins, "What Constitutes a Model Municipal Lodging House," *Proceedings of the National Conference of Charities and Correction* (1904), 155–66

the number rose to 105,564 in 1908; and the 78,392 lodgings given in 1913 rose to 452,361 in 1914. The Municipal Lodging House closed in 1918–19 because of lack of applicants during wartime prosperity, but it did not reopen during the hard winters of 1920–21 and 1921–22. Many destitute men, who would otherwise have been inmates of the Municipal Lodging House with the medical attention, sanitary sleeping quarters, and other assistance for rehabilitation which it offered, became instead "regular feeders" at the "bread lines" and permanent patrons of Hogan's "flop." There seems to be no doubt that the absence of municipal provision made for an increase of promiscuous begging and injudicious almsgivings.

Many other institutions and agencies regularly or sporadically extend assistance to the homeless man. Yet, in perhaps no other field of social work is there more overlapping and duplication of effort, or so low standards of service. For example, the missions and some of the churches, working independently of one another, boast that they feed and clothe the needy, but they make little or no effort to distinguish between those who do and those who do not deserve assistance. Consequently, the missions lay themselves open to exploitation by the homeless man. A constructive program for rehabilitation demands the co-ordination of the efforts of all agencies now engaged in serving his needs.

THE HOMELESS MAN AND RELIGION

The missions, and for that matter, the welfare agencies are unpopular with the habitués of Hobohemia. The hobo, in his songs and in conversation, shows unmistakably his aversion to all efforts to remake his character or to reshape his destiny. This feeling of antipathy is naturally strongest with the adherents of the I.W.W. who come in competition and conflict with the mission worker.

With full recognition of the cynical reaction of the average hobo to the mission, it cannot be denied that thousands of homeless men are converted every winter, and that a certain proportion of these, how large no one knows, lead permanently changed lives. The mission touches the inner life of these men in a way that no social agency or organization has ever done, or perhaps can do.

Even the homeless man has aspirations above the satisfaction of his physical wants; he desires to live in a larger, more complete sense. The I.W.W., with its radical program of changing "things as they are," appeals to the restless and rebellious spirit of youth. But the broken man, or the old man who has given up hope, finds comfort and peace in adapting himself to "things as they are." Religion to him is just this change of attitude, "making oneself right with God." While the young man is confident that he can right what is wrong in this world, the old man looks to the next world to compensate for the inequalities and injustice of present existence.

APPENDIX A
SUMMARY OF FINDINGS
AND RECOMMENDATIONS

THIS study has pictured the life and the problems of the group of homeless migratory and casual workers in Chicago. It now remains to sum up the findings of the investigation and to outline the recommendations which seem to flow from the facts.[1]

FINDINGS

1. The homeless casual and migratory workers, while found in all parts of the city, are segregated in great numbers in four distinct areas: West Madison Street, Lower South State Street (near the Loop), North Clark Street, and Upper State Street (the Negro section).
2. The number of homeless men in these areas fluctuates greatly with the seasons and with conditions of employment.
3. The concentration of casual and migratory workers in this city is the natural result of two factors: (*a*) the development of Chicago as a great industrial community with diversified enterprises requiring a variety of unskilled as well as skilled laborers, and (*b*) the position of Chicago as a center of transportation, of commerce and of employment for the states of the Mississippi Valley.
4. The homeless men in Chicago fall into five groups: (*a*) the seasonal laborer, (*b*) the migratory, casual laborer, the hobo, (*c*) the migratory non-worker, the tramp, (*d*) the non-migratory casual laborer, the so-called "home guard," (*e*) the bum. Groups *b*, *c*, *d*, and *e* constitute what are known in economic writings as "The Residuum of Industry." In addition to these groups of the homeless casual and migratory workers are the groups of seasonal laborers and the men out of work, which expand and contract with the periods of economic depression and of industrial prosperity.

[1] The findings and recommendations of this study were prepared by the Committee on Homeless Men of the Chicago Council of Social Agencies and its report accepted by the Council.

5. The causes which reduce a man to the status of a homeless
   migratory and casual worker may be classified under five
   main heads as follows:

   a) *Unemployment and Seasonal Work:* these maladjustments
      of modern industry which disorganize the routine of life
      of the individual and destroy regular habits of work.

   b) *Industrial Inadequacy:* "the misfits of industry," whether
      due to physical handicaps, mental deficiency, occupa-
      tional disease, or lack of vocational training.

   c) *Defects of Personality:* as feeble-mindedness, constitu-
      tional inferiority, or egocentricity, which lead to the
      conflict of the person with constituted authority in
      industry, society, and government.

   d) *Crises in the Life of the Person:* as family conflicts, mis-
      conduct, and crime, which exile a man from home and
      community and detach him from normal social ties.

   e) *Racial or National Discrimination:* where race, national-
      ity, or social class of the person enters as a factor of
      adverse selection for employment.

   f) *Wanderlust:* the desire for new experience, excitement,
      and adventure, which moves the boy "to see the world."

6. To satisfy the wants and wishes of the thousands of homeless migratory and casual workers at the lowest possible
   cost, specialized institutions and enterprises have been
   established in Chicago.   These include:

   a) Employment agencies.
   b) Restaurants and lodging-houses.
   c) Barber colleges.
   d) Outfitting stores and clothing exchanges.
   e) Pawnshops.
   f) Movies and burlesques.
   g) Missions.
   h) Local political and social organizations, as "The Indus-
      trial Workers of the World" and the "Hobo College."
   i) Secular street meetings and radical bookstores.

7. Chicago as the great clearing house of employment for the
   states of the Mississippi Valley naturally and inevitably
   becomes the temporary home of men out of work for the
   entire region.   The following appear to be the facts in
   regard to the workers and the conditions of employment:

a) Fluctuations of industry, such as seasonal changes, and of unemployment, force large numbers of men into the group of homeless migratory and casual workers.

b) At the same time, the homeless migratory and casual worker develops irregular habits of work and a life-policy of "living from hand to mouth."

c) Employment records indicate that the lower grade of casual workers prefer work by the day, or employment by the week or two, to "permanent" positions of three months or longer.

d) The Illinois Free Employment offices, efficiently administered with simple but well-kept records and with courteous treatment of applicants, placed 50,482 persons in the year ending September 30, 1922, mainly in positions in and near Chicago.

e) The private employment agencies dealing with the homeless man, about fifty in number, which are, in general, poorly equipped, with the minimum of record keeping required by law and with inconsiderate treatment of applicants, place about 200,000 men a year in positions, for the most part, outside of Chicago.

f) The law relating to private employment agencies as approved June 15, 1909, in force July 1, 1909, and as amended and approved June 7, 1911, in force July 1, 1911, appears not to be enforced in two points:

    i) the requirement that sections three (3), four (4), and five (5) of the law be posted in a conspicuous place in each room of the agency; and

    ii) the return to the applicant of three-fifths of the registration and other fees upon failure of applicant to accept position or upon his discharge for cause.

8. The health and hygiene of the homeless migratory and casual worker is of vital concern not only for his economic efficiency but also because of the relation of his high mobility to the spread of communicable diseases.

9. The homeless migratory and casual workers constitute a womanless group. The results of this sex isolation are:

a) No opportunity for the expression and sublimation of the sex impulse in the normal life of the family.

b) In a few cases, the substitution for marriage of free unions more or less casual, usually terminated at the will of the man without due regard to the claims of the woman.

c) The dependence of the greatest number of homeless men upon the professional prostitute of the lowest grade and the cheapest sort.

d) The prevalence of sex perversions, as masturbation and homosexuality.

10. The attraction for the boy of excitement and adventure renders him peculiarly susceptible to the "call of the road."

a) Hundreds of Chicago boys, mainly but not entirely of wage-earning families, every spring "beat their way" to the harvest fields, impelled by wanderlust, and the opportunity for work away from home.

b) Of these a certain proportion acquire the migratory habit and may pass through successive stages from a high-grade seasonal worker to the lowest type of bum.

c) The boy on the road and in the city is constantly under the pressure of homosexual exploitation by confirmed perverts in the migratory group.

d) Certain areas of the city frequented by boys have been found to be resorts and rendezvous for homosexual prostitution.

11. While the majority of the homeless migratory workers are American citizens of native stock:

a) They are in large numbers for practical purposes disfranchised because they seldom remain in any community long enough to secure legal residence.

b) They constitute a shifting and shiftless group without property and family, and with no effective participation in the civic life of the community.

c) According to statements from police authorities they contribute but slightly to the volume of serious crime.

d) Both on the road and in the city, they are at all times subject to arbitrary handling and arrest by private and public police and to summary trial and sentence by the court.

e) The attitude of Chicago, like that of other communities toward the homeless man, has been a policy of defense intrusted to the police department for execution.

12. Social service to the homeless migratory and casual worker has for the most part been remedial rather than preventive; unorganized and haphazard rather than organized and co-ordinated.

   a) Professional beggars and fakers exploit public sympathy and credulity for individual gain to the disadvantage of the men who need and deserve assistance.

   b) The missions and certain churches feed, clothe, and provide shelter for several thousand men during the winter months.

   c) The Dawes Hotel, the Christian Industrial League, and the Salvation Army hotels provide lodging at a low charge.

   d) The Salvation Army maintains the Industrial Home with workshops which accommodate a limited number of men.

   e) The United Charities and the Central Charity (Catholic) Bureau, although concerned mainly with family relief, give certain forms of assistance to the homeless man.

   f) The Jewish Social Service Bureau maintains a department for homeless men, which acts as a referring agency to two shelter houses.

   g) The American Legion and other patriotic organizations have provided assistance of various types to the ex-service man out of employment.

   h) The Municipal Lodging House, which closed its doors in 1918, has not been reopened, despite the evident need of the winters of 1920–21 and 1921–22.

   i) The Cook County agent provides free transportation to non-residents to place of legal residence and refers residents to Oak Forest Infirmary.

   j) The county and city hospitals and dispensaries provide free medical care.

   k) Unco-ordinated effort of the organizations for service to the homeless man has resulted in duplication of activities, a low standard of work, and the neglect of a constructive program of rehabilitation.

RECOMMENDATIONS

The findings of this study indicate conclusively: (a) that any fundamental solution of the problem is national and not local, and (b) that the problem of the homeless migratory worker is but an aspect of the larger problems of industry, such as unemployment, seasonal work, and labor turnover.

NATIONAL PROGRAM

The committee approves, as a national program for the control of the problem, the recommendations suggested by the studies on unemployment and migratory laborers contained in the *Final Report of the Commission on Industrial Relations* (pp. 114–15; 103):

1. The enactment of appropriate legislation modifying the title of the Bureau of Immigration to "Bureau of Immigration and Employment" and providing the statutory authority and appropriations necessary for—

   a) The establishment of a national employment system,[1] under the Department of Labor, with a staff of well-paid and specially qualified officials in the main offices at least.

   b) The licensing, regulation, and supervision of all private employment agencies doing an interstate business.

   c) The investigation and preparation of plans for the regularization of employment, the decasualization of labor, the utilization of public work to fill in periods of business depression, insurance against unemployment in such trades and industries as may seem desirable, and other measures designed to promote regularity and steadiness of employment.

2. The immediate creation of a special board made up of the properly qualified officials from the Departments of Agriculture, Commerce, Interior, and Labor, and from the Board of Army Engineers to prepare plans for performing the largest possible amount of public work during the winter, and to devise a program for the future for performing, during periods of depression, such public work as road building, construction of public building, reforestation, irrigation, and drainage of swamps. The success attending the construction of the

[1] The United States Employment Service established in 1918 requires adequate appropriations for its efficient functioning.

Panama Canal indicates the enormous national construction works which might be done to the advantage of the entire nation during such periods of depression. Similar boards or commissions should be established in the various states and municipalities.

3. The Interstate Commerce Commission should be directed by Congress to investigate and report the most feasible plan of providing for the transportation of workers at the lowest reasonable rates, and, at the same time, measures necessary to eliminate the stealing of rides on railways. If special transportation rates for workers are provided, tickets may be issued only to those who secure employment through public employment agencies.

4. The establishment by states, municipalities, and, through the Department of Labor, the federal government, of sanitary workingmen's hotels in which the prices for accommodations shall be adjusted to the cost of operation. If such workingmen's hotels are established, the Post Office Department should establish branch postal savings banks in connection therewith.

5. The establishment by the municipal, state, and federal governments of colonies or farms for "down and outs" in order to rehabilitate them by means of proper food, regular habits of living and regular work that will train them for lives of usefulness. Such colonies should provide for hospital treatment of cases which require it.

The Chicago Plan for the Homeless Man

For the local situation and for such action as lies in the hands (a) of the citizens of this community, (b) of the city of Chicago, (c) of Cook County, and (d) of the state of Illinois, this committee recommends:

I. As a Program for Immediate Action—

1. *The establishment of a Municipal Clearing House for Non-Family Men.*

   a) *Purpose:*

      i) To provide facilities for the registration, examination, classification, and treatment of homeless

   migratory and casual workers in order, on the
   basis of individual case-study,

   ii) To secure by reference to the appropriate agency
   emergency relief, physical and mental rehabilitation, industrial training, commitment to institu-
   tional care, return to legal residence, and
   satisfactory employment.

b) *Organization:* The Clearing House will maintain the
following departments:

   i) *Information Bureau:* to provide information in
   regard to employment, public institutions, social
   agencies, indorsed hotels, and lodging-houses, etc.

   ii) *Registration:* by card, giving name, age, occupation, physical condition, reference, residence,
   nearest relative or friend, number of lodgings,
   disposition, and all other information.

   iii) *Vocational Clinic:* to provide medical, psychiat-
   ric, psychological, and social examination as a
   basis of treatment.

   iv) *Records Office:* to record findings of examination,
   to clear with other agencies, local and national,
   and to enter recommendations and results of
   treatment.

   v) *Social Service Bureau:* to provide for both immediate and after-care service for the men under the
   supervision of the Clearing House.

c) *Personnel:* to consist of director, clerical force, inter-
viewers, social workers, and experts, as physician,
psychiatrist, psychologist, and sociologist.

d) *Intake of Clearing House:* registrants to be referred to
the Clearing House by:

   i) *Citizens*, to whom homeless men have applied for
   relief.

   ii) *Missions*, where food or lodging have been
   received by homeless men.

   iii) *Charities.*

   iv) *Travelers' Aid Society.*

   v) *Local organizations.*

    vi) *Police Department:* closing of police stations to lodgers and provision for supply of such applicants with tickets of admission to the Clearing House; direction by police to the Clearing House of persons found for the first time begging.

    vii) *Courts, police stations, House of Correction, and county jail:* provision to every homeless man or boy upon discharge with ticket of admission to Clearing House guaranteeing three days' liberty with food, lodging, and an opportunity for honest employment.

e) Classification: As a result of examination in the Vocational Clinic the men will be divided for treatment into three groups: (1) boys and youths, (2) employable men, and (3) unemployable men. The unemployable will be further divided into: (i) the physically handicapped, (ii) the mentally defective, (iii) alcoholics and drug addicts, (iv) the habitually idle, (v) the untrained, and (vi) the aged.

f) Treatment: Upon the basis of the preceding examination and classification, the men will be given the following services:

    i) Those in need of emergency relief, temporary lodging, meals and bath, by the agencies in the field and by the Municipal Lodging House (when reopened).

    ii) Those in need of clean clothes, free laundry work at the Municipal Laundry (to be established).

    iii) Those who are proper charges of other communities and who may be better cared for there, transportation from relatives or from Cook County agent.

    iv) Those in need of medical service, treatment at the Cook County Hospital, Municipal Tuberculosis Sanitarium, or dispensaries, and observation at the Psychopathic Hospital.

    v) For the unemployable physically disabled, education as provided in the Chicago plan for the

physically handicapped (under consideration by
the state in co-operation with private agencies).

vi) For the unemployable but physically able-
bodied, individual arrangements for industrial
education.

vii) For the aged and permanently physically dis-
abled, placement in the Oak Forest Home.

viii) For the employable, references with vocational
diagnosis and recommendation to the Illinois
Free Employment offices and other employment
agencies.

ix) For persons under the supervision of the Municipal Clearing House, when desirable, individual
case work and after-care.

x) For incorrigible vagrants and beggars for whom
no constructive treatment is provided in the
program for immediate action (see constructive
treatment in "Program for Future Action")
commitment to the House of Correction.

g) *Administration:* The Clearing House to be administered by the city of Chicago under the City Department of Public Welfare; the director of the Clearing
House to be also superintendent of the Lodging House
and of the Municipal Laundry and the Municipal
Bath House, a physician on full time to be assigned
by the City Department of Public Health, a psychiatrist and psychologist by the state criminologist of
the State Department of Public Welfare.

h) *Advisory Committee:* Under the auspices of the
Chicago Council of Social Agencies, an advisory committee to the director of the Clearing House be
organized to be composed of public and private
agencies and civic, philanthropic, commercial, industrial, and labor organizations, co-operating with the
Clearing House.

i) *Financing:* An appeal to be made at once to the
city council for funds to equip and maintain the
Municipal Clearing House, Municipal Lodging House,
Laundry and Bath House, to provide for the following
budget:

Tentative Annual Budget for Caring Adequately for Homeless Transient Men in Chicago

Clearing House	Maximum*	Minimum
Rent of headquarters, including light and heat.....	$ 2,500.00	....
Heat and light in free quarters..................	....	$ 1,000.00
Equipment......................................	1,000.00	1,000.00
Office supplies, stationery, printing, etc	500.00	500.00
Staff:		
Superintendent.............................	6,000.00	4,000.00
Assistant...................................	2,500.00	....
Six interviewers and field workers.............	9,000.00	....
Two interviewers and field workers.............	....	4,000.00
Two stenographers...........................	2,400.00	....
One stenographer............................	....	1,500.00
Physician (part time)........................	1,800.00	....
Psychiatrist (part time)......................	1,800.00	....
Director of vocational guidance...............	4,000.00	....
Janitors....................................	1,800.00	1,800.00
Total	$33,300.00	$13,800.00

* The maximum budget represents expenditures in the event headquarters cannot be secured free of rent, services of physician and psychiatrist cannot be secured from city and Institute for Juvenile Research, and at a time when a full staff will be necessary.

2. *The reopening of the Municipal Lodging House* under the following conditions (adapted from "Program for Model Municipal Lodging House," by Raymond Robins):

   a) *Administration:* under the City Department of Public Health in close affiliation with the Clearing House for Homeless Men.

   b) *Purpose:* to provide free, under humane and sanitary conditions, food, lodging, and bath, with definite direction for such permanent relief as is needed for any man or boy stranded in Chicago.

   c) *Registration and preliminary physical examination:* made in Clearing House a condition to admission.

   d) *Standard of service:*
      i) Sanitary building.
      ii) Wholesome food.
      iii) Dormitories quiet, beds comfortable and clean.
      iv) First-aid treatment: vaccination, bandages and simple medicaments furnished free.

    v) Isolation ward for men suffering from inebriety, insanity, venereal diseases, etc.

    vi) Fumigation of lodgers' clothing, including hat and shoes, every night.

    vii) Nightly shower bath required.

3. *The establishment of a Municipal Laundry and a Municipal Bath House by the city of Chicago:* to be operated in close affiliation with the Municipal Clearing House.

4. *Utilization of existing facilities for industrial training:* Co-operation with existing educational institutions for the vocational training of boys and youths and of the physically handicapped, mentally defective, and industrially inadequate who are unemployable but willing to work. (See "Program for Future Action.")

5. *Employment agencies:*

    a) The extension of the service of the Illinois Free Employment office.

    b) The enforcement of the law relating to private employment agencies: the requirement that sections three (3), four (4), and five (5), of the law be posted in a conspicuous place in each room of the agency; and the return to the applicant of three-fifths of the registration and other fees upon the failure of applicant to accept position or upon his discharge for cause.

    c) The further study of private employment agencies and of labor camps in order to provide the homeless man with adequate protection against exploitation.

6. *Public health and housing:*

    a) The further building of sanitary workingmen's hotels with low charge for accommodations.

    b) The maintenance and raising of standards of cheap hotels in Chicago through rigid inspection and tightening of requirements.

    c) Medical examination, inspection, and supervision of men in flops, together with vaccination and hospitalization of needy cases.

7. *Vagrancy Court:* the reorganization of the Vagrancy Court for the hearing of cases of incorrigible vagrants and beggars on the basis of the investigations of the Clearing House.

8. *Protection of the boy:*

   a) Prevention of aimless wandering through the provision of wholesome and stimulating recreation, through the extension of all activities for boys, and through the further development of vocational education and supervision. The Vocational Guidance Bureau of the Board of Education should be removed to an area of the city free from unwholesome contacts.

   b) An educational campaign organized through the Mid-West Boy's Club Federation should be carried on in all the boys' organizations in Chicago showing the danger of "flipping" trains and playing in railroad yards. The National Safety Council has a great deal of material which could be used in such a campaign.

   c) Co-operation with such organization as the Brotherhood of Railway Trainmen, the special police organizations of the railroads, the Lake Carriers Association, and automobile clubs, in a program to prevent boys wandering away from home. Pamphlets should be prepared for distribution, asking for co-operation and enforcement of working certificate regulations in this and other states, child labor laws, juvenile court laws, etc.

   d) The enlistment officers of the army, navy, and marine should demand the presentation of a birth certificate in all cases in which they doubt the age of the applicant.

   e) The co-operation of the managers of the hotels and lodging-houses in an effort to keep boys under seventeen out of the hotels in the Hobohemian areas, or at least to use their influence in preventing boys and men from rooming together.

   f) Because most of the contacts the boy has with tramps are unwholesome, the police should not permit boys to loiter or play in the areas most frequented by the tramp population; namely, West Madison Street, South State Street, North Clark Street, and adjacent territory. Parents ought to be made aware of the nature of the contacts the boy has with the tramp in these areas and in the parks.

g) The assignment of special plain-clothes policemen experienced in dealing with vagrants to the parks and other places in which tramps congregate. They should be instructed to pick up and hold in the Detention Home any boy under seventeen years found in company with a tramp.

h) More strenuous effort should be made to occupy the leisure time of boys who frequent the districts in which the tramps congregate. It is the boy with leisure time who is the most susceptible to the unwholesome contacts. Supervised recreation should be carried on to an extent that boys who play in Hobohemian areas might be attracted to other sections. When school is not in session a more extensive program of summer camps might help.

i) Since the Juvenile Court of Cook County is equipped to investigate the cases of vagrant boys under seventeen in Chicago, and return them to their homes, all vagrant boys apprehended by anyone in the daytime should be reported to the chief probation officer, Juvenile Court. Vagrant boys over seventeen should be directed to the Clearing House.

j) After five o'clock vagrant boys under seventeen should be turned over to the police who will take them to the Detention Home, from which home they will be taken to the office of the chief probation officer the first thing in the morning.

k) Whenever a boy under seventeen is taken in custody by the police, because of contact with tramps, or whenever a boy is held as a complaining witness against a tramp, he should always be reported to the Juvenile Court. It is the responsibility of the court to put the boy in touch with some proper individual or agency, so that he will be adequately supervised and befriended in the future.

9. *Publicity and public co-operation:* the education of the public through news items in the daily press and editorial comment; public co-operation through tickets of admission to the Clearing House providing food and lodging in the Municipal Lodging House constantly to

be distributed through societies, institutions, hotels, business offices, churches, clubs, housewives, and other citizens.

II. A PROGRAM FOR FUTURE ACTION—

1. *That a bond issue* be submitted for approval to the voters of the city of Chicago providing for the erection of adequate buildings for a Municipal Clearing House, Municipal Lodging House, and Municipal Laundry and Bath House.

2. *That an Industrial Institute* be established by the state of Illinois in Chicago for the vocational training of the physically handicapped, mentally defective, and industrially inadequate, who are unemployable, but willing to work.

3. *That a State Farm Colony for Industrial Rehabilitation* be established by the state of Illinois for the compulsory detention and re-education of unemployables, such as beggars, vagrants, petty criminals, who are unwilling to receive industrial training.

4. *That a Department of Industrial Training of the House of Correction* be opened, pending the establishment of the State Farm Colony for Industrial Rehabilitation, for the commitment and re-education of unemployables, such as beggars, vagrants, and petty criminals.

APPENDIX B
DOCUMENTS AND MATERIALS

CHAPTER I.   HOBOHEMIA DEFINED

115. *Summary of a Study of Four Hundred Tramps*, Nels Anderson, summer, 1921.
124. An evening spent on the benches in Grant Park; description of men and their talk.
135. *A Study of Eight Cases of Homeless Men in Lodging Houses*, R. N. Wood, December, 1922.
145. An unpublished paper on the hobo, "Along the Main Stem with Red," Harry M. Beardsley, March 20, 1917.
146. *Chicago's Hobo Area*, Sherman O. Cooper, December, 1917.
157. *Chicago's Hobo District*, Melville J. Herskovits, December, 1919.
159. Comparative statistics for the three wards in which Hobohemia is located, 1910–20.

CHAPTER II.   THE JUNGLES: THE HOMELESS MAN ABROAD

1. "A Day in the Jungles," A. W. Dragstedt, a hobo who knows the jungles.
76. "Job Hunting via Box-Car in the Northwest," *Hobo News*, Bill Quirke, September, 1921.

CHAPTER III.   THE LODGING HOUSE: THE HOMELESS MAN AT HOME

2–3. Recital of an evening spent by Nels Anderson in a flophouse, April, 1922.
70. Statistics: Bridewell population, lodging-house patrons, registered voters.
79. *Report of Visit to Ten Gambling Houses in Hobohemia*, Nels Anderson, January 1, 1923.
105. Casual worker, ex-soldier, twenty-eight, few days in town, lost money in gambling-house.
151. *A Dozen Hotels in the Loop*, George F. David, August, 1922.

CHAPTER IV.   "GETTING BY" IN HOBOHEMIA

4. Jewish hobo, parasitic philosophy, middle-aged, begs from Jewish agencies in all cities.

5. Transient dreamer, twenty-seven, known to many agencies in different cities.

6. Boy in teens, Jewish, moves with ease from agency to agency, good solicitor.

7. City bum, twenty-four, petty robber, works occasionally, jail experience.

8. "Fat," a panhandler with a self-justifying philosophy, works on favorable jobs.

9. Englishman, forty-one, paralyzed arm, alcoholic, mendicant, was a bricklayer.

89. Faker, Bulgarian, forty-five, plays deaf and dumb, "works" restaurants.

90. Home-guard bum, sixty-nine, works at odd jobs, often mendicant, drinks some.

95. Ex-soldier, funds about gone, going East for work, clean, sober, "working" charities.

97. Boy tramp, eighteen, left home to avoid school, wants to be engineer, works.

98. Two young men temporarily without money and work, adjusted in a few days.

102. City bum, thirty-five, talkative, lazy and unkempt, mendicant much of time.

103. Away from family for work, gets money from wife, loafs, later returns home.

104. Jewish tramp, sells papers, tin worker, served time in jail for wife desertion.

111. Loafs, fat, unattractive, works some, not welcome home; his family send him money.

112. Well-to-do sister ashamed of him, sends him money; he calls it "borrowing."

113. Beggar with a philosophy, condemns peddlers who beg part of time, works occasionally.

123. Spanish war and world-war veteran, forty-six, compensation, tries to go to school.

131. Description of life with the "slum proletariat" by one of them.

152. *Mendicancy in Chicago*, Melvin L. Olsen, December, 1919.

155. *Case Studies of Beggars in Chicago*, Joseph Arnsdorff, December 16, 1919.

161. Statement from the secretary of the Mid-City Commercial Association on the hobo problem.

CHAPTER V.   WHY DO MEN LEAVE HOME ?

10. Pioneer hobo and tramp, "played all the games," fifty-six, blames self for misspent life.

11. Belgian, fifty-eight, coal miner, lumber jack, Chicago in winter, single, seldom penniless.

12. Pioneer hobo, fifty-one, perhaps dying, miner's "con," away from home (Ohio) thirty years.

13. Migratory worker, single, fifty-six, ever restless, mines, sea, harvest, sheep shearer.

14. Anemic man, lung trouble, textile worker, light work only, hopes open air will help.

15. Beggar, peddler, one leg, industrial accident, justifies begging and drink.

16. Migrant, would settle down, drinks, loses jobs, single, getting old, health failing.

17. "Dope" user, weak, anemic, poorly clad, dirty, beat way from Boston.

18. Old man, seventy-eight, poor-farm and hospital experience, mendicant, lives on fifty or sixty cents a day.

19. Restless young man, twenty-four, no permanent desires, carpenter, capable, sober, congenial.

20. Restless young worker, easily bored by the monotony of a job.

26. Irish, ex-soldier, ex-sailor, twenty-seven, sings, wants to study music, ex-secretary of "Hobo College."

27. Feeble-minded, left home in war time, odd jobs, in town often, often in missions.

28. Pessimistic, imaginative, unstable, about forty-five, fair worker.

29. Periodical drinker, quarrelsome when drunk, otherwise good worker.

30. College man, twenty-seven, ex-salesman, left wife, homosexual experience, avoids work.

31. Chronic drinker, stockyards worker, seldom migrates, many arrests, away from wife twelve years.

32. Boy tramp, sixteen, on way to Texas, from Ohio, parents dead, only brother a soldier.

33. Left home when jilted by girl, too sensitive to return, very transient.

34. Returned home after jail experience, humiliated, left home, away for several years.

35. Ex-soldier, as small-town boy left home in crisis, stayed away to make bluff good, twenty-two.

36. Boy left home in fear of punishment from father, returns occasionally.

37. Migrant because of trouble over woman, about thirty, dare not return, radical.

38. Became migratory to avoid paying alimony, dare not return, about forty.

39. Boy tramp, nineteen, egotist, traveled much, works little, gambles, jail record.

40. Oldest boy becomes runaway, twenty, other boys in family follow, dislikes father.

CHAPTER VI.   THE HOBO AND THE TRAMP

41. Scotchman, thirty-two, single, ex-soldier, sailor, nurse in winters, casual in summer.

42. Deck hand summers, migrant to South in winter, single, generally sober.

43. Carpenter, casual, often discharged, would settle but losing efficiency by drink.

44. Old man, fifty-eight, plasterer, fair worker but casual, has ceased migrating, sober.

45. One-time harvest hand, seldom leaves Chicago, peddles trinkets, gambles.

46. Romantic tramp, revels in wandering, carries tiny camera, seeks notice, does not work.

86. Recital of experiences of boy tramp, now a doctor in Chicago.

91. Russian, able-bodied hobo, about thirty-five, clean, sober, works in and near Chicago.

92. Boy, eighteen, on way home (Indiana) from winter in West, plans to leave tramp life.

100. Congenial, irresponsible man of twenty-five, sober, clean, very transient, works as porter.

109. Runaway boy from Hammond, Indiana, sixteen, in Hobohemia looking for work, very worldly wise.

CHAPTER VII.   THE HOME GUARD AND THE BUM

47. City bum, twenty-three, in missions when broke, works as teamster, "got" religion once.

48. Wife deserter, drinks, loiters on "stem," odd jobs, formerly pig killer.

49. Ex-pugilist, single, forty-five, now mission "stiff," works on docks in summer, alcoholic.
50. Health ruined by drink, thirty-two, light jobs, baker, farms in summer, Chicago much of time.
72. Crippled in industrial accident, sixty-two, family grown, would care for him, drinks.
78. Classification of types of homeless men submitted by Mr. Wirth of Jewish charities.
127. Classification of tramps, hobos, and other types of homeless men by Dr. Ben L. Reitman.

CHAPTER VIII.   WORK

73. Pioneer type, fifty, seldom comes East, miner, prospector, lumber jack.
77. Man forced to be idle by hard times, learned to get along, later refused work.
83. Old man, fifty, single, winters in Chicago, farm jobs in summer, drinks some.
93. Laborer, migrant, forty-four, becoming radical on account of work shortage, had some money.
94. Ex-soldier, twenty-seven, without funds but hopeful, hustling worker.
96. Boy tramp, twenty, reformatory record, traveled much in three years.
114. Brought cattle from Wyoming to Chicago, lost all with women and drink, still happy.
134. *Study of Employment Agencies and Labor Placement Problems*, E. H. Koster, August, 1922.
158. *The Unemployed and the Unemployable in Chicago*, Rupert R. Lewis, December, 1917.
160. Statistics of the Chicago Free Employment offices for the year ending September 30, 1922.

CHAPTER IX.   HEALTH

106. Ex-soldier, released from army hospital, gets compensation, drinks much.
107. Italian bricklayer, rheumatism, gets aid from union, family in Italy, sons in war.
108. Mental case, talks to self, attracts much attention on street, loud and vulgar.

117. Teamster, thirty-six, raised in slum, unemployable with locomotor ataxia, peddles pencils.

121. Chicago boy, does not go home, needs medical attention for feet and eyes, gambles.

122. Boy tramp, great wanderer, homosexual, intelligent, two years on road.

139. Mortality statistics for Hobohemia for 1922, non-resident cases.

147. Communication of Dr. Herman N. Bundesen, commissioner of public health, concerning the health and medical care of the homeless man in Chicago.

CHAPTER X. SEX LIFE

51. Middle-aged woman, character on West Madison Street, feeds cats, scolds everyone.

52. Street faker, aspires to be actor, jail experience, free-union experience.

53. Boy tramp, going West, travels without difficulty but is often accosted by perverts.

54. Homosexual case, boy involved, man died in jail while awaiting trial.

55. Bum who works on docks and boats, involved in boy case, Bridewell for term.

81. Four boys in Grant Park, each with jail and tramp experience.

82. Case of boy in teens, tramp, "flirting" with men in Grant Park.

87. *Cases of Venereal Disease Due to Homosexual Infection*, Dr. Ben L. Reitman.

110. Boy tramp, nineteen, exploited by perverts, decidedly feeble-minded, on way home (Indiana).

120. Young man, twenty-two, well dressed, homosexual prostitute, loafs in Grant Park.

125. Observations upon the unnatural attachments of some homeless men and boys.

141. Wife deserter, left home to enable her to divorce him.

142. Statistics showing marital condition of homeless men.

153. *The Sexual Life of Habitual Wanderers*, J. L. Handelman, August 22, 1919.

CHAPTER XI.   CITIZENSHIP

56. Case of a transient voter showing difficulty hobo has of voting.

57. Hobo's affair with police in Kansas, hobo bitter against police.

58. University of Iowa student and police, fair observer, has been hobo, letter to writer.

59. Recital of hobo and private police in Ohio, narrator has settled in Chicago.

80. Report of visit to police court, hobos tried at rate of one a minute, August 28, 1922.

85. *Report of Two Weeks' Commitment to the Cook County Jail,* Nels Anderson, May, 1922.

149. Case of police persecution.

162. Newspaper clippings on the death of Martin Talbert in a Florida convict camp.

CHAPTER XII.   HOBOHEMIAN PERSONALITIES

22. Marxian socialist, soap-boxer, dogmatic and undiplomatic, would educate "slaves."

25. Dreamer, poet, migrant, critic, very changeable, good family, single, ex-soldier.

75. Pamphlet on Mike Walsh published by himself, states his policies and achievements.

126. Character sketch of J. E. How, "Millionaire Hobo," also correspondence with Nels Anderson.

CHAPTER XIII.   THE INTELLECTUAL LIFE OF THE HOBO

23. Tries to write saleable songs and novels, sober but gambles, single.

116. Leader in hobo organization, writes for *Hobo News*, carries I.W.W. card.

119. Hobo philosopher, carrys bundle, sells pamphlets about self, sleeps in parks.

129. Thirty-one copies of the *Hobo News* containing various types of hobo literature.

150. Manuscript on "What the Hobo Reads," Daniel Horsley.

CHAPTER XIV.   HOBO SONGS AND BALLADS

130. Collection of hobo songs and poems made by Nels Anderson, forty-one selections.

CHAPTER XV.   THE SOAP BOX AND THE OPEN FORUM

21. Soap-boxer, scientific bent, takes self and message seriously, calls it "education."

24. Single-tax advocate, about fifty, living away from family, sells Ford's *Weekly*.

60. Notes on an afternoon's series of talks on the soap box on Madison Street.

138. Debate, "Hobo College" v. students from the University of Chicago, "Kansas Industrial Courts," April 12, 1923.

140. *Study of "Hobo College" in Chicago*, Charles W. Allen (teacher at college), 1923.

CHAPTER XVI.   SOCIAL AND POLITICAL ORGANIZATIONS

61. Co-operative movements among hobos, experiences of John X. Kelly, now in Chicago.

74. Financial statement of the I.W.W., May and June, 1922.

84. Conversation with an I.W.W. who was once a steady migratory worker, old soldier.

CHAPTER XVII.   MISSIONS AND WELFARE AGENCIES

62. "Visit to Bible Rescue Mission," Nels Anderson's experience, spring, 1922.

63. *Salvation Army Revival*, Sherman O. Cooper.

64. Case of "X" at the Bible Rescue Mission, bears public testimony to former badness.

65. Ex-bum and wife deserter, graduate foreign university, steady man now.

66. Mission worker, "saved" twenty years ago, was alcoholic and a failure, in business now.

67. German, Madison Street bum, came into mission to get warm, got religion, left old life.

68. Ex-drunkard, often thrown out of mission, finally got converted and is a new man.

69. Young man, mission "stiff," easily converted, became a "backslider" next day.

71. Wife deserter, mission hanger-on, clean, erect, active but avoids work.

99. Letter by Bill Quirke to *Hobo News* on missions in Los Angeles. He assails missions.

118. Ex-soldier in Legion headquarters, trying to get job on strength of army experience.

143. *Study of Missions and Mission Characters*, L. G. Brown, 1923.
156. *A Study of Missions*, H. D. Wolf, August, 1922.

APPENDIX A.   SUMMARY OF FINDINGS AND
RECOMMENDATIONS

128. Unpublished materials by Nels Anderson, covering his study of 400 tramps, 230 typewritten pages.
144. *Study of 110 Runaway Boys in Chicago Detention Home*, F. C. Frey and B. W. Bridgman, 1922.
148. "Outline of Program for the Prevention and Treatment of Vagrancy," prepared by the Committee on Relief of the Chicago Council of Social Agencies, and submitted to the Executive Committee of the Council, June 13, 1918.
154. Responses to requests for information on the homeless man problem from social agencies in the larger American cities.

APPENDIX C
BIBLIOGRAPHY

HISTORY AND SOCIOLOGY OF WANDERLUST AND VAGRANCY

AYDELOTTE, FRANK, *Elizabethan Rogues and Vagabonds* ("Oxford Historical and Literary Studies"). Oxford: Clarendon Press, 1913. Pp. 187.

FLORIAN, EUGENIO, *I Vagabondi Studio Sociologico-guiridico, Parte prima, L'Evoluzione del Vagabondaggio.* Torino, 1897. Pp. 1–124.

HUTTEN, JOHN CAMDEN, *The Book of Vagabonds and Beggars.* Translated and printed in England by Hutton, 1860.

JOFFROY AND DUPOUY, *Fugues et Vagabondage.* Paris: Alcan, 1909. Pp. 368.

MARIE, A. A., AND MEUNIER, R., *Les Vagabonds.* Paris: Giard and Brière, 1908. Pp. 331.

MARIET, "Le vagabondage constitutionnel des dégénérés" (continued article), *Annales medicopsychologique,* 1911–12.

MAYHEW, HENRY, *London Labour and the London Poor.* London: Griffin, 1862. Pp. 504.

PAGNIER, ARMAND, *Du Vagabondage et des Vagabonds, Étude Psychologique, Sociologique et Medico-legale.* Lyons, France: 1906.

PARKER, CARLTON H., *The Casual Laborer.* New York: Harcourt, Brace & Howe, 1920. Pp. 199.

RIBTON-TURNER, CHARLES J., *A History of Vagrants and Vagrancy and Beggars and Begging.* London: 1887. Pp. 720.

SPEEK, PETER A., "The Psychology of the Floating Workers," *Annals of the Amer. Acad. of Pol. and Soc. Science* (Philadelphia), LXIX, 72–78.

TANNENBAUM, FRANK, *The Labor Movement.* New York: Putnam, 1921. Pp. 259.

THANET, OCTAVE, "The Tramp in Four Centuries," *Lippincotts,* XXIII (May, 1879), 565.

TUGWELL, REXFORD G., "The Gypsy Strain," *Pacific Monthly Review,* III, 177–96.

WILMANNS, KARL, *Zur Psychopathologie des Landstreichers.* Leipzig: Barth, 1906. Pp. 418.

WILMANNS, KARL, "Psychoses among Tramps," *Centralblatt für Nervenheilkunde,* December, 1902.

THE LABOR MARKET AND INDUSTRIAL MOBILITY

BAKER, OLIVER E., *Seed Time and Harvest, Bull. United States Dept. of Agric.*, No. *183*, March, 1922.

BRISSENDEN, PAUL F., "Measurement of Labor Mobility," *Jour. of Pol. Econ.*, XXVIII (June, 1920), 441–76.

BRISSENDEN, PAUL F., AND FRANKEL, EMIL, "Mobility of Industrial Labor," *Pol. Science Quar.*, XXXV (December, 1920), 566–600.

DEVINE, EDWARD T., "The Shiftless and Floating City Population," *Annals of the American Academy of Soc. and Pol. Science*, X (September, 1897), 149–64.

FRY, LUTHER C., "Migratory Workers of Our Industries," *World's Work*, XL (October, 1920), 600.

Immigration Commission, Reports of, *The Floating Immigrant Labor Supply* (*Immigrants in Industry*), 25 parts, XVIII, 331–525. Senate Reports, Washington, 1911.

LESCOHIER, DON D., *The Harvest Worker, Bull. United States Dept. of Labor*, No. *1020*, April, 1922.

LESCOHIER, DON D., *The Labor Market*. New York: Macmillan, 1919. Pp. 338.

SLICHTER, SAMUEL H., *Turnover of Factory Labor*. New York: Appleton, 1919. Pp. 460.

THE PROBLEM OF UNEMPLOYMENT AND VAGRANCY

BEVERIDGE, W. H., *Unemployment: A Problem of Industry*. London: Longmans, Green & Co., 1909. Pp. 317.

BLISS, W. D. P., *What Is Done for the Unemployed in European Countries. United States Labor Bull.* No. *76* (1908), pp. 741–934.

BOOTH, WILLIAM, *The Vagrant and the Unemployable*. London: 1909. Pp. 79.

DAWSON, W. H., *The Vagrancy Problem*. London: P. S King & Son, 1910. Pp. 270.

HUNTER, ROBERT, *Property*. New York: Macmillan, 1912. Pp. 380.

KELLY, EDMOND, *The Elimination of the Tramp*. New York: Putnam & Sons, 1908. Pp. 111.

Laws of Various States Relating to Vagrancy.

LAUBACH, FRANK C., *Why There Are Vagrants*. New York: University of Columbia Press, 1916. Pp. 128.

LEWIS, BURDETTE G., *The Offender, and His Relations to Law and Society*. New York: Harper, 1921. Pp. 380.

LEWIS, O. F., "Vagrancy in the United States," *Proceedings of the National Conference of Charities and Corrections* (1907), pp. 52–70.

MARSH, BENJAMIN C., "Causes of Vagrancy and Methods of Eradication," *Annals of the Amer. Acad. of Pol. and Soc. Science*, Vol. XXIII, No. 3, pp. 445–56. Philadelphia: 1904.

Massachusetts Association of Relief Officers, *Report on Best Methods of Dealing with Tramps and Wayfarers*, 1901.

"The Men We Lodge," *Report of the Advisory Social Service Committee of the Municipal Lodging House*. New York City: Dept. of Public Charities, 1915. Pp. 42.

NICHOLS, MALCOLM, "National Aspects of the Transient Problem," *The Family*, III (June, 1922), 89–91.

OSTWALD, HANS OTTO, *Die Bekämpfung der Landstreicherei*. Stuttgart: R. Lutz, 1903. Pp. 278.

Report of the Commissioner of Public Affairs. Portland, Ore.: Wood Yard, 1915.

Report of the Mayor's Committee on Unemployment. New York City: 1917. Pp. 132.

WOLFE, ALBERT B., *The Lodging Problem in Boston*. Boston: Houghton Mifflin, 1906. Pp. 200.

THE I.W.W. AND THE CASUAL LABORER

BROOKS, JOHN GRAHAM, *American Syndicalism*. New York: Macmillan, 1913. Pp. 264.

BRISSENDEN, PAUL F., *The I.W.W.: A Study of American Syndicalism*. New York: University of Columbia, 1920. Pp. 438.

HOXIE, R. F., "The Truth about the I.W.W.," *Jour. of Pol. Econ.*, XXI (November, 1913), 785–97.

I.W.W. Song Book. Chicago: The Equity Press, 1922.

Preamble and Constitution of the I.W.W. Chicago: General I.W.W. Headquarters, 1921. Pp. 69.

ST. JOHN, VINCENT, *The I.W.W., Its History, Structure and Methods*. Chicago: The Equity Press.

TRIDON, ANDRÉ, *The New Unionism*. New York: Huebsch, 1913. Pp. 198.

MATERIALS FOR THE STUDY OF THE HOBO AND THE TRAMP

BROWN, EDWIN A., "*Broke*," *the Man without a Dime*.   Chicago: Brown & Howell, 1913.   Pp. 370.

DAVIES, WILLIAM H., *Autobiography of a Super-Tramp*.   New York: A. A. Knopf, 1917.   Pp. 345.

ELLIS, HAVELOCK, *Studies in the Psychology of Sex: Sex Inversion*. II, 391.   Philadelphia: Davis, 1915.

FORBES, JAMES, "Jockers and the Schools They Keep," *Charities Survey*, XI (1903), 432.

FLYNT (WILLARD), JOSIAH, *My Life*.   New York: Outing Publishing Co., 1908.

FLYNT (WILLARD), JOSIAH, *Tramping with Tramps*.   New York: Century, 1899.   Pp. 398.

HOWARD, OLIVER OTIS (Maj. Gen., U.S. Army), "The Menace of Coxyism," *North Amer. Rev.*, CLVIII (1894), 687–96.

KEMP, HARRY, *The Cry of Youth*.   New York: Mitchell, Kennerley, 1914.   Pp. 140.

KEMP, HARRY, *Tramping on Life*.   New York: Boni & Liveright, 1922.   Pp. 438.

KNIBBS, H. H., *Songs of the Outlands*.   New York: Houghton, Mifflin Co., 1914.   Pp. 73.

LINDSAY, VACHEL, *Handy Book for Beggars*.   New York: Macmillan, 1916.   Pp. 205.

LONDON, JACK, *The Road*.   New York: Macmillan, 1907. Pp. 224.

LONDON, JACK, *War on the Classes*.   New York: Macmillan, 1905.   Pp. 278.

McCOOK, J. J., "A Census of Tramps and Its Revelations," *Forum*, XV, 753.

McGREGOR, TRACY W., *Twenty Thousand Men*.   Detroit: McGregor Institute, 1922.   Pp. 29.

MULLIN, GLEN, "Adventures of a Scholar Tramp," *Century Magazine*, Vol. CV (February and March).

SERVICE, ROBERT W., *The Spell of the Yukons*.   New York: Barse & Hopkins, 1907.   Pp. 99.

WYCKOFF, W. A., *The Workers: The East*.   New York: Scribners, 1897.   Pp. 270.

WYCKOFF, W. A., *The Workers: The West*.   New York: Scribners, 1898.   Pp. 380.

STUDIES OF THE HOMELESS MAN IN CHICAGO

ANDERSON, NELS, "Cases Studies of Homeless Men in Chicago" (typewritten manuscript in office of Chicago Council of Social Agencies and Department of Sociology, University of Chicago).

ANDERSON, NELS, "The Juvenile and the Tramp," *Journal of Criminal Law and Criminology*, Vol. XIV (1923–24).

"The Chicago Municipal Lodging House for Men," in the *Report and Handbook of the Department of Health of the City of Chicago* (1911–18), pp. 1076–81.

"Fifty Cheap Lodging Houses," *First Semi-Annual Report of the Department of Public Welfare of Chicago* (March, 1915), pp. 66–73.

FOLEY, R. W., "The Shifting Population of Homeless Men and the Cheap Lodging House" (typewritten manuscript of twenty-nine pages in Department of Sociology, University of Chicago).

Report to the Mayor and Alderman by the Chicago Municipal Markets Commission on a Practical Program for Relieving Destitution and Unemployment in the City of Chicago, December 28, 1914.

ROBINS, RAYMOND, "What Constitutes a Model Municipal Lodging House," *Proceedings of the National Conference of Charities and Correction* (1904), pp. 155–66.

SOLENBERGER, ALICE W., *One Thousand Homeless Men.* New York: Russell Sage Foundation, 1911. Pp. 374.

STEAD, WILLIAM T., *If Christ Should Come to Chicago.*[1]   Chicago: Laird & Lee, 1894. Pp. 463.

[1] The first chapter describes the homeless-man areas of 1893.

INDEX

"A No. 1," 100
Adler, Herman M., 73
Agencies, conflicting policies of, 15
Alcoholism, 66, 67, 134–35
American Express, 166
American Legion, 260
Ashleigh, Charles, 205
Association of hobo with women, 138
Associations: I.B.W A., 230, 235–40;
    I.W.W.,230–35; J.P.A.,ix; M.W.U.,
    230
Atkins, Brigadier J. E., 171, 180–81
Attitude of perverts, 148

Ball, Charles B., 260
Ballot, hobo regard for, 153
Barber colleges, 37–38
Barrel-house, 27
Begging, 47, 49, 50
Bills of fare on "stem," 34
Bloch, Iwan, 144
Boarding companies, 130–31
Bookstore, 38
Borrowing, 49
Boy tramp, and perversion, 145; and
    wanderlust, 83
Boyd, Charles J., 120
Boys and tramp life, 85
Bread lines, 258
Brennan, Pat, 208
"Bughouse Square," 9–10
Bum, the, 98

"Carrying the banner," 53
Catholic charities, 259
Christian Industrial League, 27–28,
    260
Chicago, a winter shelter, 12–13
Chicago labor exchange, 12, 110
Chicago plan for homeless men, 271–79
Chicago Urban League, 259
Civil authorities and tramp, 163–64
Clearing house for homeless men, 122,
    136
Clothing stores, 35–36
"Coffee an'" level, 40
Cooking in jungles, 22–23
College," "Hobo, 172, 173, 174, 175,
    177, 227, 237

Construction work, 107
Court experience of hobo, 165–66
Criminal, hobos not, 164–65
Crises in life of person, 77–79
Crop moving, 107
Cubicles or "cages," 30

Dawes, General C. G., 28
Day in the jungles, 21–25
Dragstedt, A. W., 25 n., 171, 177–78,
    212
Drug addicts, 67–68, not hobos, 69

Educating the proletariat, 219
Egocentricity, 74–76
Ellis, Havelock, 144
Employment agencies, comparison of,
    115–17; private, 111–12; public,
    114–16
Employment service, need of, 122
Evangelists and soap-boxers, 217

Faking, street, 43
Farmer-Labor Party, 152
Flops, co-operative, 238–39
Flynt, Josiah, 94, 146
Fortune-tellers, 39
"Free-lance" speakers, 216, 218
Free-union marriages, 141–42

"Getting by," a game, 57, meaning
    of, 40–41
Giovannitti, Arturo, 201
Grafts, old and new, 44
Grant Park, in summer, 11
Greenstein, "Mother" 139, 171, 183–
    84

Handicapped men, 125–28
Harvey-Dammarell hotels, 28–29
Harvey-McGuire hotels, 28
"Hat trick," the, 45–46
Hazards of casual work, 129
Health Department, 131, 132, 133
Healy, William, 70
Hill, Joe, 208, 209
Hobo, definition of, 87–89; and drink,
    135; and exposure, 136; health in

[293

town, 131–33; hostility to in small
town, 26; institutions, 15; names
for, 93; nativity of, 150–51; origin
of, 88; pioneer, and frontiersman,
92; poor beggar, 49; and religion,
262; status of, 167; voting, 151–
52; what he reads, 187–89; worker,
91
Hobohemia, defined, 3
"Hogan's Flop," 31–33
Home, why men leave, 61 ff.
Home guard, 96–97; types of, 100–101
Homeless men, and the law, 154;
mostly unmarried, 137
Horsley, Dan, 171, 175–77
Housing problem, 39
How, James Eads, 88, 172, 174, 175,
239

I.B.W.A., 230, 235–40; Holding Committee, 237–38; origin of, 235–36;
program of, 236–37
Industrial attractions, 62; fishing,
107; ice-harvesting, 108; lumbering, 108; sheep-shearing, 107–8
Industrially inadequate, 65
Industry, changes in, 62–63; hazards
of, 65–66
I.W.W., 230–35; literature list, 187–
88; methods and appeal, 232–34;
origin of, 230; periodicals, 191;
program, 231; treatment in Chicago, 235; treatment by Ku Klux
Klan, 191

"Jack rolling," 5, 51–52
Jewish Social Service Bureau, 259
Job hunting, 109
Jobs sold, estimate of, 111
Jockers, 103
Johnson, Glenn R., 72
Jungle, buzzard, 103; a day in, 21–
25; democracy in, 19; laws of,
20–21; location and types of, 16–
17; on lake front, 10; trial in,
24–25; womanless, 18
Juvenile Protective Association, ix

Kelihor, T. T., 160
Kelly, John X., 171, 173–74, 242,
243–46

Kemp, Harry, 196, 199
"Killing time," 215–16
Klein, Nicholas, 88
Knibbs, H. H., 198

Lady barbers, 38
Langsman, Charles W., 171, 178–79
Laubach, F. C., 126
Leadership in Hobohemia, 184
Lescohier, Don D., 119
Library privileges, 185
Life, loss of, 161–62
Light work, 129
Living, cheap in city, 13
Lodging-houses, municipal, 127, 134,
260–61; quasi-charitable, 27–28;
sanitary conditions of, 131–32;
types of, 27

Medical attention, free, 13; on the
job, 130
Melis, Lewis, 206
Mental tests, 71–73
Migratory Workers' Union, 230; 240–
41; aims and objects, 241, 247
Miller, H. A., 82 n.
Missions, 250–58; converts of, 253–
54; competition between, 250;
migratory national, 252; perma-
nent local, 251; soliciting funds,
252; "wild cat," 253
Mission stiffs, 98, 103
Mobility, complicates problem, 15;
effects of, 120, 248–49; of handi-
capped men, 128
"Mooching," 50
Movies and burlesque, 37
Mullenbach, James, 260
Municipal Lodging House (Chicago),
260–61; (New York), 127, 134
Mushfaker, 99
Myers, Dr. Johnston, 171, 181–83

National program, 270
Negro hobos, 8
New York Central Railroad, 166
News, Hobo, 177, 185, 186, 187, 192

Odd jobs, in city, 41
Old men, 69

"One Big Union," 231
Open forums, 226–28
Organizations among hobos, 230; failure of, 247–49

"Panhandling," 50
Park, R. E., 82 n.
Partnerships among hobos, 147
Passing the hat, 223
Patriotism, 151
Pawn shops, 36
Peddling on street, 42
Personal degradation, 57, 65
Personality, defects of, 72–76
Perversion among tramps, 144–47
Pintner and Toops, 71, 72 n.
Poems and ballads, 194–214; "Away from Town," 199–200; "Beaten Men," 205; Bum," "The, 201–2; Bum on the Rods and the Bum on the Plush," "The, 202; Dishwasher," "The, 201–2; Gila Monster Route," "The, 194–96; "Harvest War Song," 208; Hobo Knows," "The, 203; Hobo's Last Lament," "The, 212; "Men That Don't Fit In," 204; "No Matter Where You Go," 213–14; "Nothing to Do But Go," 198–99; "One Day; Some Way," 205; "Optimism," 213; "Portland County Jail," 211; Preacher and the Slave," "The, 210; Slave Market," "The, 206–7; Tramp," "The, 209; Tramp Confession," "The, 196–98; Wanderer," "The, 206
Police, encounters with hobos, 156–58; methods of, 155, 160, 164; private, 155; types of, 154–55
Poorhouse, aversion of hobo to, 56;
Population, turnover in Hobohemia, 13–14
Program for future action, 279
"Proletariat," 176
Property, destruction of, 161
Prostitutes, "second raters," 143
Prostitution, 142–43
Punk, 99, 103

Queen, Stuart A., 26 n.

Racial discrimination, 81
Radical press 186
Raid on jungles, 23–24
Railroad yards, 8
Reitman, Ben L., 87, 102, 134 n., 143, 171, 172–73
Religion, practical, 182; and love, 179; and work, 180
Restaurants and lunchrooms, 33–35; sanitary conditions of, 35
Robins, Raymond, 260
Rountree, B. Seebohm, 64 n.

Sabotage, 121
Saloons, 38–39
Salvation Army, 27–28, 250, 260
Scissor Bill, 99
Seasonal fluctuations, 63
Seasonal workers, 89–90
Second-hand clothing, 35–36
Service, Robert W., 203
Sex isolation of hobo, 144, 149
Seymour, James, 200
Short jobs, 118–19
Sickness and disease, 133
Soap-boxers, ethics and tactics of, 222–24; and opinion, 228–29; his rôle on stand, 229; versatility of, 224–26
Social center for hobos, 11; in the jungles, 16, 26
Solenberger, Alice W., 9 n., 71, 87, 125–26
Solidarity, the Industrial 190–91
State farm colony, 277
Stealing, petty, 51
Street speaking, 216–20; lectures, 220
Strike jobs, 120–21
Summary and findings, 265–79

Terman, L. M., 71 n.
Testimonies of converts, 256
Thornburn, Charles, 205
Tramp, the, 93–95
Tramping, a man's game, 137
Tucker, St. John, 87
Tugwell, Rexford, 82
Types, rendezvous of, 5, 7, 9; of homeless men, 105; numbers of each in Chicago, 105–6; of peddlers, 42–43

Unemployables, 104
Unemployment, 64–65
United Charities, 259

Vagrancy, explanation of, 85–86; in
    small towns, 163
Van de Water, John, 171, 179–80
Vaudeville, 37
Venereal disease, 133–34

Walsh, Michael C., 171, 174–75,
    242

Wanderlust, 82–83
Welfare organizations, 259–60
Westbrook, Warden Wesley, 165
White, Henry A., 203
Winter, "getting by" in, 52–53
Women and homeless men, 138–42
Work, a national problem, 121–22
"Working the folks," 46–47
Writings of hobos, 188–90

Younger hobos, 140–41

PHOENIX BOOKS
Sociology, Anthropology, and Archeology

P 2   *Edward Chiera:* They Wrote on Clay
P 7   *Louis Wirth:* The Ghetto
P 10   *Edwin H. Sutherland,* EDITOR: The Professional Thief, by a professional thief
P 11   *John A. Wilson:* The Culture of Ancient Egypt
P 20   *Kenneth P. Oakley:* Man the Tool-maker
P 21   *W. E. LeGros Clark:* History of the Primates
P 24   *B. A. Botkin,* EDITOR: Lay My Burden Down: A Folk History of Slavery
P 28   *David M. Potter:* People of Plenty: Economic Abundance and the American Character
P 31   *Peter H. Buck:* Vikings of the Pacific
P 32   *Diamond Jenness:* The People of the Twilight
P 45   *Weston La Barre:* The Human Animal
P 53   *Robert Redfield:* The Little Community *and* Peasant Society and Culture
P 55   *Julian A. Pitt-Rivers:* People of the Sierra
P 64   *Arnold van Gennep:* The Rites of Passage
P 71   *Nels Anderson:* The Hobo: The Sociology of the Homeless Man
P 82   *W. Lloyd Warner:* American Life: Dream and Reality
P 85   *William R. Bascom and Melville J. Herskovits,* EDITORS: Continuity and Change in African
       Cultures
P 86   *Robert Redfield and Alfonso Villa Rojas:* Chan Kom: A Maya Village
P 87   *Robert Redfield:* A Village That Chose Progress: Chan Kom Revisited
P 88   *Gordon R. Willey and Philip Phillips:* Method and Theory in American Archaeology
P 90   *Eric Wolf:* Sons of the Shaking Earth
P 92   *Joachim Wach:* Sociology of Religion
P 105 *Sol Tax,* EDITOR: Anthropology Today: Selections
P 108 *Horace Miner:* St. Denis: A French-Canadian Parish
P 117 *Herbert A. Thelen:* Dynamics of Groups at Work
P 124 *Margaret Mead and Martha Wolfenstein,* EDITORS: Childhood in Contemporary Cultures
P 125 *George Steindorff and Keith C. Seele:* When Egypt Ruled the East
P 129 *John P. Dean and Alex Rosen:* A Manual of Intergroup Relations
P 133 *Alexander Heidel:* The Babylonian Genesis
P 136 *Alexander Heidel:* The Gilgamesh Epic and Old Testament Parallels
P 138 *Frederic M. Thrasher:* The Gang: A Study of 1,313 Gangs in Chicago (Abridged)
P 139 *Everett C. Hughes:* French Canada in Transition
P 162 *Thomas F. O'Dea:* The Mormons
P 170 *Anselm Strauss,* EDITOR: George Herbert Mead on Social Psychology
P 171 *Otis Dudley Duncan,* EDITOR: William F. Ogburn on Culture and Social Change
P 172 *Albert J. Reiss, Jr.,* EDITOR: Louis Wirth on Cities and Social Life
P 173 *John F. Embree:* Suye Mura: A Japanese Village
P 174 *Morris Janowitz:* The Military in the Political Development of New Nations
P 175 *Edward B. Tylor:* Researches into the Early History of Mankind and the Development
       of Civilization
P 176 *James Mooney:* The Ghost-Dance Religion and the Sioux Outbreak of 1890